Praise for *Warrior*

"Dr. Tick proposes a groundbreaking new approach to combat-trauma treatment that transcends mere assimilation back into functional civilian status. He presents a truly holistic understanding of PTSD and explains why society must acknowledge and embrace warriors' wounds as our own. A must-read for veterans, their families, counselors, and all healers." **LARRY MALERBA, DO**

Author of *Green Medicine: Challenging the Assumptions of Conventional Health Care*

"Dr. Tick's approach to healing eclipses today's world of symptom management. *Warrior's Return* goes beyond living on the 'life raft' and addresses the deeper level of healing that firmly plants veterans back into the fertile ground of life, living, and making a difference." **ROBERT CSANDL, MHS**

Vietnam veteran and executive director of Treatment Trends, Inc./Veterans Sanctuary

"So much attention is given to the symptoms of returning soldiers with little for the wounding of their hearts. Dr. Ed Tick, author of *War and the Soul* and director of Soldier's Heart, has worked for more than three decades to develop and apply a model for not just treating post-traumatic stress disorder (PTSD), but for actually healing the condition at the origin of the wound. In his first book he mapped out the inner world of the combat survivor with a portrait of the soul at war and now, with his newest writing, *Warrior's Return,* he provides a detailed holistic, cultural, and spiritual understanding of PTSD and the way home through the restoration of the spiritual warrior. As a combat veteran myself, Dr. Tick's work has been invaluable in my return home and for a new life after war. Modern diagnostic procedures have not offered much for a problem that historically has existed through many millennia. However, now veterans from all wars, past and present, have the information needed with this amazing approach." **JOHN WESLEY FISHER, DC**

Vietnam veteran and author of *Angels in Vietnam, Not Welcome Home,* and *The War After the War*

"Ed Tick has counseled thousands of wounded warriors. He has studied the warrior in history. He knows the ancient archetypes of warriors and war. No politician should send soldiers to war without reading this book. All of us who care about our warriors should read this book. *Warrior's Return* is a unique contribution. It will change your understanding of the warriors who protect and defend us." **MICHAEL LERNER**

President of Commonweal and author of *Choices in Healing: Integrating the Best of Conventional and Complementary Approaches to Cancer*

"A poignant and beautiful masterpiece that I could not put down. *Warrior's Return* goes to the heart and soul of the warrior's experience—and how the individual, community, and country can transform inwardly shattered protectors into valued and healed contributors in society. A must read for Service members, their families, helpers, and the nation's citizens—all of whom share responsibility for sending our sons and daughters off to war and bringing them all the way home again."

GLENN R. SCHIRALDI, PHD, LTC (USAR, RET.)
Founder of Resilience Training International and author of *The Post-Traumatic Stress Disorder Sourcebook, The Complete Guide to Resilience,* and *The Resilient Warrior*

"As a field battalion surgeon in Vietnam, I returned with PTSD, a term which then did not exist. Neither did the methods of healing in this brilliant book. Had they existed, my journey might have been smoothed, along with the suffering of thousands of war veterans since then. The brutal truth is that war often devastates the victors as well as the defeated. Physical wounds may heal, but psycho-spiritual wounds can fester for a lifetime. Dr. Edward Tick understands the causes and cure of these problems as clearly as anyone I know. *Warrior's Return* is a masterful follow-up to his groundbreaking *War and the Soul.* These books constitute the Bible for understanding and treating war trauma. We owe it to our returning warriors to master the wisdom in these two volumes.

LARRY DOSSEY, MD
Battalion surgeon, Viet Nam, and author of *One Mind: How Our Individual Mind Is Part of a Greater Consciousness and Why It Matters*

"*Warrior's Return* should be required reading. This is a raw and honest book explaining what happens when men and women are sent to war. At the same time, the book is filled with inspiration and hope. The cross-cultural stories that Dr. Edward Tick shares are deep and rich. What is so inspirational is how Dr. Tick offers a psychospiritual approach that heals and restores the heart, soul, and spirit of our veterans. This is a powerful and important book that offers a comprehensive vision to assist veterans' reintegration into community."

SANDRA INGERMAN, MA
Author of *Soul Retrieval: Mending the Fragmented Self*

"The French novelist Antoine St. Exupery once wrote that what is most important is not what is visible, but what is invisible—an insight that Dr. Ed Tick would wholeheartedly agree with in regards to the wounds of war veterans. His invaluable new book, *Warrior's Return,* is an ecology of war's invisible wounds, both those of the warriors themselves and that of the culture that pretends to support their hero-warriors in the name of patriotism, but for the most part prefers their soul wounds to remain invisible. Finally, here is a book that makes the darkness in our warriors' souls visible—and then provides a map that offers hope and direction to bring those souls home again."

PHIL COUSINEAU
Author of *The Art of Pilgrimage* and editor of *Beyond Forgiveness: Reflections on Atonement*

"Ed Tick is probably the world's leading authority on warrior cultures and the warrior's path through the life span. Readers will find here an understanding of the psychological wounds of war as a human universal rather than as a psychiatric condition, followed by an account of the necessary requirements for the warrior's personal transformation and the successful return home. The suggestion is that psychiatric and psychological care are effective only to the extent that they meet the profound human truths discussed in this book. Veterans who read Tick's work will find meaning and dignity even in their darkest places."

ROGER BROOKE
Veteran of South African Special Forces, professor of psychology, and director of military psychological services at Duquesne University

"A masterpiece from one of our wisest elders for understanding the complex dimensions of war trauma. In drawing from an essential recognition of the warrior (and healer) archetypes, Dr. Tick provides a scholarly map that should be essential reading for all trauma therapists, and by the institutions that are entrusted to treat our military. By addressing these soul wounds, we can begin to provide the deep healing that our returning warriors deserve. This is, as a nation, our sacred duty to those who have risked life and limb to defend us."

PETER A. LEVINE, PHD
Author of *In An Unspoken Voice: How the Body Releases Trauma and Restores Goodness* and *Waking the Tiger: Healing Trauma*

"Our warring nation has become skilled at healing many of the physical wounds our men and women receive in war. However, we are not as skilled at healing the invisible wounds that reside in their hearts and their souls. Dr. Edward Tick's vital work utilizes multicultural healing rituals to welcome our veterans back from battle, to make sacred the powerful initiations they experienced, and to help them take their honored place as soul warriors who personify strength, resilience, and hard-won wisdom."

KARLA MCLAREN
Author of *The Language of Emotions* and *The Art of Empathy*

"*Warrior's Return: Restoring the Soul After War* is a provocative, transcending, and solidly researched analysis of how cultures across time have both successfully and unsuccessfully addressed the inevitable traumatic wounding from war and violence. Ed Tick's lucid writing style embeds veterans' narratives, historical lessons, and compelling insights to unveil a prescriptive model for how society can effectively assist warrior populations throughout the cycle of initiation, restoration, and returning to society—making it one of the most powerful and profound accounts of war, warriorhood, and healing ever written."

MARK C. RUSSELL, PHD, ABPP,
Commander US Navy (Ret.) and director of the Institute of War Stress Injury, Recovery, and Social Justice at Antioch University

"*Warrior's Return* prepares readers for the realities of war's lingering impact and encourages us all to confront what it really means to recover from injury, both physical and invisible. Dr. Tick does a great job of telling the individual stories of our veterans, in modern times and throughout history, and the challenges that emerge as warriors return home and must adjust to a new set of circumstances and realities. This book is a must-read for any veteran, loved one, or citizen who wants to learn how spiritual guidance can assist in the transition back from combat operations."

DENNY HECK
Congressional Representative, Washington

"Edward Tick's enlightening portrayal of America's 'throwaways'—our returning soldiers—gives a much-needed voice to the sad epidemic confronting our veterans. He courageously explores the PTSD crisis and draws light to the support systems that fail our warriors. Although he sheds light on a bleak reality, his words and message are full of hope and possibility. As a colleague also committed to serving first responders, I couldn't be more thankful for this book and its clear and powerful message.

LISA WIMBERGER
Founder of the Neurosculpting Institute and author of *Neurosculpting* and *New Beliefs, New Brain*

"Finally someone has displayed enough compassion to give returning warriors a scientific way of dealing with their trauma. *Warrior's Return* is a book important enough for everyone to read."

ARUN GANDHI
President of Gandhi Worldwide Education Institute

"After finishing Ed Tick's new book, *Warrior's Return,* all I can say is 'Wow.' Ed takes a well-rounded and holistic approach to continued healing and growth for veterans after coming home from battle, and his depth and drive to continue working with the military are truly inspiring."

MICHAEL MCCAWLEY
Chaplain (Major), US Army

"*Warrior's Return* is an invitation to take the long journey through war to a 'warrior's return.' Dr. Tick beckons the reader to think deeply about the warrior and offers insight and a rich, hopeful lexicon that will assist in our individual and corporate desire to overcome and heal the 'soul wound' of war. This book will inspire, challenge, teach, and guide those who have served and suffered and those who want to help them."

MIKE LEMBKE
Chaplain (Colonel), US Army

"Ed Tick's book *Warrior's Return* is a wake-up call that instills a gut-level understanding of the unacceptable horrors of war and the inevitable soul-scarring that impacts our courageous soldiers and our society. Clearly, no one ever wins, at any time, during war. Ed shows a pathway of healing that can forever break this traumatic cycle of horror that impacts us all. Prayerful Music has the power to help heal the spiritual wounds of our courageous veterans and bring a lasting peace to their hearts."

JONATHAN ELIAS
Composer and music producer of *The Prayer Cycle* and *Path to Zero* albums and president and founder of Elias Arts

"*Warrior's Return* is an engaging and healing journey into the great soul-suffering that our returning veterans face. Ed Tick wisely and compassionately reveals the invisible horrors of PTSD and calls to the heart that our concept of war as a means of settling differences has never worked and will never work. *Warrior's Return* is a must-read for any legislator or military officer involved in making a decision to place soldiers into the battlefield."

STEVE ROBERTSON
Founder/CEO of ProjectPeaceOnEarth.org and author of *The Power of Choice: Success and Your Life Purpose*

"Dr. Ed Tick never tries to be something he is not—he is an authentic soul. Like some medicine men from other cultures, he stands apart from those he serves. He has mastered the art of sitting quietly in the dark with warriors and has found ways to honor their words, experiences, and pain. *Warrior's Return* is an anecdotal road map that does not point the way *back*—for there is no way back—but *forward and through,* to a place of wholeness. These words bring light into the darkness for any warrior who has stumbled to find his or her way home, or for anyone who has ever loved such a warrior."

KEVIN TURNER
Chaplain (Brigadier General), assistant chief of chaplains, US Army

"This is a beautifully written and profound book. This provocative work has the type of universality and breadth one finds in the works of Joseph Campbell and Carl Jung. It probes the wisdom of the ancient Greeks, the teachings and rituals of our Native American heritage, the assessments of leaders such as President Lincoln and General Sherman, and the reflections of our modern-day warriors. Not only will the reader acquire a deeper understanding of what it means to be a warrior, what it means to be in war and how the war experience transforms a warrior, but it also provides compelling approaches to help heal the warrior's soul, spirit, and mind when she/he returns from war. This is an important work. It should be read not only by all professionals tasked with treating the returned warrior, but by the family and friends of warriors, by the politicians who make policies affecting warriors and decisions on whether to send our warriors into combat, by those given the responsibility to prepare our men and women for combat, and by anyone who believes they should have a voice in determining whether we send troops into combat or how we care for and treat our warriors when they return from war."

MARNIE LO BAUGH, PHD
Clinical and neuropsychologist, and

LES LO BAUGH, ESQ.
Attorney, Vietnam veteran, and advisory board member for SupportVetsNow.org, Hiawatha Institute for Indigenous Knowledge, and ProjectPeaceOnEarth.org

"We are a warrior society. The men and women who go to 'war' are our warriors. *Warrior's Return* is not at all about what you think it is going to be about. Edward Tick's holistic approach to welcoming our veterans home—not just with thanks and parades, but with communities waiting to receive, tend, integrate, and fold them back into the tribe—is a soul's view of a conscious and connected humanity that cares for and includes all its members. *Warrior's Return* is for us all and for our communities. It inspires us to repair our wounded world and become 'refuge and sanctuary' for all who work for the good of the whole."

BERYL BENDER BIRCH
Cofounder of GiveBack Yoga and author of *Yoga for Warriors*

WARRIOR'S RETURN

ALSO BY EDWARD TICK

Nonfiction

Sacred Mountain: Encounters with the Vietnam Beast (1989)

The Practice of Dream Healing:
Bringing Ancient Greek Mysteries into Modern Medicine (2001)

War and the Soul: Healing Our Nation's Veterans
from Post-Traumatic Stress Disorder (2005)

Poetry

The Golden Tortoise: Viet Nam Journeys (2005)

The Bull Awakening: Poetry of Crete and Santorini (2014)

To learn more about Edward Tick's pioneering work
with veterans and to see the film *Healing a Soldier's Heart,*
visit healingasoldiersheart.org

WARRIOR'S RETURN

RESTORING THE SOUL AFTER WAR

EDWARD TICK, PHD

BOULDER, COLORADO

Sounds True
Boulder, CO 80306

Published 2014

Cover design by Rachael Murray
Book design by Beth Skelley

All the stories and quotes herein are true and are reprinted with permission. Stories not referenced were received through personal communications from survivors. If a full name is given, it is a real name used with permission by a survivor who wishes to stand in public witness. When only first names are given or anonymity is maintained, it is to protect confidentiality.

Printed in the United States of America

Library of Congress Cataloging-in-Publication Data
Tick, Edward.
Warrior's return : restoring the soul after war / Edward Tick, PhD.
pages cm
Includes bibliographical references.
ISBN 978-1-62203-200-6
1. Veterans—United States—Psychology. 2. Veterans—Mental health—United States.
3. Post-traumatic stress disorder—United States. 4. War—Moral and ethical aspects.
5. War—Psychological aspects. I. Title.
UB357.T53 2014
616.85'21200973--dc23

2014019975

Ebook ISBN 978-1-62203-224-2
10 9 8 7 6 5 4 3 2 1

For Kate Dahlstedt, my beloved,
who never falters,
whose work this is as well;
and
For all Warriors whose wounds speak truth

The descent to Hell is easy;
Death's gate stands open night and day;
But to retrace our steps, to climb to the air above,
Hoc opus, hic labor est,
This is our life-work, this our labor.

VIRGIL, *Aeneid*

Contents

INTRODUCTION A Call to the Nation . . . ix

PART I **The War After the War**

CHAPTER 1 The Universal Warrior . . . 3

CHAPTER 2 The War After War . . . 23

CHAPTER 3 War Wounds Us All . . . 35

CHAPTER 4 Arena for the Soul . . . 57

CHAPTER 5 The Journey Through Hell . . . 79

CHAPTER 6 The Invisible Wound Today . . . 95

PART II **Bringing Our Warriors Home**

CHAPTER 7 War Trauma and the Social Contract . . . 119

CHAPTER 8 The Wound: A Holistic Understanding . . . 141

CHAPTER 9 Wounding and Identity . . . 149

CHAPTER 10 The Transformational Journey . . . 165

CHAPTER 11 Lessons from the Chiefs of Old . . . 175

CHAPTER 12 Religion and Spirituality for War Healing . . . 193

CHAPTER 13 The Path of Warrior Return . . . 205

CHAPTER 14 Spiritual Comfort and Healing for the War-Wounded . . . 219

CHAPTER 15 Redemption of the Wounded Warrior . . . 237

REVEILLE Of Warriors and Doves . . . 253

Acknowledgments . . . 261

Notes . . . 263

Index of Veterans' Testimonies . . . 281

Index . . . 283

About the Author . . . 299

INTRODUCTION

A Call to the Nation

In Norse mythology the king-god Odin gave an eye for wisdom. What if this wound is the eye we pay for wisdom and the path to it? Can we understand traumatic wounding not as unjust and horrible occurrences that victimize us and should not have happened? Rather, can we understand it as a pathway to initiation and transformation that, in spite of our suffering, can become our great teacher and gift?

Our concern is the invisible wounding from war. The physical wounds are most visible to our veterans who deserve first concern. But in truth we are all wounded. Grandparents, parents, siblings, children, friends, neighbors, care providers, teachers, taxpayers are all caught in war's long and crushing tentacles. Our entire society reels in pain, exhaustion, despair, and debt. Look closely. All lives are affected and we all need be concerned.

Many civilians do not think war has touched them until they remember that their grandfather was in World War II, their nephew in Bosnia, or their neighbor's daughter in Iraq. Or that the suicide in their neighborhood was by a despairing veteran for whom life should have been just beginning. Or that the national debt from the war economy squeezed the hope and finances out of their struggling family's meager resources. War touches us all. We must awaken to how.

Our challenge is this: how do we turn war's inevitable wounding and suffering into wisdom and growth that truly brings warriors home and benefits us all?

THE WARRIOR

The warrior is a foundational archetype in psyche and society. The warrior is the inner spirit and public persona that protects, energizes, motivates, and guides us. We steer ourselves toward its ideal. There are great variations in different societies' warriors, but the archetype is universal. Each individual and culture, aware or not, develops the inner psychospiritual warrior as well as its outer military, political, and social roles.

Many individuals and classes throughout history and the world have striven after the warrior ideal, noted for qualities such as devotion, courage, strategic thinking, leadership, action, service, and sacrifice. Picture Minutemen, Spartans, Knights Templar, Zulus, Incas, Vikings, Samurai. Conjure the Lone Ranger and Tonto, Robin Hood and his Merry Men, King Arthur and the Knights of the Round Table, hobbits and dwarves trekking through Middle-earth. And think of warriors' distortions, their shadow expressions, in quests for power, wealth, fame, land, or revenge. Think of the Nazi S.S. and Taliban terrorists, of Macbeth and Darth Vader.

The Warrior archetype is built into us and awakens as part of our psychospiritual development. It does not disappear as we age. Rather, it is meant to evolve, be integrated with our other core archetypes, and inspire and empower us throughout the life cycle. Without our inner warriors, we are incomplete and weakened.[1] Our society and we are more complete and mature to the degree that we successfully embrace and develop our inner warrior and the moral and protective outer role meant to serve the best in a society.

Key practices necessary to nurturing the warrior and protecting its morality, strength, integrity, and beauty include Initiation, Restoration, and Return. Initiation is the process whereby our old self dies and a new, more mature, and wiser self evolves in its place. Restoration refers to bringing back the energies, beliefs, motivations, commitments, and loves of those who have been to war and may be depleted or disillusioned to the point of despair and brokenness. We restore spirit. Return refers not just to bringing troops out of harm's way but to complete homecoming for the whole person in body, mind, heart, and soul with meaning, honor, respect, and reintegration into community. When we practice these aright—and it is possible—we fill our communities with honorable, noble, wise elders who in turn serve and mature the society and its most needy.

WHERE HAVE ALL THE WARRIORS GONE?

Many caring professionals, citizens, and institutions strive to respond to the needs of troops and veterans. In spite of these sincere attempts, the massive VA health-care system, and innumerable programs and techniques, we hear constant disturbing reports of ongoing, increasing, and abject suffering. We will examine these in depth; for now let us remember the astronomical suicide, substance abuse, divorce, child abuse and neglect, illness, and accident rates, and the unemployment, homelessness, and other life struggles that we hear about every day, that millions of survivors live with as their daily fare.

Warriors are meant to be strong, noble, beautiful, and able to serve for protection, enlightenment, and guidance all their days. Yet the American landscape is littered with victims suffering traumatic wounding we do not know how to heal.

The wars in Iraq and Afghanistan have caused three major invisible wounds" to service people at epidemic levels. These so-called "signature wounds of our modern technological wars are Post-traumatic Stress Disorder (PTSD), Military Sexual Trauma (MST), and Traumatic Brain Injury (TBI). These three wounds, often occurring in combination, create such a complex of transformed and troubled thinking, feeling, perceiving, and behaving that the afflicted person can become lost for life with devastating personal, familial, and social consequences. Too often both veteran and family despair over any possible healing or homecoming, and the costs to society are astronomical. Far greater numbers of new and older veterans die from suicide, "accidents," or stress-related diseases than were killed during their wars. These consequences will be examined in the opening chapters.

This is the ecology of war's invisible wounds: multitudes of disabling symptoms among millions of survivors; public ignorance about their causes, occurrences, and needs; government denial or resistance to diagnosis, treatment, and support; lack of wisdom or resources to address the wounds; and ignorance about and lack of success in how to effectively tend them. We are, in psychologist Paula Caplan's phrase, "a war-illiterate society."[2] Everyone agrees that our troops and veterans deserve a return to productive and creative lives after service. The question remains: how?

Traumatic wounding from war and violence has been with us since ancient times, and we will examine their prevalence and treatment throughout history. For our exploration of how we transform war's suffering into wisdom and blessing for survivors and society, we must ask fundamental questions about our contemporary understanding of war trauma.

Let us begin with questions about this wound. The right questions alter the ways we understand war and its consequences and provide guidance in how to respond to our survivors in ways that provide direction for true restoration and homecoming.

By now we have all heard of Post-traumatic Stress Disorder (PTSD), the name first given traumatic wounding by the American Psychiatric Association in 1980 and so popularized that it is well known, heavily reported, and commonly diagnosed. But what if what we call PTSD today were not an individual medical or psychological pathology and its sufferers were not doomed to helpless breakdown causing chronic struggle and suffering?

Both military service and combat are transformational experiences. Wounding to the psyche accompanies war. Survivors are transformed into someone and something else. What if what we call PTSD today were the troubling and troublesome shape of their new, untended, and incomplete identities? What if it represents their struggles to be reborn into someone new and different out of the hell-fires of war? What if the proper questions to ask focus less on veterans and more on *our* collective responsibilities regarding war? What if significant reasons our veterans suffer in epidemic numbers lie, to paraphrase Shakespeare, "not in the veterans but in ourselves"? What if the sources of traumatic breakdown are in society; in our beliefs and practices; in the reasons and ways we prepare for and make war; and in the ways we neglect or fail our troops before, during, and after service? What if veterans are carrying our collective war wounding alone because it is denied and disowned by society at large? What if this causes them to collapse into the massive wound to the body politic that belongs to us all? What if, instead of asking, "What is wrong with our veterans?" we asked, "What is the *real* cause of military PTSD? What happened to their brains, biochemistry, and thinking? What helps them readjust, reduce their symptoms, and reenter civilian society again? In short, how do we treat *them*?"

We can indeed conceive of healing, growth, and restoration for our invisible war wounds to our veterans and society. We must not be content with, at best, difficult readjustment to a lifelong condition.

Instead of focusing on fixing our veterans or getting their symptoms under control, we must ask, "How can *we* bring *our warriors* home?"

MY SEARCH FOR WAR-HEALING WAYS

I began working with Vietnam War veterans in the 1970s, before the modern diagnosis of PTSD was created. My first vet patient had been stationed stateside, and he sent troops to war and received back the wounded and dead. Never overseas, he suffered nightmares; anxiety attacks; substance abuse; rages; promiscuity; high-risk, antisocial behavior; and employment and relationship instability.[3]

From this beginning I saw what war had done to my peers—those who had fought, those who had been part of its huge machine even from a distance, and also many who did their best to protest or avoid it. It was my war too.

Many of us heard our World War II fathers referring to "the war." Many with Vietnam vet fathers or grandfathers grew up hearing that conflict called "the war." Troops returning from Iraq and Afghanistan refer to "the war."

Every war manifests universal conditions that we find in every other war. "The war" is Ares or Mars, the god of war who delights in slaughter, drives us to our worst, demands of us our best, and seems to never leave us. My parents' war was World War II, my generation's was Vietnam, my children's Iraq and Afghanistan. In our rush to be relevant and help our new veterans, we must remember: wars do not end; their suffering and killing go on and on long after bullets stop flying.

Every war is "the war." Every survivor has known its god-power. Every war and survivor can become our teacher.

I wanted to serve our veterans as a "home-front doc," a healer. I wanted, as much as possible for someone who wasn't there, to see what they had seen and learn what they knew. I was also seeking my initiation and inner warriorhood and the service that might evolve it.

Vets tested me to be sure my motivations were true and full of integrity, that I could "take it," that I wasn't trying to profit off their war stories.

Then they took me—in memory, story, emotion, dream, relationship, adventure, and service—to where their souls had been blasted and scorched and were still stuck. My great challenge became to discover what we might do to heal their crippling and pervasive wounds.

I worked as a psychotherapist with many veterans, advised veteran's organizations, helped create crisis response teams, and trained agency counselors. Most importantly, I spent innumerable hours with vets in and out of counseling settings. Over many a pizza I listened to their stories, attended their meetings, participated in their causes, and shared their challenges. I became part of what constitutes an extensive subculture of American society. Vets initiated me into a world very different from civilians'. I could not have known it existed without their need, welcome, and guidance. Working to help facilitate and complete their journey changed me.

By the mid-1980s I was convinced that war's invisible wound is not only caused by the massive stress that alters neurological, emotional, and cognitive functioning. These changes, to be sure, are real and severe. But the invisible war wound is also holistic and complex. It impacts and transforms every aspect of our being. It is, in essence, spiritual, moral, and communal.

The protest movement had declared, "Bring the boys home." Though still young in years, these veterans were sad, lonely, hurt, angry, and exhausted old men. They were back on home soil but psychologically and spiritually not home. I found it intolerable that so many of my vet peers seemed condemned to an adult life of chronic suffering and alienation with likely early deaths. It is the utmost betrayal for any country to send its sons and daughters into slaughter for unjust reasons and afterward abandon, neglect, and mistreat them, and then leave them in a bereft and condemned condition for the rest of their lives. Since the world has had so many wars large and small throughout history, it must be that some other cultures found ways to bring hope and healing to those afflicted by war and maintained better faith with their warriors.

I have been on a search into world traditions that continues to this day, studying war and the warrior from cultures the world over and throughout the ages. I travel this continent and the globe to visit enclaves of warriors and survivors from different cultures. I study warrior remnants, ruins, and testimonies from other cultures and times. I question veterans from other countries to compare their culture's experiences with ours. I facilitate reconciliation meetings between former battlefield foes and atonement practices for those who have destroyed and want to restore.

I concluded that our modern conception of traumatic war wounding and healing is woefully inaccurate and inadequate. It must be revisited, reconceived, and restored, as we will present herein. Dr. John Fisher, chiropractor and combat veteran, laments, "There is still so little known about PTSD after all this time." And Dr. Michael Uhl, psychologist and combat vet, declares, "There is no *cure* for PTSD."

My previous book *War and the Soul* presented an understanding of the inner psychospiritual wounding from war that today we call PTSD. *War and the Soul* offered a complete portrait of the combat survivor. It introduced "soul wounding" and "moral trauma" as meaningful and usable contemporary concepts. It mapped the survivor's inner landscape using myth, ritual, custom, tradition, history, cross-cultural studies, first-person testimony, and decades of clinical experience. It concluded with a partial presentation of the necessities of return from warfare.

Since publication in 2005, *War and the Soul* has garnered influential military, veteran, professional, academic, clinical, and civilian audiences. Troops, chaplains, and mental health officers use it to sustain and guide those in the combat zone. My greatest honor is to hear from troops downrange who testify that the book helped them survive the combat zone and from veterans at home who say they put down the shotgun and instead found hope and direction.

In response to the explosion of interest and need and our national veteran care crisis, my partner Kate Dahlstedt and I founded the nonprofit organization Soldier's Heart in 2006, dedicated to healing the invisible wounds of war. Soldier's Heart has developed an international network of thousands. Through psychospiritual growth, identity transformation, community involvement and education, intensive retreats, pilgrimage, and other practices, we facilitate and teach warrior's return to achieve a full and successful homecoming and restoration. Our dilemma—once we accurately understood the inner world of combatants—was: how do we use this portrait to bring not just readjustment or symptom reduction but true healing and homecoming?

Warrior's Return demonstrates the stages of the full return journey for war survivors as it has been practiced across cultures and in history, myth, and psyche. It completes the map of the warrior's journey home after both combat and further wounding on the home front, and it teaches how to use it. It reports on the place of the warrior in society; the response to returning warriors in other cultures, historical and world mythological and religious traditions; the reasons for the absence of PTSD in post-war Viet Nam; and other new and relevant findings. It applies these to a cross-cultural, humanistic, and nonpathological understanding of war trauma and recovery.

In its focus on the combat experience, *War and the Soul* is akin to the *Iliad*. In its focus on the return journey, *Warrior's Return* is like the *Odyssey*. *Warrior's Return* offers a new and complete mapping of the warrior's life journey, the return journey from service, and how to understand and work with war trauma based on these findings. We equally address individuals, families, communities, the nation and our international community, and both the military and civilians. *Warrior's Return* thus works on all levels for military, professional, and popular audiences and on both theoretical and practical levels, with applications and implications for a new, holistic, hope-filled, and heart- and soul-centered understanding of war trauma and its healing.

Warrior's Return demonstrates how, once we understand the comprehensive and soul-based inner wounding as traditional warrior cultures did, we can learn to bring our warriors home in ways that transcend our helplessness and despair at healing war's invisible wounds to successfully facilitate growth, transformation, and restoration.

HEALING, GROWTH, AND RESTORATION AFTER WAR ARE POSSIBLE

When we understand that invisible war wounding is inevitable and it is everyone's responsibility to tend it, then our attitudes, relationships, and responsibilities to veterans change and we can find both new and time-honored directions for hope.

Michael Phillips was a truck driver through dangerous and embattled territory in Viet Nam. He earned the nickname of "Magoo" and still proudly uses it. "Not too many years ago," Magoo says, "I was a penniless, unemployed, homeless-for-the-fourth-time, broken, suicidal, and very unhealthy Vietnam-combat veteran." He had been a drug addict for over thirty years and an alcoholic for over thirty-six. After four decades, he had "become a train wreck" and finally asked for help from the Veterans Administration. Overcoming numerous roadblocks, he persisted and was provided life-saving assistance by the VA. Magoo says, "Without having the opportunity to go to the White City VA, known as the SORCC (Southern Oregon Rehabilitation Center and Clinics), my drug and alcohol abuse along with my mental state would have very likely ended my life one way or another, possibly by suicide either deliberate or accidental." At White City, Magoo learned about the physiology and emotions of PTSD and skills for symptom management and self-care. We first met "by accident or providence" when I lectured at a college campus near the facility. Due to be released within the month, he stated, "Now that I know how to manage my PTSD, what am I going to do? I've got too much time, an empty apartment, an adequate disability check, but nothing else."

Since that first meeting, Magoo has studied *War and the Soul*, attended veteran healing retreats that my Soldier's Heart organization staff and I lead based on that book, and traveled back with me to Viet Nam twice. Now Magoo volunteers at his old facility, lectures on veterans' issues in his community, and is featured in media appearances. He has lost weight, become an eloquent public speaker, and seeks involvement in community affairs. In 2011, in advance of our group return to Viet Nam, Magoo traveled alone to Korea where he met with their veterans, conducted comparative research on the impact of war for both countries, and opened doors for collaborative projects between American and Korean veterans. In 2013 he visited World War II sites and cemeteries across the Pacific, meeting with veterans of both sides where they had served.

Magoo and I have worked together outside a traditional therapy context to transform his condition into an honorable wound that is a source of strength and growth. In a few years Magoo has transformed into a spiritual warrior, which, he says, is "a title that will guide me in service for the rest of my life." He summarized: "The twenty-eight months I spent at SORCC saved my life. The incredibly timely introduction to

Soldier's Heart prior to my discharge showed me a purpose for my life. My participation with Soldier's Heart has given meaning to my life. And the journey continues . . . "

Magoo is one of countless veterans of World War II, Korea, Vietnam, Iraq, Afghanistan, and America's numerous unknown secret or forgotten small wars who have successfully transformed their invisible wounds from causes of severe breakdown to sources of wisdom that, in turn, serve society and promote healing and peace. *Warrior's Return* tells us how.

Warrior's Return reveals the necessary stages for warriors coming home. These philosophies and strategies can bring our troops and veterans healing and restoration in mind, heart, and spirit. Most trauma-healing strategies are externally derived for stress or symptom reduction or cognitive reformulation and are applied *pro forma* to veterans. These strategies are often guided by healers who may have little or no experience in working with the military or veterans, have greater curiosity about their methodology than about warriorhood, or do not appreciate how unique and different from civilian experience both military service and combat are.

In contrast, *Warrior's Return* presents a vision and path for transforming the invisible wounds of war. This vision derives from my intimacy and three and a half decades of successful healing work with wounded warriors and survivors from every major and most minor conflicts Americans have been involved in since the Spanish Civil War. It also grows out of my work with veterans from other cultures and my lifelong study and participation in the worldwide warrior tradition. My venues in working with troops and veterans include our biggest military bases and hospitals; intimate, intensive healing retreats; Native American reservations; remote, ramshackle motel rooms; the streets where the homeless live; and old battlefields overseas among former foes.

Our goals in healing veterans must not be limited to symptom management, stress reduction, altering brain chemistry, or learning body–mind cooperation. While these can reduce suffering and stabilize adjustment, we accomplish restoration and homecoming through psychospiritual transformation of the veteran in cooperation with community so that meaning, soul, and spirit are restored; the identity is enlarged; the warrior–civilian rift is healed; and moral trauma is rectified. When these occur, the wound can dissipate and an elder spiritual warrior can return.

Warrior's Return maps the philosophical, psychological, social, and spiritual dimensions of successful veteran restoration. It covers the universal dimensions of military and war experiences. It presents a world history and philosophical, cultural, and cross-cultural examination of invisible war wounding and its response and treatment throughout time. It offers a holistic understanding of warrior's invisible wounds, an explication of what warriorhood is in both traditional and modern terms, and a demonstration of how modern militaries and societies too often fail or betray the warrior ethos, resulting in moral trauma and collapse. It reveals the hidden social contract that exists between the warrior and society and the dire consequences to both when this contract is betrayed. It demonstrates how to transform traditional concepts of spiritual warriorhood into a guiding vision and practice that work for veteran restoration today. It maps the necessary conditions for the warrior's return journey from the battlefield to home. It presents the spiritual, religious, mythological, historical, cultural, psychological, and spiritual dimensions of war healing that can inspire, guide, and support a successful homecoming through identity transformation, soul restoration, community reconciliation and restitution, and psychospiritually based "Post-traumatic Growth."

No society is healthy without a healthy, functioning elder warrior class leading the way into a future of hope, responsibility, true security, and peacemaking based on the transformational wisdom and healing gained from ordeal. Following the psychospiritual portrait of the inner world of the combat veteran presented in *War and the Soul*, *Warrior's Return* gives hope and direction to our nation and world and to our ailing troops, veterans, and their families by mapping this homeward journey to restoration and how to walk or guide it.

PART I

The War After the War[1]

This war is eating my life out.

ABRAHAM LINCOLN

CHAPTER 1

The Universal Warrior

Once a warrior always a warrior[1]

After half a year in Afghanistan, twenty-year-old Marine rifleman Michael Abattello and his team went on yet another dangerous patrol. They drove several Humvees through a remote village surrounded by stark mountains where US Marines had been attacked before.

The mountains had been shaped over centuries, stones cleared and piled into waist-high walls, slopes flattened and plowed as arable terraces.

A boy about ten years old popped up from behind a wall. He stared and pointed at the Marines, then turned and ran along the lowest terrace.

One Marine yelled, "Shoot him! He's running to tell the enemy." Children might be scouts, lookouts, forced to carry guns, or wired with bombs. Another said, "They've fooled us this way before."

Michael jumped out of his Humvee. "Guns down!" he commanded. "He's only a boy. I'll catch him." He turned to his battle buddy Joe. "Marines don't kill innocent children. C'mon!"

They ran up the long terraces in blistering sunlight, the boy looking back, Michael and Joe straining in full uniform and equipment to catch up. "It'd be easier to shoot," Joe panted. "He's a child," Michael answered.

The Marines reached the summit. No enemies. No shooting. No boy. There stood an old barn, door swinging. "He must be in there with the bad guys," Joe said. "It's a trap. Blow it!"

"We don't know that," Michael said. "Cover me. I'm going in."

Rifle pointed, Michael squeezed into the barn. Only scattered hay and farming tools. "Clear and empty," he called. Joe entered, eyes darting.

A wooden ladder led to a hayloft. A sprinkling of hay trickled to the floor.

"There," Joe yelled and pointed his rifle.

"Down!" Michael ordered. "I'm going up."

"Perfect ambush," Joe argued. "You're dead."

Michael climbed the ladder. "C'mon up," Michael called from the loft. "It's safe." Joe climbed and stood beside Michael. Nothing but a pile of pale yellow hay.

"They must be hiding in there." Joe fixed his bayonet. "I'll get them before they get us." He prepared to stab his blade into the hay.

"No!" Michael said. "If it was an ambush, they'd have shot us already."

Michael shouldered his gun and separated the long, thick, yellow stalks. Deep in a hay cave, he saw small hands and feet, then legs and arms, then little bodies. Huddled inside was the boy. Next to him, clinging tightly together, were two small girls and a teenager dressed in a burka.

Michael laid his gun on the floor and signaled Joe to do the same. He said in Pashto, "Hello, children. Peace be with you. Don't be scared. We're your friends."

Slowly the children stood up. The girls were only five or six years old. The boy was between them, the teenager behind, tall and dignified in her dark robe.

Sunlight poured through cracks in the barn roof. A soft dust cloud rose from the yellow hay. The light from the sun filtered through the dust, filling the loft and surrounding the children in a golden halo.

The burka-robed teenager spread her cloaked arms around the children standing in the halo. Michael blinked and stared. His heart squeezed. Joe shrugged and looked at the floor.

There before him, bathed in golden light, Michael saw Mother Mary, Shekinah, Quan Yin. He saw the Divine Mother of all religions and all peoples caring for, protecting, and showering mercy and kindness on all living beings.

Michael spoke to the children. The boy was the only brother of these three sisters. The enemy had told them that Marines were devils who hurt and tortured children. The boy only ran to protect his sisters.

Michael took off his helmet. "See," he said with a smile, "I'm not a devil. Marines are your friends. We're here to help you. We want you to be safe, to have good food and schools and good lives. Come. Let us take you home."

The Marines and children emerged and descended the terraces. Michael and Joe introduced the children to their smiling squad, who escorted them home.

Worried, robed parents ran out to meet them. The entire family was safe. They served tea and sweets to the Marines and all together shared a joyous reunion.

Michael visited this family often. He played with the children and taught them some English. He helped the family with its farming chores and learned about goat care from them. He became the children's uncle.

Now back in America, Michael often thinks of his Afghani family. His heart is still drenched in the golden light of that day on the distant mountain when, in the midst of war, he acted rightly and was given the defining vision of his life.

Short months after high school graduation, the day after 9/11, Michael enlisted to defend our nation after attack. He loved the Marine Corps and its warrior tradition. He practiced to be a superior rifleman, trusting that commanders and country would use him for the good. He learned Pashto, and in Afghanistan, he wandered among the people. He tried to save rather than destroy when possible.

Michael is not just a Marine. He is a warrior. In his behavior in Afghanistan and his love of our nation, he exemplifies the warrior tradition.

But war wounded Michael. His body is full of shrapnel. He can no longer dance and cannot bend some fingers. He has constant back and limb pain. He has had nightmares, broken relationships, and sleep disorders, and he felt displaced, threatened, unwanted, and unsuitable for ordinary life in America. He saved those children and others, and in battle he refused medical care and a Purple Heart in order to remain beside his comrades. Yet Michael was never honored, thanked, or recognized, and he fought for years for a disability rating.

Michael had to fight and kill. He witnessed wild dogs devouring dead bodies. He saw the visage of the war god in mangled comrades, civilians, enemy fighters, and the Afghan land. "War is sick," Michael said. "The only way to survive it is to become as sick yourself as the situation surrounding you. War makes everyone sick."

Why did right action not protect Michael from long-term pain? How did he travel from honorable warrior in the combat zone to broken, alienated, and unseen at home? How did he become a throwaway rather than "first among citizens"? And how is it that in Michael and uncountable millions the noble warrior tradition has so devolved? Why do we have broken and wounded warriors scattered throughout the rancorous nations around the globe rather than a world community filled with honorable and wise elder warriors guiding us all toward peace?

UNIVERSALITY OF THE WARRIOR ARCHETYPE

Warrior is a Spiritual Form, a recurring ideal or archetype. It is built into both psyche and society. It has characteristic images, patterns, stories, and values that are given unique shape by its host cultures. It resurfaces in individual lives throughout history and across cultures. We learn this from history, the social sciences, literature, the arts, mythology, and sacred writings. We learn it from our elders, children, and veterans. We learn it from those who serve, no matter what the politics, economics, or motivations behind their deployments.

I stood beside an elderly man named Alberto in a Puerto Rican village. We leaned on a harbor railing and gazed at the sea. I noticed a chain hanging around his neck and disappearing beneath his T-shirt. "You still wear your dog tags?" I asked.

"How do you know?" he retorted, surprised.

"That chain is unmistakable."

"Only for those who get it," he answered. Eighty-year-old Alberto is a Korean War combat veteran. He yanked his tags out of his shirt and dangled them between us. "Once a warrior always a warrior." He grinned.

"*Es verdad*," I affirmed. "True! The change is forever, and we wish to serve all our lives. You've been in the real thing. May I ask what you think of our recent wars?"

"Lies, stupidity, immorality!" Alberto barked. "We never should have gone. But I'm waiting for the president to phone. Even though the wars are wrong, I'd go tomorrow. I should die so our children and young warriors can live."

Warriors have been a mainstay of civilization for at least the last 5,000 years, since the dominance of the patriarchy, sedentary agricultural societies, and recorded history. They were educated, trained, and initiated by elders, and they experienced life-threatening ordeals. They served their people by protecting them during conflict, by acting aggressively toward competitors, and by playing important roles throughout their life cycles. With rare exceptions, warriors have been a part of almost every culture we know.

Early written evidence of mature and developed warriorhood stretches as far back as one of the first known works of literature, the Sumerian *Epic of Gilgamesh*. Gilgamesh's kingship dates to around 2700 BCE, the inscribed poem to around 2000 BCE. It narrates a warrior-king's battles against cosmic forces and tells of brotherhood found and lost forever in battle. A warrior, mortally wounded by a wild creature, warns his surviving royal comrade, "I have seen things as a man / and a man sees death in things" and "You'll be alone and wander / looking for that life that's gone or some / Eternal life you have to find."[2] Initiation, inevitable change and loss, awareness of death, the necessity to conquer "the beast," carrying the burden and sorrow alone, the search for meaning and the sacred—these are eternal aspects of the Warrior archetype spoken to us from over 4,000 years ago.

We know of more than 14,600 wars waged in the 5,600 years of recorded history.[3] The only cultures that have not had warriors are those that have been isolated from other human societies. Examples are Greenland, which has never known war, and tribes deep in the Amazon jungles that have not had to compete with neighbors for resources. In contrast, many tribal cultures through the ages—including those in "wide-open spaces" like American forests and plains, African savannas, or New Guinea jungles—have lived in competition and developed complex warrior traditions to initiate their young, protect their people, define identities and boundaries, gather resources, nurture children, and aid the elderly. Even in great spaces, the warrior will surface and serve.

THE INNATE WARRIOR ARCHETYPE

Ted began protesting as he came of age during the Vietnam War. Awakening to the hidden dangers and collaborations within our "military-industrial-government complex,"[4] he became a lifelong peace activist. Seen at almost every regional protest march, he rarely missed protesting policies he thought unjust.

Ted had two sons. In order to raise them to be noncompetitive and protected from violence, he forbade them to play war games or own anything resembling a weapon. Even water guns were banned.

Ted's sons and their friends organized their own black-market operation. They smuggled toy plastic guns onto his property, hid them in bushes, under trees, in basement cubbies. The neighborhood boys went out of their way to "play guns" with Ted's sons, especially at their home when Ted was away.

My wife, Kate, and I made sure that our son, Gabriel, knew many veterans growing up. He heard their stories and respected them. We did not forbid Gabriel's play with guns but wanted him to be educated about the realities he was playing with.

One day Gabe and his friends were playing "Vietnam War." I had "played guns" growing up, so I understood. But seeing his little friends and him shooting each other with plastic M16s and AK-47s as pretend GIs and Viet Cong upset me.

"Gabe," I said one day when he was seven, "the real versions of those weapons killed my friends and the Vietnamese."

"We like being warriors, Dad," he explained. "But don't worry. I know the difference between play and the real thing."

I was proud that Gabriel knew that difference at an early age. It was in part because he knew veterans and counted some among his closest uncles and elders. Ted, in contrast, so mistrusted the Warrior archetype that he tried to ban its expression in his children. Ted did not recognize that he was as committed, devoted, energized to his own mission of protest as any warrior. He, too, had an inner striving to protect our community against further violence. In essence Ted was a warrior for peace.

These stories illustrate what millions of parents have observed. Take the toy gun away and the child will use a stick or finger instead. The Warrior archetype is natural, innate, and deep. It is a source of extraordinary energies and passions. Its core values are protection and preservation of its community. It offers identity and belonging in a strong brother- and sisterhood. It will awaken and find means of expression whether we recognize it or not, whether we encourage or inhibit it. When we discourage it, we may unwittingly make it even stronger as it seeks disguised means of expression. Like it or not, almost all societies have warriors and we each have an inner warrior. The archetype, its psychospiritual importance, and its social role need and deserve attention, support, education, training, practice, and expression.

WHAT IS A WARRIOR?

Sgt. Maj. Lou Rothenstein was one of our earliest intelligence officers to serve in Vietnam. As an IO, he was responsible for "winning the hearts and minds" of local people and gathering information about the enemy. He declares, "For me, Warriorhood is living by an ethos—a code of honor—a creed. It is a way of living life." Warriorhood is a pathway through life with a set of expectations, norms, behaviors, and values that must be fulfilled and guided by a high moral code of conduct. This is what the Native American tradition meant by "warpath," better understood as the lifelong Warrior's Path.

Codes must accompany warriorhood, necessitated by the core of violence in the warrior's life. The code or creed provides the warrior an ethical foundation for conduct based on right relationships to society, the killing arts, and other human beings against whom he or she must fight. Lt. Colonel van Rooyen is the former commanding officer of South Africa's 1 Parachute Battalion. He was in the war zone for fifteen years. Asked how, after so many years in combat, he managed to sleep at night, he replied, "I never did anything that was not militarily necessary."[5] On modern battlefields Colonel van Rooyen echoed various warrior codes, including the Samurai, whose code is never to fight in personal anger. Such codes, military ethics professor Shannon French explains, serve as "moral and psychological armor that protects the warrior from becoming a monster in his own eyes."[6]

Our ancestors recognized this need. In our Biblical roots we find guidance for limiting destructiveness and healing traumatic losses. Since humanity will tend to act with selfishness, cruelty, or immorality, the Commandments were necessary; the Lawgiver realized this human tendency toward evil and the need to limit and shape it for the good. The Old Testament contains rules for practicing humane warfare, codified in Deuteronomy 20. It appeared approximately 3,000 years before the Geneva Conventions, yet its tenets have not been honored to this day.

Each branch of the US military has a creed memorized by its recruits, and each branch trains and promotes its version of the warrior culture and ethos. The *Rifleman's Creed*, for example, is the oath memorized by every US Marine since it was first written in World War II. The essence of Marine service is in being on the ground in direct contact with the enemy. The Creed is meant to provide unshakeable guidance through the difficulties of combat. It states in part, "My rifle is human, even as I am human, because it is my life. Thus, I will learn it as a brother. I will learn its weaknesses, its strengths, its parts . . . I will keep my rifle clean and ready, even as I am clean and ready. We will become part of each other." The US Army's *Soldier's Creed* begins, "I am an American soldier . . . a Warrior . . . " The Army's warrior ethos embedded in the Creed is again meant to be a solid foundation of guiding values and actions: "I will always place the mission first. I will never accept defeat. I will never quit. I will never leave a fallen comrade."

Such codes may be universal. *Bushido* was the famous warrior code and ethos of the Samurai that govern every aspect of a warrior's life "from root to branch." The fictional Robin Hood gave his men a code, popularized as "rob from the rich and give to the poor." Even the Nazi S.S. had their code, equating honor with duty and declaring obedience and the willingness to die.

According to Roger Brooke, former South African paratrooper and now professor of psychology, for warriors "the spiritual core of submission and dedication to a moral authority greater than one's self is at the heart of things." Chaplain Kevin Turner, a Special Forces officer for two decades and now one of four generals of the US Army Chaplaincy, focuses on the strength and determination necessary for warriorhood and the protection it offers: "The highest calling of a warrior is when they stand, even unto death, in the defense of one who has been knocked down." Greg Walker retired from Special Forces in 2005 and is himself a Wounded Warrior. Greg found his "new normal" and lives in meaningful recovery, and he now advocates for Operation Iraqi/Enduring Freedom/New Dawn veterans. To express the essence of warriorhood, Greg quotes Shakespeare's *Henry IV*, part 2: "Care I for the limb, the thewes, the stature, bulk, and big assemblance of a man! Give me his spirit." A Green Beret who operated in dangerous and secretive circumstances, Greg declares, "It is the sacred Spirit of the man or woman that ultimately creates, sustains, and endures in combat and afterward—whether that combat is physical, moral, spiritual, or mental in experience and effect."

The Warrior archetype has characteristic traits when active and healthy. Paul Henderson spent twenty-three years in the Army, twelve of those in Special Forces and two more in Special Operations. He was in command for a decade, rose to the rank of Lt. Colonel, and is a crusading lawyer today. He analyzes the warrior's necessary traits:

> To me, there are two aspects to warriorhood. One is a state of mind. There is a transpersonal purpose whether it is to a country, a community, a family, an idea, a squad. Something bigger than the self. Purpose sustains when it is difficult to do so. It requires courage—both physical and moral. And, by "courage" I simply mean the willingness to act in the face of fear. It's certainly not the absence of fear. It is dedication to service for the sake of that service—not for glory or personal gain. Motives are important here.

The warrior's state of mind, Col. Henderson declares, is its core asset. But skills—carefully trained and painstakingly perfected—and "martial arts," are also required.

> Second, warriorhood is a set of skills. Warriors know their craft. They are technically and tactically proficient and stay current and honed. The heart of a lion will accomplish little without the training and skills to effect an outcome. Whether it is a soldier, an artist, a healer, a teacher, or even a salesclerk—the spirit of warriorhood can play out in any activity, but you have to know what you are doing. Desire and intention are not enough.

These experienced combatants do not mention killing. Lt. Col. David Grossman suggests, "It may be simply too painful for society to address what it does when it sends young men off to kill other young men in distant lands."[7] We have developed a national taboo against admitting this essence of warriorhood, leaving the veteran mistrustful of how he or she will be treated by nonveterans, fearing rejection, and hating the question, "Did you ever kill anyone?"

Traditional cultures did not hide this essential task of warriors either from young warriors-to-be or their people. Roger Shourds is a Pend d'Oreille tribal member—in his Salish language *Qlispele*—a Native American from Montana. He was a Marine in Viet Nam. His warrior name is *Kwu Kak Nupkus*, "He Who Sees the Bear." Nupkus explains his tribe's traditional meaning and preparation of warriors:

> Our word for warrior is *Sxwplstwe* (man) or *Sinmsci* (woman), which means "one who is tasked to kill and/or take blood." It was taught to the children as soon as they could understand. There was never any pretense that the warriors in battle would do anything but kill our enemies who were judged by how honorable and strong they were, which in turn would make us stronger and more honorable. There was never any hatred of the enemy. From the beginning the boys and girls who chose to walk the Warrior's Path knew that they were not going to "be all you can be" and learn new skills. They were tasked to kill to protect the Tribe.

Native American tradition stressed protection of the tribe—it was for this that warriors ultimately fought. Thus the name of the modern Mohawk Warrior Society, *Rotiskenrakete*, literally means "men who carry the burden of peace."[8]

The archetype and its psychological identity, functions, and social roles are specialized and different from the other inborn archetypes that organize our inner lives. The Warrior has its unique spirituality, stories, images, traditions, principles, and practices for nurturance, protection, development, guidance, morality, healing, and connection to "powers and principalities" beyond the individual. These are to a significant extent shaped around the most traumatizing action a person can perform: killing other human beings.

Maj. Gen. William Arnold was the US Army's Chief of Chaplains during World War II. His message to soldiers was printed in the Bible distributed to American troops. (I always carry my father's.) He counseled, "A soldier who knows the Word of God and honestly tries to observe God's law is a man of power and influence among his fellows and *exalts his military service to the high level of religious faith, courage, and loyalty.*"[9]

Chaplain Arnold voiced a profound responsibility and challenge to warriors and society. Warriorhood entails transformation and sacrifice. Army Chaplain Col. Michael Lembke declares, "It's hard not to be melodramatic when speaking of the warrior. There is little that is routine or mundane about the acts of selfless service required in 'war.'"

To explain the essence of warriorhood, Chaplain Lembke invokes the prophet Isaiah's vision of the suffering servant. "From a Judeo-Christian perspective, Isaiah 53 in specific, a warrior is the suffering servant who willingly and knowingly puts him- or herself on the path of sacrifice in armed conflict for another." In Isaiah 52:14 and 53:2–3, Isaiah's description of the servant matches that of many returning veterans:

> Many people were shocked when they saw him;
> he was so disfigured that he hardly looked human . . .
> He had no dignity or beauty . . .
> There was nothing attractive about him . . .
> We despised him and rejected him;
> He endured suffering and pain.
> No one would even look at him—
> We ignored him as if he were nothing.

Chaplain Lembke identifies the nugget of irony and challenge inherent in the warrior's calling: "And yet we will continue to ask common, ordinary men and women to do uncommon and extraordinary acts to deter war, to fight in war, and to return from war." Common people, often without adequate spiritual preparation or know-how, are challenged to elevate themselves to extraordinary conditions of service and sacrifice and must somehow *exalt* that service.

The soul is our moral center. Socrates taught that the soul is that in us that differentiates good from evil; it grows from the right choice or shrivels from the wrong. Socrates had been a warrior. In one battle he was last defending and saving the line of retreating Athenians. There he practiced the meaning of courage—an absolute moral stand unto death on behalf of others.[10] John F. Kennedy, also a combat veteran, taught that true courage is a matter of character that guides decisions and actions "subject every minute to the test of moral law."[11]

In a war that seemed as morally clear as World War II—during which troops believed they were in a necessary battle against evil forces attempting to destroy homelands, entire races, and civilization itself—exalted purpose may have been easier to grasp: we *were* attacked; the Nazis *were* committing genocide. But even during World War II, troops became exhausted and disillusioned. Allied Forces Commander General Eisenhower overheard many soldiers wondering why they were fighting this long and brutal war so far from home when it seemed to not directly concern them. Eisenhower had all battalions within fifty miles of liberated concentration camps send troops on a tour through them to be reminded of their moral purpose. He wanted every soldier to "at least know what he is fighting against."

The "warrior soul" is that part of us that wishes to serve with high honor for moral purpose. When trained or used in illegitimate, abusive, disproportionate, or immoral ways, it is wounded. When used in moral ways for immoral ends, it is in anguish. When alone and unseen in its willingness to sacrifice life, when its pain is neglected, it falls into despair. Vietnam veteran Brian Delate warns, "Remembering makes you want to forget, and being forgotten makes you want to die."[12]

We must perceive the Universal Warrior and understand that how we use our warriors—when, where, and why we ask them to serve; how we prepare them; what we ask them to do and why; how we bring them home and tend them—either harms or fulfills, wounds or develops, that universal inner presence and power. Our warriors' anguish tells us that the invisible wound is a sacred wound, a wound in our relationship to the inner warrior, the archetype. As one Iraq vet said, "We don't need complicated psychological definitions. PTSD results when your head tells you to do what your heart tells you is wrong." It is straightforward—as a warrior do you judge that you were used for good or ill, for preservation or aggression? The invisible wound results from the degree to which an individual soldier fulfills or fails to fulfill, betrays or feels betrayed by, the pursuit of the Warrior ideal.

Reflecting on the meaning, identity, roles, and challenges of warriors through the ages, a composite portrait states that the ideal warrior is:

> assertive, active, and energized . . . clear-minded, strategic, and alert . . . us[ing] both body and mind . . . Disciplined . . . assess[ing] his or her own resources or skills and those arrayed in opposition . . . a servant of civilization and its future, guiding, protecting, and passing on information and wisdom . . . devoted to causes he or she judges to be more important or greater than the self . . . A warrior knows how precious and fragile life is and does not abuse or profane it . . . [W]arriorhood must be directed toward transcendent goals . . . based upon universal principles and connected to divine and honorable powers and purposes.[13]

In brief, Warriorhood is a state of mind, heart, and spirit matched with a set of practical and physical arts that include knowledge and training in how to kill and are guided in action by a high moral code, used to protect one's people, homes, and highest values, and meant to serve and preserve life.

WARRIOR INITIATION

In traditional societies becoming a warrior was a primary form of initiation into male adulthood. It has been so for millennia. A man became a man and a contributing citizen by first becoming a warrior willing to give his life for the community. During initiation young men, and today young women, are brought face to face with life's ultimate conditions and tested to prove their readiness to serve adult roles and the society beyond themselves.

We have many examples of life-threatening initiation. Think of the Walkabout performed by Australian aborigine youth during which they spend weeks or months alone wandering the Outback. In ancient Athens military training lasted two years, and men served as permanent militia whenever needed and without pay until age sixty. Among many Native American tribes, boys accompanied and assisted warriors during their raids in order to be exposed to and trained for battle before they had to participate. These practices, undergone by almost everyone, constituted initiation. It accomplished the death of the child self and rebirth into adulthood for the individual and the provision of new mature citizens for the society. Giving back was neither optional nor reserved for the few.

Contemporary warrior initiation both replicates these universal dimensions and is uniquely challenging. Military service is one of the few roads to initiation into and training for responsible adulthood left in modern society. The military often serves well as the institution in which young women and men, many displaced or wounded from childhood, learn and practice responsible adult citizenship. This replicates the universal purpose of warrior initiation.

The United States today is transitioning our military into "a profession of arms." Our collective military force is growing smaller and will continue to shrink. It is all volunteer, highly trained, and mobile; heavily armed with and dependent on high-technology weaponry; heavily dependent on pharmaceuticals to keep stressed troops operating; and expected to endure multiple deployments. A career officer said, "I had seven tours in Iraq and Afghanistan so seven of you [civilians] would not have to go." These conditions introduce into service questions we will explore later regarding distance, purpose, resiliency, participation, awareness, approval and support, moral use and practice, and the health of our democracy. For now we understand that we have inherited this contemporary challenge. Andrew Bacevich, an Army officer for twenty-three years and now professor of history writes:

> The approach this nation has taken to wage war since Vietnam (absolving the people from meaningful involvement), along with the way it organizes its army (relying on professionals), has altered the relationship between the military and society in ways that too few Americans seem willing to acknowledge . . . In all the ways that really matter, that relationship has almost ceased to exist.[14]

Later we will explore the consequences of this "divorce."

Any modern recruit must be accepted for service, take an oath, and enter a unique and demanding contract. To make the recruit one of the warrior tribe, the military's intensive indoctrination, training, and service deconstructs the civilian identity. One Iraq combat veteran said, "They took us apart like Spartans and put us back together in their own image." Troops learn discipline and hone physical and combat skills. They surrender autonomy and individuality to complete missions and serve something greater than themselves. They learn the necessity of sacrifice, including of life itself. Troops also become highly trained killers. Many use this training, and all return to civilian life knowing how to kill. They live by devotion to their comrades in arms, commanders, units, nation, and cause. Many military values are quite positive and necessary for the betterment of society. They are often wanting in civilians who never had to learn them or give away years of life.

The initiatory function of warriorhood demonstrates that the identity and role of Warrior is private and public, internal and social, psychological and spiritual. Just as wounds are both visible and invisible, so too are the many ways that our warriors serve and preserve the social order.

THE MEANING OF TRAUMA

The word *trauma* comes directly from ancient Greek. It originally meant a puncture wound, a wound that pierces.[15] An arrow or spear wound was a trauma. Ancient wisdom, including medicine, did not separate body and soul. Instead it taught that wounds occur to both—despair, anguish, loss of faith are as real as broken limbs and stabbings. It also taught that the soul was wounded with the body and must be tended or it will remain wandering, disconnected, or harmed.

In the *Iliad*, when Achilles's battle buddy Patroclus was killed, the invisible wound that pierced Achilles's heart and undid his character was a trauma. When combat vet Richard Boes wrote, "I've got a hole in my soul"[16] or when MASH (Mobile Army Surgical Hospital) unit executive officer Captain Frank Hill wrote from Afghanistan in 2006 of "the weight that leaves a mark," they expressed the violent, painful, and lasting emotional and spiritual penetration called trauma. Trauma is rape of the soul.

In the ancient world, trauma referred especially to a wound to a living being, but it sometimes referred to hurt or damage to things as well. Herodotus used the word for damaged ships.[17] The hole blown in the destroyer USS *Cole* in Yemen on October 12, 2000, by a terrorist bomb was a trauma. The ship's physical trauma emotionally shocked and frightened the entire nation, causing widespread feelings of insecurity, rage, and grief. Though it was a small collective wound compared with the September 11, 2001, attacks, the point is that such impact is collective; the wounds are not only to survivors but spread through families and communities, cultures, and societies.

The Greeks also sometimes used the word *trauma* to indicate a defeat. This may indicate the anger, frustration, displacement, confusion, disheartedness, or waste that survivors may feel after defeat in battle or defeat of their cause. Herodotus called the Spartan defeat at Thermopylae a trauma, even though it was a willing sacrifice.

I received a message on my answering machine from an unidentified veteran. "I read your book," an angry voice declared. "You're full of crap. The only cause of PTSD is losing!" Then the phone slammed down. This veteran echoed the anguish of many over defeat or stalemate: "We were handcuffed," "We won every battle but lost the war," "The protest movement supported the enemy," "The rules of engagement favored the bad guys," "You can't put a timeline on a war."

Not just Afghan War vets but several generations of veterans felt traumatized by the fall of Fallujah in Iraq in January 2014. Adam Banotai, who fought there as a twenty-one-year-old Marine, said, "None of us thought it was going to fall back to a jihadist insurgency. It made me sick to my stomach to have that thrown in our face, everything we fought for so blatantly taken away."[18] Vietnam veteran Chuck Searcy tirelessly directs efforts to defuse unexploded bombs left in Viet Nam. From Ha Noi he wrote, "Looks like Fallujah may become synonymous with Khe Sanh in the history of tragic, wasteful, meaningless military misadventures. And the soldiers who were the pawns will suffer through the rest of their lives struggling to answer the question, 'Why?'" Searcy reflected on the impact of our recent wars on older veterans:

> The wound passes through the generations of our warriors. A friend told me that the invasion of Iraq hit him like a body blow; a debilitating recurrence of PTSD made it difficult for him to work and function for days. *Déjà vu all over again* might be a good Yogi Berra quote to apply.

Some veterans of controversial wars believe that they would not feel wounded if they had been allowed to fight for as long and as many casualties as it took to achieve a military victory, no matter the justice of the cause. These vets unknowingly share this ancient belief that losing a war is traumatizing. They may measure victory by casualty figures or believe that the only good soldier is a winner. They challenge us to examine our own moral bottom line. "Was it worth the cost?"

THE SHADOW

If we consciously, purposefully, wisely educate and prepare our young and inner warriors, if we give them healthy and creative means of expression, if we use them only for moral ends, then the Warrior archetype can develop toward the ideal to serve, protect, preserve, assert, guide, act, and complete. If we do not prepare our warriors well, if we misuse or neglect them, they may rebel, resist, refuse, act out, lose control of, or misuse their warrior training in harmful or destructive ways. They may find distorted expression in violent or antisocial behaviors, dangerous or criminal activities, gang behavior, sexual and substance abuse, or other ways, including political and military. These express the warrior's "shadow," its potential for using innate energies and drives in unconscious and destructive ways. Later we will hear of "the beast." Now we realize that the shadow exists for societies as well as individuals. Carl Jung wrote during both world wars that war is "this uprising of the unconscious destructive forces of the collective unconscious. The result has been mass murder on an unparalleled scale."[19]

As goes the individual into darkness or light, so go cultures and entire civilizations. In whatever version of wilderness we find ourselves, it will be as it always has been. We need our warriors to help guide the way through.

THE WOUNDED WARRIOR

I first met him three decades ago. Much of him looked strong and whole. His face was young, handsome, intent, with a sweep of curly hair. His thighs, torso, and arms were honed and sleek. His left arm thrust forward and his body crouched.

But both his legs were missing below the knees, both arms below the elbows. Above his rippled stomach a great gash cut across his chest, fracturing its cavity and separating his heart and left shoulder from the rest of him, now connected by a rod.

His head too had been knocked off, then restored. Though his eyes, nostrils, and mouth flared, his lips were cracked, his nose was broken, and his skin was torn.

Ravaged and exhausted body. All support knocked out from under him. Mind stunned and confused, repositioned but not restored.
Heart and body separated. Heart broken.

Yet enduring. Striving to protect to the last breath. Resolute against pain and suffering. A will that propels his body beyond its wounds. Strength and devotion that stand their ground until he can stand no more.

This was the spirit I met in a statue called "The Wounded Warrior" in Athens, Greece. Dating to about 280 BCE, it was originally from Delos, a sacred island reserved for pilgrimage and worship.

The warrior displayed his eternal qualities, his wound, struggle, strength, courage, and cry. He had served for righteous reasons—to protect his home and family—and had stood his ground to the last. He epitomizes Chaplain Turner's definition: to "stand, even unto death, in the defense of one who has been knocked down." His devotion and struggle are frozen in marble. In its deformation due to time and conquest we see the skewed mind, broken heart, schism between heart and body, and frozen cry that is the essence of war wounding. The warrior's wound, struggle, resistance, and cry belong to warriors of all times and places.

I lead veterans and survivors on healing journeys to Greece. We visit ancient warrior sites, study history, mythology, and philosophy, and we contemplate artifacts and our own stories. When veterans look on the Wounded Warrior statue they declare, "That's me. That's a portrait of exactly how I am inside." Sometimes sobs wrench out from dark depths.

They perceive a long-gone brother-in-arms and find relief in knowing that the invisible wound is as old as war itself.

In the statue they see the invisible wounded warrior in themselves. They see trauma frozen in marble "for all who have eyes" to witness.

Now we must witness our wounded warriors of today.

CHAPTER 2

The War After War

If people really knew, the war would be stopped tomorrow. But of course they don't know, and can't know.

LLOYD GEORGE, Prime Minister of Great Britain, on hearing a report from the World War I front

Daniel is tall, lanky, with bright eyes and a gift for poetry. He spends countless sleepless hours alone and is often exhausted upon waking or from routine chores. He gets sudden crippling headaches. He forgets names and confuses events and numbers. Some of his thinking abilities are deteriorating as if he were an old man. He often has searing gut pain, toilet difficulties, and is never sure what is safe to eat. All these symptoms came home with him from Iraq, where he was exposed to depleted uranium weapons and breathed their toxic dust. Daniel sadly says, "Radiation poisoning." By his late twenties he began planning for an early death.

Few of us know about our veterans' daily struggles to survive, endure, and adapt once they return home. Combat may last weeks, months, a year, or several years and deployments in today's wars. But what about the lives of the rest of our veterans and their families?

GIs are returning from our new wars with severe physical wounds that we have not yet seen in public. Entire classes of invisible wounds are coming home as well—Traumatic Brain Injury (TBI), Military Sexual Trauma (MST), and Post-traumatic Stress Disorder (PTSD). Brain injury and sexual trauma both involve PTSD to significant degrees and may have similar symptoms: insomnia; nightmares; rages; flashbacks; hypervigilance; difficulties concentrating, organizing, and focusing; intimacy and employment challenges; and more. Veterans of recent wars may have any or all of these wounds in crippling combinations. When we refer to war trauma we include all these invisible wounds.

PTSD is the name of a syndrome and its list of symptoms, not the portrait of a human being. What is the shape of a life after war? Why does the war imprint remain for a lifetime even though the time spent in its deadly zone was short in comparison? Why can't they "just get on with it"? How does the soul collapse or heal from war in all the decades after its time in "the valley of the shadow"? What will become of our new veterans like Daniel? How will they and their families fare tomorrow and in ten, twenty, thirty years if they do not receive all they need to truly heal and return home?

We must look together at the full scope of war's costs and consequences to our new wounded warriors and to our war-weary nation and world. George Washington said, "The future of our Armed Services and the future of our country will be integrally linked with how we take care of our veterans." War's costs, consequences, and the responsibility to address them belong to us all. We must embrace our veterans' wounding as ours. We will explore why this is so.

" . . . BEAUTIFUL FRIEND, THE END . . . "[1]

I hadn't seen him since the days of the combat veterans' therapy program I had directed in a remote mountain village. Then he was squat and strong, full bearded and sharp-eyed. He played guitar for hospital-bound disabled vets. He practiced Native American prayers and rituals with his Ojibwa partner. That was twenty years ago.

Now Walt was a pale sack of bones fading to nothing on the cold frame and mattress of his Veterans Administration hospital bed.

In Vietnam, Walt had been condemned to the zone he named "the place of no beauty." His yearlong tour of duty was encapsulated in his memory as an intolerable act committed without choice in an unbearable reality.

The war never left Walt. It pursued him through nightmares, suicide attempts, homelessness, guilt, despair, broken families, and failed careers.

The war had broken his heart; its unseen pain had ambushed him with three heart attacks by the time he was forty. Daniel expects an early death from radiation sickness; kidney cancer due to Agent Orange exposure was killing Walt in his late fifties.

I heard this news at a Hospice consultation. I sped to the hospital and rushed to his room. Walt was splayed under a thin sheet, motionless and skeletal. His shallow breath wheezed in and out. I sat next to him, looked into his ragged face, and took his limp hand. I waited and remembered it all, as if we had parted yesterday.

Born on Long Island, Walt was the only child of a German father who had served in the Wehrmacht, the regular German army, during World War II. He immigrated to the United States soon after. The family said that Walt was their only member born in freedom.

As a boy, Walt had been "the Nazi," "the kraut," the "bad guy" in war games he played with his friends. "I volunteered to go to Vietnam to finally be one of the good guys," he had said. "I went to earn my family's place in America. I couldn't have known how wrong I was."

Walt became a heavy machine operator during the war. Two memories returned again and again, when he was awake and in nightmares. Walt still saw, smelled, and felt the rank mud, dead leaves, stubs of trees, and blasted hillside on which he had lived, worked, and fought for a year. This "place of no beauty," as he called it, was not the country of Viet Nam but our American creation. He declared, "Any soul condemned to such a place shrivels up and dies."

His second memory was personal. To prepare for a senior officer's inspection, Walt was ordered to move rotting enemy bodies from a mass grave with his backhoe. "The stench has never left my nostrils," he confessed. "It doesn't matter that they were enemy dead or that I was following orders. I desecrated the dead. That is one of the greatest sins a human being can commit. The moment I dipped my hoe into that pile of bodies I lost my soul."

Walt came home to supportive parents grateful that he was alive. He tried college, several careers, marriage, and fatherhood. Nothing worked. He could not sleep. He wandered the continent, living in run-down motel rooms or apartments. He met a Native woman whose disenfranchised past, damaged tradition, and wandering mirrored his. Her people accepted Walt as one of their own. He practiced their spiritual ways. He prayed for those souls he had desecrated.

During his thirties he had three massive heart attacks. Each nearly killed him.

"I sinned in Viet Nam," he reiterated. "This is payback. The universe takes its due. There is no escape."

Walt survived, but his partner often returned home to find him drunk on their couch. A few times she found him with a shotgun's muzzle in his mouth.

"You were lucky," some vets in our therapy group told him. "You only had to move dead meat, not kill anyone." Others said, "You found a spiritual path. At least you've got something to believe in." A few asked for his guidance praying in the Native way. "Maybe I offered some comfort to my brothers," he had concluded. "But I failed as a man, a son, a husband, a father, an American patriot, and I've never had a career. I'm leaving behind no legacy, nothing of value."

I sat beside his hospital bed. I held his frail hand and looked into his exhausted face. His poor health was now killing him, along with lifelong despair and emptiness of meaning and legacy. This had been shaped by violence and trauma to his family in two wars over three generations on three continents. Walt's big, hope-filled heart had been shattered.

"Thank you for visiting," the floor nurse said to me as I sat in his barren room. "It's good that somebody remembers."

Walt's eyes fluttered open. I smiled and said hello.

For a long time Walt didn't answer. "Ed?" he finally asked.

"Yes, Walt. Hello . . . I'm glad to see you again but sad that it's this way."

Nothing moved but his eyes and lips. I asked if he could think, if he knew what was happening. He explained in a strained whisper that when he had the energy to stay awake, yes, he could think and was aware. But he could not even take his hand out of mine or move a leg for comfort.

"Why are you here?" he asked.

"Because brotherhood is forever," I said. "Because I remember and honor you and your story."

"Brotherhood," he mumbled. "When everything else is gone, we still have that." He paused, then asked, "But why me? There's nothing worth remembering."

"I want to thank you," I said, "for giving everything. For sacrificing everything to serve. For not dehumanizing the enemy but remembering they were people with souls too. For grieving them your entire life. For trying to give comfort to their dead and to our brother vets. For finding a way to pray again. I honor you and thank you."

A spark briefly ignited his dark eyes. "I didn't know anybody could find anything of worth in the life I've lived."

"Oh yes," I said. "Your life meant something. You mean something." He smiled faintly. "May I carry your story?" I asked. "May I tell others?"

"Yes!" Urgency flared in his voice. "Please. Give it away. Make it mean something. Maybe it can warn or protect some other poor soul."

Through his window we watched the colors fade in the evening sky. I promised I would do all I could to give his story meaning, to ensure that war would not have the final word after all. Then we said a difficult last goodbye.

Walt had wanted to redeem his family's past and earn them a home by serving their new country with honor. He had wanted a loving home where he could raise good children and continue the family line. He had wanted education and a career that gave something back to the world. His parents had wanted peace and belonging after their sad past. But it had come to this—Walt alone, fading into oblivion in an anonymous hospital bed, the end of his family line.

Eight men had been in our combat veterans therapy group in 1990. Ray had died of brain cancer and Preston of liver disease, both from Agent Orange exposure. Jim had died alone in his forties of a heart attack in his mountain cabin. At his funeral his parents had said, "Our son was killed in Viet Nam. It just took time for the war to catch up." Walt was the fourth of eight to die early of the war after the war. Two others were rated as psychologically disabled and unable to work. By the time we reached our late fifties, our group had a 75 percent post-war casualty rate, replicating the statistics for the entire generation of Vietnam War veterans. Many baby-boomers are living longer, healthier lives. In contrast, it is believed that only one-third of the 2.7 million troops who served in Viet Nam during the war are still alive. Mortality from diseases, suicides, accidents, and overdoses are significantly higher among veterans than their civilian counterparts.[2]

My four men and all the others will not appear in official statistics. Their names will never be etched on the Vietnam Veterans Memorial Wall in Washington, D.C. Are we not responsible to count as war casualties anyone who dies of its wounds no matter how long after service?

MORE WOUNDS THAN WE CAN TEND

Captain Candy was an Army mental-health officer for a brigade of 5,000 troops. She wrote me during her first Iraq deployment:

> There is never a break from the needs of these soldiers. One of mine just attempted to kill himself and ended up on a breathing machine . . . Within twenty-four hours of release from a medical unit he ate a handful of aspirins. I dealt with him all morning yesterday. I had him restrained and taken to another place. They put him back into the same conditions that caused him to overdose in the first place. I deal with emergencies like this daily without any support.

Captain Candy later reflected on the impact of service:

> I was deployed to Iraq twice. I left my family and friends and people who for the most part have no clue what this work or war feel like. I think about the troops overseas and tell myself that at least I am alive with some people who care. But the mental health needs of our troops require 24/7 coverage, and on my base there was only me. Even on leave I never escaped.

It would be tragic enough if Walt's and Candy's stories were only about veterans. But vets are not the only ones whose sacrifices and losses we must recognize. The English poet John Milton wrote, "They also serve who only stand and wait." War's aftermath reaches those who remain behind awaiting their loved one's return. Waiting is also a form of service that entails suffering and sacrifice with accompanying fear, grief, and loss. Worse, waiting can contribute to severe consequences such as depression, despair, broken marriages and families, troubled children, even death.

Terry Bell was a Ranger captain commanding a combat rifle company in the Central Highlands during the Vietnam War. He reports:

> Forty years ago my first son was born. Three days later I deployed to Viet Nam. How little I knew then of the devastating impact my war-fighting would have on my young family and myself. After twenty years, my wife divorced me—confident that I was not the man she had married. I was not.
>
> Today my son lives with his wife and my first two grandchildren. I have not seen or heard from them for nearly ten years. My heart has yearned to be reconciled with them—to be forgiven by them for bringing my war home.
>
> In 2003, I ended thirty-six years of denial and dysfunction by accepting VA care for my severe PTSD. My current wife and I learned how war's horrors had affected me and, in turn, my family. Disability compensation followed. I began to understand how pervasive combat's effects had been for forty years.

Survivors and their families whose fates replicate Daniel's, Walt's, and Terry's are found in every corner of our country and from all our wars.

VETERANS' FAMILIES

Poet Spencer Reece is the grandson of a family that moved to Oak Ridge, Tennessee, during World War II to work on the Manhattan Project. An entire secret city was created for these families, and Spencer's father grew up there. As his grandfather worked on bomb research, both he and Spencer's young father became increasingly withdrawn. His grandmother and her girlfriends became chain-smokers and heavy drinkers. When the atomic bomb was dropped on Japan, Spencer wrote about it in a poem: "everyone was quiet . . . the quiet of the exhausted and the innocent. The quietness inside my father . . . would come to define him."[3]

To comprehend the scope of challenges upon returning home from war, consider these vignettes of a few of our post-9/11 survivors and family members.

Couples

Patty, Susie, and Lisa dragged their husbands in for therapy. Each partner had gone to Iraq or Afghanistan believing in the wars. One couple lived a mile from the Flight 93 crash site in Pennsylvania on 9/11. That husband declared, "I enlisted to get revenge. They almost hit my home."

Each serviceman had become disillusioned overseas. "They weren't the real enemy," one Iraq veteran reported. "How can I behave honorably when our commander-in-chief is a liar?" A patriotic vet said, "I wanted to go after the people responsible for 9/11. But we attacked the wrong people for the wrong reasons." An Afghanistan veteran confessed, "Yes, I killed civilians. The way we treat them only makes us more enemies." And another, "They don't want us there. You can't create a democracy by violence and force."

By the time each of these Iraq or Afghanistan veterans had been home less than a year, they were drinking bottles of hard liquor daily. They were unable to attend college or work and lived exhausted from nightmares and sleeplessness. Their families felt threatened by their rages, depression, and despair. Each was unable to bond or communicate well. Each was given large doses of medications to quell symptoms. Each had a difficult time getting evaluations, benefits, treatment, or counseling. One Iraq vet reported that his VA counselor lectured him, "You're hopeless. You can't heal. PTSD will be with you for the rest of your life. Learn to live with it." The vet's response: long dreary days, increased drinking, marriage failing.

Patty, Susie, Lisa, and their families were in despair. No one knew how to talk with or help their vet. Each sometimes came home to a drunk or depressed partner threatening suicide. "Every day at work I live with the fear that I'll find him dead on the couch when I come home," Susie said.

These survivors' fear and helplessness were compounded by anger at our country. "My boyfriend left as a strong, proud, patriotic, handsome man. He came home a wrecked shell," Lisa exclaimed. "Is this what we have to live with for the rest of our lives?" Parents and in-laws offered financial assistance and places to live when their children were destitute. None of the couples foresaw having children; childlessness is yet another uncounted casualty of war. "My husband is like a sick child," Susie said. "He needs constant support and care. His rages put us both in danger. We can't bring children into this." Each spouse feared an incomplete and dependent marriage and each family feared their line coming to an end.

Parents, Siblings, and Grandparents

Spouses are not the only family members who struggle with deployment and post-deployment issues. In fact, they sometimes get more support or attention than other relations. Jo, the mother of a helicopter pilot on his fifth deployment, reported:

> Parents and siblings are impacted by war in ways that may be less obvious and are for the most part ignored or minimized by the military and civilians. We parents and siblings seem invisible. We quickly learn that the military does not consider us as "family." Longtime friends don't hang around when we are involved in wars that last this long. The military culture and wives, girlfriends, friends, and civilians often give "the silent treatment" to parents and siblings. We are excluded day in and day out as we stumble along trying to figure out how to keep our lives together with little information or support before, during, and after our loved one deploys. They ignore us and hope we stay quiet while they focus on spouses and children.

Sarah was deployed to Iraq in the medical corps. Her daughter was two when she left, three when she returned. A stranger rather than a mother came home; primal bonding had snapped. Mother and daughter are struggling to create a connection that should have been treated as sacrosanct. In addition to war grief, Sarah carries grief from lost mothering and from wounding to her child that she fears may be with them for life.

Kris, the mother of an eighteen-year-old soldier, received a cell phone call from her son in the middle of a firefight. Amidst the sounds of gunfire and explosions, Kris heard her son scream, "Mom, help! I'm shooting civilians to get the enemy. The enemy is shooting civilians to get me. The only people I want in my sights are the politicians who put us here. Someone stop it all!" Then the phone went dead. Kris did not know for several days that her son had survived the fight.

"I felt like I was there, killing those civilians," Kris cried. "My son has killed and tells me I don't know him now. What is happening to him? How can I help? What is happening to me? To our country? I don't know who we are anymore."

Joan, a soldier's sister, said that each time her brother deploys, "It is like a glass wall goes up between me and the rest of the world, and I just watch as life goes by. It is like being held in suspended animation. It is a lonely place."

One pair of grandparents in their late sixties had two grandchildren left in their care while their son and daughter-in-law both served downrange. The children cried all the time, were failing in school, had no playmates, and were plagued by nightmares and sleeplessness. "We've been to counselors and school officials," the elders reported. "Everyone knows it's the war but not what to do about it." They could find no peers with similar stories either for their grandchildren or themselves. "This war," they said, "is destroying three generations of our family."

Jo summarized the impact of being not a "military mom" but what she renames a "war mom." Her words resonate with all "war families."

> What is normal about letting a loved one go off to war? When a loved one is deployed, the "letting go" includes worry about IEDs (improvised explosive device) or RPGs (rocket-propelled grenade), being shot at or shot down, sleep deprivation, extreme temperatures, lack of food, becoming a prisoner. There is a possibility that our loved one could come home in a flag-draped coffin. Much of our lives are lived in a state of shock as we experience firsthand what war is really like. The responses we usually get from an uneducated public or from military personnel are so hurtful or inappropriate that we stop talking to anyone and remain silent. Perhaps the most heartbreaking

> experience is when parents and siblings are told that a spouse or significant other will not allow us to attend a fifteen-minute Family Goodbye ceremony or Family Welcome Home Ceremony because now they are the family. We are on a solitary journey—without a road map!

Stories like these do not commonly get media attention. There are no suicides, murders, "accidental deaths," overdoses, or war-induced illnesses. There is no criminal behavior. But there is a terrible toll in divorces, illnesses, domestic violence, abuse or neglect, promiscuity, insomnia, nightmares, unemployment, substance abuse, and other difficulties these new veterans, their families, and our nation will face. Let us examine this composite cost.

CHAPTER 3

War Wounds Us All

Wars bring scars.

BENJAMIN FRANKLIN

We have heard stories of how our wars have affected, even unto death, our old and new vets and their families. But our picture is incomplete. We must contemplate the scope of war suffering affecting us all—every community and pocketbook, our entire nation, and the world. We have more than enough stories and research to create a composite portrait of the impact of war on society.

WITNESSING THE WOUNDED SPIRIT

This book is not an interminable record of personal stories of grief and loss or disturbed, incomplete, and wasted lives among veteran and civilian populations resulting from war. It is certainly not about their statistics. Research and testimony of such losses appear in our media regularly, and many books detail throat-choking combat and survival stories. Responsible advocates, publications, and organizations strive to expose this situation to the public. In fact, we are bombarded with so many sorrowful stories that our citizenry is becoming numb. "This is what happens when you have an unengaged population whose focus starts to shift away," said Tom Tarantino of Iraq and Afghanistan Veterans of America.[1] Our troops know the nation is turning away from them. They feel misunderstood, neglected, abandoned, and betrayed. Many become desperate.

During wartime Abraham Lincoln believed "tenaciously" in the "necessity of perfect unity of popular opinion and action."[2] In contrast, Andrew Slater, in combat in both Iraq and Afghanistan, said, "Iraq was the first major war that wasn't a national experience, but something a particular piece of America went through."[3] When we are not united as a nation in pursuit of a necessary, shared goal demanding collective sacrifice; when we feel helpless in changing or responding to war's crises and casualty lists; when it does not express our values and beliefs; when a society is internally in turmoil over the righteousness or necessity of a military action; when we seriously question whether our leaders are telling us the truth, leading us astray, or pursuing unjust ends, then any of us may become a depressed casualty.

The wound that today we call PTSD may not be primarily to the individual but to the body politic, the nation's soul. Individual servicemen and women who enact the nation's policies may collapse because they are made to carry the collective wound as though it were their individual pathological condition to be treated and endure. We expend much time, effort, and resources on symptoms. We diagnose, then attempt to eradicate or control them. We thus overload individual vets with responsibility for their own suffering and miss the full portrait of war.

We do not treat war's invisible wounds effectively because for many reasons we do not understand them accurately. We have inherited the trance and denial, what Robert McNamara called "the fog of war." The misinterpretations of our times prevent us from seeing what is in front of us.

The United States has been involved in an endless series of wars and smaller violent military engagements since its founding and in every generation. Though most Americans are only aware of our major wars, the fact is that the United States has been in some form of armed conflict in almost every year of its existence, with only about a dozen years, including the Great Depression, free of violent military action.

Many of our parents, grandparents, and great-grandparents were traumatized in wars and by violence and oppression in their countries of origin. Some may have gained admittance or citizenship to America by serving in the military. Our ancestors passed on the impact of collective and unhealed trauma as if it were the normal flow of life. We are all inheritors of transgenerational trauma. Not only in American history but also for the last 5,000 years of human history war has been so common that we have accepted it as normal and ignored its extensive consequences. We do not know what humans, or a society, or American society untraumatized by war look like. Many believe that war is inevitable.

Neither have we studied war, warriorhood, or post-war healing in other cultures or eras. Rather, we measure everything against recent American experience and our scientific, technological, economic, and consumerist mindset.[4] Further, people are generally shy, scared, or reluctant to engage veterans where they hurt. Finally, "Nobody likes to talk about war," said Chaplain Col. Michael Lembke. "Civilians don't and soldiers don't. But we have to do it, and we know our citizens are not watching."

But we can let "the spirit" of war trauma speak to us. If we listen and understand it aright, if we truly let our veterans and their wounds have their say, we may hear what they are trying to tell us. Then we may develop a vision and respond in ways that restore and transform.

And how do survivors want us to hear them? Not as disabled or less, not as throwaways, not with our complicated explanations of psychological and cerebral malfunctioning, but as whole people with honorable and necessary stories that must be shared. In her poem "Sentry," veteran healer Kate Dahlstedt voiced this attitude, which she offers to all survivors in our restoration work with veterans:

I look into your soft eyes as you hold up your tattered shield—
to keep me from seeing . . .
The Beast
fangs dripping . . .
and you with nowhere to run . . .

But don't think I can't hear
the desperate howl behind your silence,
the crashing of your heart on the jungle floor.

It is you I really want to see,
even when it hurts . . .

I ache to hold your broken heart,
and sing and rock and rest . . .
So, I keep vigil outside your door . . .
humming the ancient Warrior Song
all night long.[5]

WAR SURVIVORS: HUMAN PORTRAITS

"Would you bring a gladiator home to meet your parents over dinner?" challenged one Special Forces vet. When war is our subject we may be contemplating a "gladiator," not a person of ordinary stature and experience to whom we readily and comfortably know how to relate.

Contemplate a composite portrait of war's survivors. Meet these women and men. Listen to their stories. Keep your heart open to the statistics we must hear and do not let them numb you; they represent countless human stories. Many troops and veterans still see dead children and smell burning flesh. They stare in horror at the legions of the slain. They are in shock at the results of war and also at learning what they, and every one of us, are capable of doing. They are in shock at betrayal and abandonment by the homeland they served. Their minds are in confusion as to who they are now. They cannot get their bearings in this civilian world so different from the military culture and wars in which they served.

Listen to their parents, spouses, and children. Spouses are in despair. They don't understand their vet partner. They don't understand why ordinary life does not satisfy, why he or she feels closer to other vets than to family, why their vet does not appreciate the sacrifices they made to wait at home alone. They don't know how to engage their vet in healing. They are often victims of abuse who tolerate it hoping that love and loyalty will heal what war took away. They wonder where the husband, wife, parent, or child they sent off to war has disappeared to—and why someone they do not know has returned.

Children cry or hide during parents' rages and cower during screaming nightmares. They can't concentrate in school. They have inexplicable behavior problems and lack friends facing similar challenges. Adult children of vets discover that they have "holes in their hearts" from missing parenting.

About the quality of life in our modern war zones, Captain Candy wrote from Iraq, "I hate this place . . . I hate being here and putting up with all the crap. I can't say anything to anyone so I have to keep it all inside . . . There is so much anger and rage here . . . Reminds me of *Lord of the Flies* at times."

About PTSD, Ayelet Burman-Cohen, an Israeli air force vet who after service became a photographer covering military funerals, writes:

> PTSD is our legend, our hell, our Garden of Eden.
> PTSD is collecting us into her long arms.
> We are both captive and holding on . . .
> We belong to it, we love it . . .
> And we fall asleep hiding in the breath of war.[6]

About growing up with a father who was a World War II concentration camp liberator, Leila Levinson writes, "I absorbed my father's terror and carried it with me into adulthood, into the home I created with my husband and children." Leila concluded sixty years after the war, "Our whole family is Hitler's victims also."[7]

About the struggle to come home, Iraq vet and songwriter Jason Moon sings,

> How do they expect a man to do the things that I have
> and come back and still be the same? . . .
> The child inside me is long dead and gone.
> I'm somewhere between lost and alone,
> trying to find my way home."[8]

THE COSTS

Suicide

We have horrifying numbers of suicides from our recent wars. Yet as bad as the reports are, the suicide rate among veterans is likely much higher. Many after-conflict deaths result from self-inflicted wounds, accidents, legal or illegal drug overdoses, or alcoholism—with no messages left behind.

In my region there have been several recent suicides. A middle-aged father found his nineteen-year-old son hanging in their basement just weeks after returning from Afghanistan. The son left a note saying he could not live with the memories of what he saw and did in the war. In another family a husband and wife were both National Guard officers. The husband deployed while his wife waited at home. Upon his return she deployed. The woman soldier became depressed. Overseas she was put on antidepressants, which were revoked when she left. "We don't want you to go home a medical statistic," she was told. Upon returning, she committed suicide. Her death was said to be from depression, not PTSD.[9]

Family members and caregivers can be at risk. Captain Candy reports that she had to take especially good care of family survivors at home on the one-year anniversary of the funeral of a soldier she helped bury. "I was so afraid the dad was going to harm himself," she says. The next night the father almost shot himself. Captain Candy "could tell he was hurting," and she went beyond her duties to visit the family off base and do follow-up interventions for several days. She counseled the family that it is healthy to feel painful emotions but not to end your life.

These are not isolated cases. Overall in the United States, approximately one in four people who commit suicide are veterans.[10] Every year as of 2007, over 1,000 veterans being treated within the Veterans Administration system, and 5,000 in total, commit suicide.[11] The suicide risk for all male veterans from any war is more than double that of the civilian population.[12] The risk for young veterans, aged seventeen to twenty-four, is four times higher.[13]

During the Vietnam War, about 58,200 service people died in the war. Of that number, 382 were in-country suicides.[14] Since the end of the Vietnam War, at least twice and perhaps three times as many veterans have committed suicide as were killed during the conflict.[15]

Forty-nine thousand veterans committed suicide between 2005 and 2011.[16] Among recent returnees, reports about their suicides come from every corner of the United States as well as from other countries with troops in combat in Iraq and Afghanistan.[17] In Iraq alone, one in five noncombat deaths were due to suicide.[18] Now Army suicide rates set records as the highest ever. In 2006 almost one-third of its ninety-nine suicides occurred in Iraq and Afghanistan. Failed relationships, legal and financial troubles, work stress, and deployment time all contributed. By May 2007, 107 troops had committed suicide while in country.[19] The magnitude of the problem prompted the Army to begin records of suicide attempts for the first time. There were almost 1,000 in 2006.[20]

The United States has had more than 6,000 total combat deaths in Iraq and Afghanistan, but twenty-two veterans are committing suicide every day, almost one an hour.[21] Now more than 6,500 veterans kill themselves every year, a far higher toll than the total number killed in the full lengths of the Iraq and Afghanistan Wars combined.[22] The suicide rate for women who deployed tripled between 2003 and 2008 to 15.2 per 100,000.[23] The year 2012 was the worst to date for active duty military suicides. In all our military branches, 349 service members took their own lives compared with 295 combat deaths.[24] This accounts for more GI suicides in one year in Afghanistan than in the entire Vietnam War. This increasing trend has been documented for, among others, British veterans of both the Falkland Islands and First Gulf Wars, Norwegian troops in United Nations forces in Lebanon, and some countries involved in the Balkan Wars.[25] In these modern wars many more veterans die from suicide *after* their wars than were actually killed in combat during them. Troop suicide is "now more lethal than combat."[26]

Accidental Deaths

He was my parents' childhood friend, a year or two older than them. During World War II he joined the Air Force, completing twenty-five bombing missions in Flying Fortresses over Europe in a service that had a 50 percent casualty rate. He died in a motorcycle accident within a week of returning home. "Everyone knew it was suicide," my mother said.

Many veterans die in violent ways after violent service. Accidents ("unconscious suicides") and criminal activity ("death by cop") may have military or combat-generated components. Iraq and Afghanistan veterans have a 75 percent higher rate of fatal motor vehicle accidents than nonvets. They are more at risk in the months following deployment, and those serving multiple tours are the highest risk.[27] "Accidental deaths" may mean that the terrible veteran suicide rate is even higher than we know. Nobody can be sure how many of these incidents are "accidents."[28]

Homicide and Criminality

Ken grew up on Long Island, enthusiastically joined the military after high school, and served a full combat infantry tour in Afghanistan. He returned home, was discharged, and soon entered college in an upstate city.

One dark night, an armed street gang attacked Ken in his apartment building. He grabbed a kitchen knife for defense and backed the intruders onto the street. They surrounded him. He "went on automatic," took a defensive position, and fought as he had been trained for combat. He slew one attacker.

At Ken's trial the judge declared that military history was irrelevant and refused to allow expert testimony. Ken was sentenced to prison for manslaughter.

Veterans are involved in homicide and other violent criminal activities in significantly higher numbers than their civilian counterparts.

In June 2001 the United States government resumed the use of the death penalty. Two of the first federal executions were of Gulf War veterans. First was Timothy McVeigh, the convicted Oklahoma City bomber. The second was Louis Jones, convicted of raping and murdering a servicewoman. He was a decorated Special Forces veteran who had parachuted under fire into Grenada, was a frontline combatant in the first Gulf War, and had PTSD. Jones appealed directly to President Bush for clemency based on his exposure to nerve gas and suffering from the Gulf War syndrome. His appeal was rejected.[29] In England in 2006, forty-one-year-old Gulf War veteran David Bradley murdered his uncle, aunt, and two cousins, then turned himself into the police. Years earlier he had reported his inability to cope with memories of four comrades' deaths during his 1991 service in the Gulf War.[30]

"No one tallies the number of soldiers and veterans in the criminal justice system," declared one report chronicling six murders by Iraq combat vets. "So it's impossible to know how many criminal cases involving Iraq war veterans are pending."[31] I have served as a defense witness for troops and veterans with firearms, assault and battery, destruction of property, substance abuse, and murder charges when their crimes may have been related to combat service and its resultant PTSD.

As of 1998, according to the Department of Justice, out of a national veteran population of over 25 million, 225,000 veterans were held in federal and state prisons. About 56,500 were Vietnam War-era veterans and 18,500 were Persian Gulf War-era vets. Of these, 20 percent reported serving combat duty and 16 percent were dishonorably discharged. Among other findings: veterans were more likely than nonvets to be in prison for a violent offense; alcohol was more likely to be involved in veteran crimes; while the number of veterans in the United States was declining, the number in prisons was rising; sex offenders constituted one-third of the prisoners held in military correctional facilities; veterans had less extensive previous criminal records and were more likely to report mental illnesses than civilians.[32] By 2004 the Department of Justice found that 57 percent of imprisoned veterans were incarcerated for a violent offense, a rate 10 percent higher than nonveterans.[33] More recent Department of Justice statistics estimate 223,000 veterans in prison, most from the Vietnam War era.[34]

Great Britain's wars in the Falklands, Northern Ireland, the Persian Gulf, Bosnia, Iraq, and Afghanistan have combined to create "shockingly high numbers of veteran soldiers in the prison population."[35] A 1994 study found that 41 percent of all British veterans had spent some time in prison.[36] Recent studies from the UK conclude that young men who "served in the British military are about three times more likely than civilians to have committed a violent offense." Contributing factors were violent behavior before enlisting, combat duty, witnessing traumatic events during deployment, misusing alcohol afterward, and age of deployment. Men under thirty were at significantly higher risk.[37] It seems irrefutable that war abroad contributes to violent and criminal activity at home.

Substance Abuse

It is tragic yet true that many veteran organization posts and chapters serve as "watering holes"—a place to gather to drink, tell stories, and escape from the alienating civilian world. Troops and vets need time and space to be alone together. And from time immemorial vets have used drinking and drugging to loosen the tongue and cope with the pain of war memories.

Many veterans use legal and illegal substances for relief from physical and emotional pain, depression, despair, helplessness, and other conditions, turning to such relief in higher percentages than nonvets. The Substance Abuse and Mental Health Services Administration reported in 2003 that on a monthly basis more veterans used marijuana, were heavy alcohol users and received more treatment for substance abuse than comparable nonveterans.[38] Additionally, general alcohol use, driving while intoxicated, and smoking were all significantly higher among vets.[39] The US government estimated that in 2002 and 2003 two million veterans, 8 percent of all veterans, abused alcohol or illicit drugs.[40] Army research found that alcohol misuse rose from 13 percent to 21 percent among soldiers one year after returning from Iraq and Afghanistan.[41] Countless troops testify that they were given many drugs downrange to cope with combat zone difficulties—to go to sleep, to wake up, to get psyched for high-intensity combat, to not feel pain, to forget acts they judge to be wrong. They returned home dependent or addicted.

Marriage Difficulties and Divorce

I worked with David, a Navy Seabee whose homecoming was to an empty house. His wife took their two children and all their belongings and left just before he arrived home. David's welcome home was only a note from his wife saying she could tell he was developing PTSD downrange and did not want to live with or expose their children to it. "In Iraq I did all I could to hold myself together," he said. "Picturing my family got me through. But I felt something vital, my soul, just fly out of me when I opened the door on that emptiness." David wrote a single poem upon return: "This is what I got for going to war / A handful of medals, nothing more . . . " and, "I can't love my medals / They'll never love me . . . "

Like the other issues we have named, marital difficulties and divorce rates are higher among veterans. I have worked with veterans who have been married and divorced not just twice but three, four, and even five times. Their rages, hypervigilance, sleep disorders, mistrust, difficulty communicating, domestic violence, sexual hungers or abstinence, substance abuse, and closest intimacy with other veterans and their dead rather than family members all contribute to the erosion of the marriage relationship.

Army researchers have found that soldiers with anger and aggression issues increased from 11 percent to 22 percent, and those planning to divorce their spouse rose from 9 percent to 15 percent after time in the combat zone.[42] Studies have shown that "since the mid-nineteenth century, wars have delayed, accelerated and undermined American marriages . . . " World War II veterans were more likely to divorce than nonvets, the risks greater for those who saw combat and those who entered service later in life.[43] Among all veterans, "the marriages of the men who actually served in combat were sixty-two percent more likely to end in divorce or separation."[44]

Korean War vets have had a 26 percent higher likelihood of divorce than their nonveteran counterparts,[45] the highest rate overall of recent American wars. Among Vietnam veterans, shortly after that war ended, the President's Commission on Mental Health concluded, "Thirty-eight percent of the marriages of Vietnam veterans broke up within six months of their return . . . "[46] This indicates the degree of vulnerability intimate relationships experience immediately upon return of a spouse from the combat zone. One study found that over 70 percent of Vietnam veterans with PTSD and their partners reported significant relationship distress compared with only about 30 percent of the non-PTSD couples. These couples reported that "they had more problems in their relationships, more difficulties with intimacy, and had taken more steps toward separation and divorce than the non-PTSD veterans and their partners. The degree of relationship distress was correlated with the severity of veterans' PTSD symptoms, particularly emotional numbing."[47]

Iraq and Afghanistan Veterans of American (IAVA) noted "a brief but significant spike in divorce rates at the start of the Iraq War."[48] The Army divorce rate doubled between 2001 and 2004 . . . officers' marriages were particularly hard hit.[49] These data only included troops still serving—not the almost 700,000 Iraq and Afghanistan veterans "who have left the military and who, without the social safety net associated with active-duty military life, might be more likely to divorce."[50]

Impact on Children

Christal Presley grew up with a veteran father who spent his days locked in his room vacillating between depression, alcohol abuse, and rage. She felt lonely, unloved, isolated. She relentlessly picked scabs, was tortured by nightmares, and had serious problems performing, concentrating, or behaving in school. She and all her family members kept their father's service and their suffering a closely guarded secret. Christal has recently been pioneering the awareness that adult children of veterans have special identities, wounds, and needs.

Whether children lose a parent during service or must adjust to family difficulties during deployment and upon return, troops' and veterans' children may suffer from the impact of war.

During the Vietnam War 95,992 children lost a parent while 39,422 women became widows.[51] By 2007 more than 19,000 children had a parent wounded since September 11, and 2,200 children had lost a parent in Afghanistan or Iraq.[52]

Deployment may increase the rate of child abuse. One study found that rates of child abuse at Texas military bases doubled soon after deployments began.[53] Another found that having a spouse in a combat zone vastly increased the rate of maltreatment of children. The majority of abuse and neglect was perpetrated by the civilian spouse left behind, demonstrating the degree of stress that partners live with and the ripple effect it has through families.[54] We must also contemplate the strain on children of having a parent in the war zone or torn apart afterward. One Muslim wife of a man imprisoned in the Serbian concentration camps wrote about their son, "When he eats he always puts a plate and silverware next to his place and says, 'This is for my dad' . . . He doesn't eat well, and he's lost a lot of weight. He only eats when I tell him to for your sake . . . He's already too grown up."[55]

War's wounds can accumulate over time and impact children born after their parents' wars. Bob, a Marine in Viet Nam, and Lynn, an in-country nurse, were both exposed to Agent Orange. Lynn's children and grandchildren have congenital defects and learning disabilities associated with dioxin, which passed on to her daughters through her breast milk. Bob's granddaughter was born with defective kidneys due to his exposure. He died in January 2014 at age sixty-one from related cancers.

In Viet Nam, 35,000 babies are born every year with severe birth defects due to Agent Orange spraying more than four decades ago. Since the Vietnam War's end, to date more than 50,000 people have been killed in Southeast Asia and 70,000 maimed by mines and bombs America left behind.[56] In the United States too, as we hear from Bob and Lynn, Agent Orange birth defects appear in children or grandchildren of veterans.

War may even affect us in the womb, across the generations and unconsciously. The trauma field now recognizes transgenerational trauma, also referred to as collective, historical, cultural, or ancestral trauma. Jungian analyst Dr. Roger Woolger, famous for his development of past-life regression therapy, reported the impact of war on his own development *in utero*.[57] Dr. Woolger was conceived in England during World War II. The family lived about eighty miles south of London under the flight path for German bombers that, harried by British fighter planes, often ditched their bombs to make a quicker retreat. The bombs sometimes fell on their town. Dr. Woolger confessed that he had a strong and irrational fear of fire that had no source other than this wartime experience. His phobia, he declared, is evidence of war's impact even on developing fetuses and the "psychic residue" it leaves in whomever it touches.[58]

Children of veterans often have nightmares, deep fears, severe anxiety, social and school troubles, attention difficulties, and other symptoms of secondary trauma, which confirms transmission across the generations. I treated a family in which a son turning eighteen dreamed in exact detail the battles his father had been in during the Vietnam War. But the father had never told his son these stories.[59]

Unemployment

The daughter of a Vietnam veteran accompanied me to Viet Nam years after the father had abandoned the family. Just before our trip she found him drunk and homeless on California streets. He repudiated her advances and cursed her for finding him in his fallen condition. In three of four Iraq veteran marriages I have recently counseled, the husband was unemployed and abusing substances, while the wife worked. The families needed financial support from parents just to obtain shelter. The one employed veteran is older and the only one able to return to a predeployment profession.

Unemployment and homelessness occur among veterans in greater numbers than among civilians. One early study found that the unemployment rate for all Vietnam–era veterans was significantly higher than for nonveterans, with even higher rates for disabled veterans and for those who actually served in Southeast Asia.[60] From the Gulf War era, according to the Department of Labor, as of summer 2005 the unemployment rate among the 3.9 million veterans was 5.2 percent, 0.5 percent higher than nonveterans. But young vets, ages eighteen to twenty-four years old, had an unemployment rate of almost 19 percent, double that of young nonveterans.[61] In 2007, then Veterans Affairs secretary R. James Nicholson declared that for young Iraq and Afghanistan veterans the unemployment rate was about 15 percent, "or roughly three times what it is overall in our economy."[62] By 2008 that rate rose to 19 percent. By 2010 the unemployment rate for the same group surpassed 21 percent, almost 5 percent higher than for their nonvet peers.[63] Recent statistics for 2012 are comparable: 20 percent of eighteen to twenty-one-year-old vets are unemployed, 3.6 percent higher than their nonvet peers, with post-9/11 vets showing a 9.9 percent unemployment rate, 2 percent higher than nonvet peers.[64]

Homelessness

At least 200,000 veterans are homeless, living on the streets or in shelters, constituting one-third of the American adult population of homeless.[65] Twice that number experience homelessness during some portion of the year.[66] The government's first in-depth study of veteran homelessness found that 16 percent of the homeless are vets, though they number less than 10 percent of the adult population. The US rate of homelessness is twenty-one per 10,000 people, compared to thirty-one for veterans.[67] During 2009 more than 136,000 veterans spent time in shelters; those on the streets were uncounted.[68] A recent study counted 62,619 homeless veterans on a single night in January 2012, of whom more than 5,000 were women.[69] Eight percent of our homeless veterans every night are women,[70] and their homelessness rate is more than double that of their nonveteran peers.[71] Seventy percent of homeless vets have psychological or substance-abuse problems.[72] In Great Britain during the mid-1990s, one-quarter of the homeless were veterans.[73]

Health Issues

In just the last three months of this writing, I attended the funeral of one veteran and supported another during his last months of life. During this same period three veterans dear to me became ill with diabetes, Parkinson's disease, cancer, and other war-related illnesses.

Veterans are threatened with weakening, disabilities, chronic illnesses, premature aging, and early death. Their care is of perpetual concern and the associated costs are astronomical. Veterans with PTSD appear more susceptible to various illnesses and physical and psychological conditions. One study found that "patients with PTSD were more likely to have osteoarthritis, diabetes, heart disease, depression, obesity, and elevated lipid levels."[74] Studies show links between PTSD, Traumatic Brain Injury (TBI), and substance abuse as well as correlations between these and homelessness.[75]

As the veteran population ages, so will the medical needs, complications, and costs of their care. PTSD symptoms are common "in a substantial minority of older veterans in primary care."[76] The numbers also increase when we consider the Gulf War syndrome, radiation illnesses from uranium exposure during recent wars, and toxic herbicide exposure during the Vietnam War that result in a host of illnesses. These numbers vastly increase again when we add TBI and Military Sexual Trauma (MST). The most recent statistics on sexual assault in the military claim that there were 26,000 abuse incidents in our armed forces during 2012, up from 19,000 in 2010;[77] at least 20 percent of active duty woman soldiers have been sexually assaulted as well as a higher number of male troops.

Disability Payments and Costs

I have known Ed B. for decades as a community leader, church deacon, and veteran activist. A World War II Marine, Ed fought in the Pacific. I helped him at age eighty-eight prepare his disability appeal for the first time. "These new wars and the obscene concept of 'endless war,'" he said, "have made me reevaluate my entire adult life. Looking at the younger veterans and their troubles, I can see the negative impact war had on me."

Considering disability claims alone, in my region PTSD disability claims from all veterans increased 300 percent from the start of the Iraq War to the present.[78] Nationwide VA claims increased almost 80 percent over five years—from 120,265 in 1999 to 215,871 in 2004. During the same period benefit payments jumped nearly 150 percent, from $1.72 billion to $4.28 billion.[79] Disability and survivor benefits soared in 2007 to 81 percent above 2000 levels, increasing $15.4 billion to a total of $34.3 billion. The VA predicts that these payments will increase to $59 billion by 2016.[80]

The costs of caring for disabled Iraq and Afghanistan vets has been estimated at $2.3 billion annually, with another $2 billion paid annually to 169,000 disabled Gulf War veterans, totaling $4.3 billion a year.[81] Regarding TBIs from the Iraq War, in 2006 Nobel-prize-winning economist Joseph Stiglitz explained that the cost of care for a single troop during the critical phase of recovery can exceed a million dollars, and the cost of care for the lifetime of brain-injured troops alone could reach $35 billion. The true cost of the Iraq War, when post-service medical and disability costs are factored in, will be one to two trillion dollars.[82]

According to the Department of Veterans Affairs, as of January 2013 there were over 3.51 million veterans on government benefit rolls.[83]

The long-term debilitating effects of war are not problems that will go away with time. The costs to our society and the world must be counted in terms of human lives and health, family tragedies and dissolutions, failed marriages, parenthood and careers, harm to the social network through lost employment, sexual abuse, substance abuse, domestic violence, crime, incarcerations, disastrous health consequences, and care costs. The magnitude of these problems will increase as troops return from the Middle East, veterans age, and the United States struggles with the economic, social, historical, moral, and psychospiritual aftermath of war.

GUATEMALA: PORTRAIT OF A TRAUMATIZED NATION

Though we focus primarily on the American experience of war trauma, it is critical to recognize that entire nations and civilizations become traumatized. Wounding is transmitted through culture and history and gives shape to a people's national character. When we can see what has happened to others from such a history, it may inspire us to realize the degree of national wounding we suffer.

Miguel Rivera carries the blood of mixed ancestry; his family has been Spanish, Mayan, and Polish for centuries. He emigrated to the United States, where he serves as social activist and change agent, working with dispossessed populations. He offered this portrait of Guatemalan national trauma:

> Guatemala was immersed in a long, bloody, and bitter civil war from 1954 to 1996. During those forty-two years of warfare, there was a gradual dehumanization of individuals due to relentless and continuous violence. It became acceptable to find mangled dead bodies in the streets and people getting kidnapped, tortured, and robbed on a daily basis. A certain numbness appeared that has continued to grow, reflecting collective hopelessness.[84]

This violence and numbness were grieved by Mayan poet Humberto Ak'abal:

> Today saplings are slashed,
> the screams of children
> don't affect anybody, nobody cares:
> the sky opens its mouth and swallows
> the shout that drowns death.

Guatemala's suffering from violence began long ago, explains Miguel Rivera.

> The native population has been subjected to exploitation and domination in one form or another since the arrival of the first Europeans in 1523. Plantation owners and Christianizing missionaries suppressed indigenous life in all of its forms, creating a sterilization of the culture.

The poet feels his entire land crying:

> Birds from the ravines:
> come and weep with me,
> my sadness is big
> and the wound hurts . . .

He struggles to find justice in such an oppressive universe:

> Lord of the skies,
> lord of the earth:

where are you when these things happen,
why do you favor the murderers . . . ?[85]

Miguel Rivera continued:

> During the years of the Civil War many political factions fought each other and as many as five different rebel groups. The military and private militias were funded by the oligarchy. They massacred innocent civilians and kidnapped, tortured, and terrorized political prisoners, artists, writers, doctors, lawyers, teachers, and students—all forms of educators. This left a void throughout the country. Members of religious orders, charity workers, and members of the press were kidnapped, tortured, and killed. The military often posed as rebels in order to create confusion.
>
> As conflict continued, people began to rob and kidnap as a way of making a living due to poor economic conditions. Even after the 1996 peace accords there was no abatement of violence due to the influx of repatriated gang members from the US and drug cartels that set up operations in the country.
>
> There is little or no accountability on the part of individuals in positions of authority, as is the case of many military men responsible for the deaths of thousands. When people speak up demanding justice, they are retaliated against and killed, as happened to Bishop Juan Gerardi, the founding director of the Guatemalan Archdiocese's Office of Human Rights.

Miguel summarized the traumatic impact on any country:

> A country suffering from constant waves of violence is reflected by a high level of numbness and disorientation in the people. The infrastructure is unattended. There is no reliable system of laws. The courts are corrupt, making the

law of the gun prevail where common sense and respect
for human life had been the norm.

Finally both Miguel and Humberto declared hope in the original values of the people and restoration of their spirit. From Humberto:

We are poor but work hard,
our sin is being honest.
We live in misery and sadness
and even so
our culture
is our resistance.

Miguel, as well, finally relies on the resilient spirit of his land and people. "In spite of all these adversities and more, it is amazing to find in the land and its people an incredible heart and a hope for life."[86]

ON "PTSD"

From here on, in our journey of restoration, I will strictly limit use of the terms *Post-traumatic Stress Disorder* or *PTSD*, primarily citing them if they are part of a quote or official report. I take this step for several reasons.

Post-traumatic Stress Disorder is a modern term that was first introduced into the psychiatric literature in 1980. Most people have heard of combat fatigue and shell shock from the world wars. In fact, the condition has been given more than eighty names since ancient times, demonstrating its near universality.[87] Traditional cultures often named and treated it as a spiritual wound needing community response. We will explore these principles for understanding trauma and its healing later. Now we suspend our dependence on the modern term and work toward a new interpretation of the wound.

"Post-traumatic Stress Disorder" is a medical and psychiatric term, updated but not significantly altered in its ongoing inclusion in the diagnostic manual. PTSD is now sometimes referred to as (1) PTSI—Post-traumatic Stress Injury, a term preferred by the Department of Defense and aligned with the newly popular term "moral injury," which we discuss later; (2) PTS—Post-traumatic Stress, dropping the "D" or "disorder" to reduce stigma and "psychologizing" but also to emphasize biochemical changes and treatment; (3) Operational Stress Disorder, as it is called in some military circles where Operational Stress Control is of critical concern and the damage is believed to be to the "brain and mind." The wound is also known as Operational Stress in Canada and elsewhere, emphasizing that severe stress and concomitant challenges arise during military service. Many people assume that PTSD is a mental illness. Many assume that its victims should be referred to medical and health personnel for medication and treatment and that trauma healing and recovery have little to do with the general, unaffected population. We will retain "PTSD" where it occurs in quotes and references as it is the most commonly used referent today. But we will emphasize, expose, and cleanse the invisible wound without attributing pathology.

To be traumatized is to be wounded—in visible or invisible ways. War wounds are inevitable. Warriors return transformed, both wounded and enlightened, displaced, and confused regarding civilian life. They also return matured, skilled, and experienced in the ways of surviving in hell. Every aspect of their functioning—mental, physical, emotional, spiritual—operates differently, according to warrior and war zone survival needs. They essentially come home as different people than they were when they left us. In the core sense of the term, they have been initiated; their old self has died and a new self has emerged.

We are nostalgic. We want back the loved one who went to war. But war, like life, is a one-way journey. Warrior and military values and traits become so deeply embedded in troops that they never fully return to former civilian identities. They do not often consider themselves damaged, certainly not mentally ill, and they feel misunderstood when so judged. Therapeutic efforts aimed at restoring their previous identities commonly fail. Colonel Eric Olson, retired chief chaplain of the New York State National Guard, declares simply, "We're not crazy. We're not sick. We're different!" David Pierce, who served aboard our nuclear-armed ships in the Persian Gulf during Desert Storm, said, "I'm not damaged or wounded. I'm just different—as if I am now egg-shaped rather than round."

We must understand our warriors for who they are now, who they have become, how they understand and experience themselves. Army Chaplain George Tyger, who served in Afghanistan, insists "don't wish / I had never gone to war / War has not scarred me for life / It has made me more . . . "[88] Successful tending efforts affirm that the women and men before us are indeed different—in mind, heart, experience, values, and philosophy. A soldier's or veteran's psychology is not a distorted or disordered version of civilian identity. It is an identity itself.

We must not attribute pathology to veterans' military and war-transformed condition nor assume that it is a disturbed health condition requiring medical treatment. Instead we recognize that we are responsible to learn, and help veterans learn, who they are now and how they have become "more."

Leonard Cohen wrote, "A scheme is not a vision." We must understand and respond to our veterans, not merely with schemes and techniques aimed at fixing their illnesses and disorders, retraining their brains, supporting their disabilities, or reducing their symptoms. The label of PTSD points us in these directions. In contrast, we can bring a vision and determination for healing that arises from our wisdom, war literacy, hearts, and souls. Many traditional cultures considered their warriors "first among equals" because of the maturity they had gained and values learned. We must see our warriors as "more" and help them live into it. And we must walk the long and demanding moral and spiritual journey home together.

We will refer to the wound, contemplate and respond to it as war's expected, inevitable, and invisible psychospiritual and cultural legacy, and we will learn how we can embrace and use it to guide our growth and service trajectory through life.

WARS BRING SCARS

We need to see the struggle to survive and heal, in John Fisher's words, "the war after the war . . . the second two-thirds of my life . . . so vexed by that single year" in combat.[89] We need to see the struggles of our families, friends, neighbors, and brother and sister citizens. We need to overcome our denial that we have no part in its source, damage, or pain, and no responsibility for its tending. We need to correct our vision of the American landscape.

We tend to focus on American veterans and casualties, trying to stitch together our own broken people and society. But limiting our scope misleads us. Here is testimony from ninth-century China that sounds like an encounter of today:

> The way is long, the body overburdened;
> Foodless, he journeys the thousand *li* to his home,
> Tearing his hair and sobbing before the old city walls,
> While the autumn wind pierces his golden scars.[90]

War hurts. It causes wounding to the deepest dimensions of our humanity. These wounds carry pain that will not and should not go away. In this sense the invisible wound is not a negative, certainly not a disease. A war-traumatized person is not mentally ill but a wandering soul—lonely, isolated, misunderstood, in anguish and trapped in "the valley of the shadow." The wound is proof that as a result of war we will be different forever. It is also proof of our humanity, that we are caring, vulnerable people who cannot go through zones of hell with impunity and cannot harm others without harming ourselves. Rather, we will be deeply and permanently affected by immersion in war and will need and deserve immeasurable doses of love, wisdom, attention, kindness, patience, guidance, and tending.

Our veterans yearn to come home; "nostalgia" and "homesickness" were early names given the invisible wound. Veterans, their loved ones, and survivors through the ages need us to understand and respond to the invisible wounds of war in ways that are radically different, more humanistic, holistic, and engaging of the Warrior archetype and ethos and the community than anything we currently do. We must interpret war's trauma and relate to our veterans in ways that demonstrate that we "get it" and engage the heart, soul, and civilian community.

"Wars bring scars," said Benjamin Franklin. It is always so.

CHAPTER 4

Arena for the Soul

War is a solemn religious matter.

GERONIMO

In its fullness and health the Warrior archetype is a strong, beautiful, noble, guiding, and protective inner presence and public role. We have seen how wounded, damaged, lost, and distorted it has become and how many veterans, loved ones, and community members suffer as a result. How did we move from a psychospiritual-social presence meant to inspire, protect, teach, and serve to our landscape characterized by so many broken warriors whose lives are laced with tragedy, devastation, and alienation?

We must next understand war as an archetypal force and grasp its most challenging and difficult dimensions.

WAR AND TRUTH

In 490 BCE Aeschylus was thirty-five and already a dramatist when he fought with his city-state of Athens against the invading Persians at Marathon. There his brother Cynegirus was killed while attempting to seize an enemy ship by the stern. Aeschylus went on to fight in other fierce battles of his times.[1] Like legions of combat veterans through the ages, Aeschylus met the "bloodthirsty God of Battle Rout" whose nourishment is murdered men, who harvests death from the field of doom.[2]

For the rest of his life Aeschylus used poetry to write about war. He invented tragedy and used it to examine the experience of war. He witnessed the sufferings of all victims, including foes. He needed to expel and express, externalize and order, grieve and shrive. The tragic vision teaches that suffering is inevitable and must be embraced, but we can act nobly, shape beauty, and squeeze wisdom and meaning from our anguish.

Aeschylus wrote his own epitaph. He wanted to be remembered as an Athenian, the son of Euphorion, and a Marathon warrior. That was all. No mention of literary accomplishments but only of home and valorous duty.

Twenty-five hundred years ago Aeschylus said, "The first casualty of war is truth."

We must heal that casualty.

THE ARCHETYPE OF WAR

War itself is an archetype. It revisits humanity in almost every society and generation. It is an endlessly repeated power, story, pattern, and influence in human history. Its tales repeat in millions of lives spent on the battlefield and distorted and destroyed by it.

Once the war god surfaces in a population, he dominates human psyche and society in irresistible ways: exerting a hypnotic power; banishing reason, proofs, explanations, and cautions; driving people to see their neighbors as dangerous and evil and to seek their demise; not ending until its powers are exhausted and a train of destruction remains in its wake. War is a Beast that dwells in the human heart and soul. Under proper conditions it possesses us until it or we are spent.

Most religions and mythologies have deities of war, put its powers in Divine hands, or offer explanations for its purpose in the Divine plan. Many, including our root Western traditions, believed that war was one of God's tools for enforcing the righteous path. On the battlefield faithful fighters and nations were rewarded. Faithless ones were punished with suffering, death, and loss.

War exposes us to the raw elements, cosmic powers, ultimate dimensions, and most difficult moral dilemmas of our existence. It changes everything regarding how we think, feel, and sense; how we sleep and dream; how we act or fail to act; how we do or do not fit into society; what we value and believe; how we love and make love; how we experience beauty, goodness, harmony, order, respect, reverence, and awe. In short, war—the god-power and archetype—transforms our relationships to humanity, society, Divinity, and ourselves. All these are traits of the heart and soul.

THE UNIVERSALITY OF WAR, SOUL, AND TRAUMA

War's reshaping of our essential selves, our souls, is our core concern. At its worst the reshaping is into one who is shattered, wasted, angry, rebellious, unable to participate in society, perhaps violent, even wanting to kill or die. At its best, reshaping may be into an identity that is wise, compassionate, mature, creative, strong, generous, and devoted—bringing great boons to society.

War inevitably breaks our hearts. At worst our hearts may be shattered by grief, pain, fear, and rage. They may be flooded with despair. We may go cold inside, seek revenge, lose the desire to love or live, even come to believe that we deserve death and eternal punishment. At best our hearts are opened, softened, and made more receptive, flooding with love, compassion, and the drive to give meaningful service.

The reshaping of woman or man into warrior is dependent on the warrior's preparation and code. It is dependent on the traditions out of which it was born and operates. It is dependent on the particular cause for which warriors fight and for which they are asked to take life and offer their own. It is dependent on the number, length, intensity, and kinds of traumatic experiences before service and while in the military and the war zone. And it is dependent on a society's use of and care for its warriors before and during service and deployments and for the rest of their life span.

Violent trauma impacts us on every level from personal to global, from the individual through the family, community and nation; across generations; in cultural, religious, ethnic, and archetypal influences; in our arts, social structures, natural environment; and in our religious beliefs and practices. This is recognized in the trauma field where we seek to help challenged populations around the world with wounds, the sources of which are not primarily individual but collective, historical, cultural, transgenerational, ancestral, and ecological.[3]

Most religious, spiritual, and ethnic traditions have deities, heroes, and legends of war. Almost all modern nations have known war. The United States has had nine major wars and more than fifty others since our founding,[4] with more than 1,186,000 military deaths since the American Revolution.[5] One scholar has called the United States "a country made by war."[6]

Commander Mark Russell was a Navy psychologist and military trauma expert with over twenty-six years of service. Now a professor of psychology, Russell states,

> In the aftermath of the Second World War, US Army Chief of Staff General Dwight D. Eisenhower gave this candid explanation for the 1.1 million neuropsychiatric casualties, "In seeking the many causes of psychiatric disability in order to correct them, we must put first the absence of prewar planning to prevent and to treat them. This blunder was made by the War Department and the technical service of the Medical Department, and was ignored by the profession of psychiatry."[7] Tragically, after every major American war since the twentieth century, military leaders, including this generation, have similarly admitted to neglecting well-documented lessons of war trauma, as basic as the need for adequate planning and preparation, directly contributing to a cycle of preventable wartime behavioral health crises that have occurred on average of every eight to twelve years throughout United States history.[8]

None of this is new. Western civilization's founding epics—the *Iliad* and the Old Testament—are "war bibles" of utmost brutality. In the Western tradition, as presented in Genesis, the first murder was a fratricide, and brother has been killing brother ever since. We have been taught for millennia that violence and its traumatic aftermath have been with us since our beginnings and so the propensity toward violence, "the war god," "the beast," must be built into human nature.

WOUNDED ROOTS

The Biblical and Greek are the twin root traditions of the Western world. They birthed and shaped our cultures and civilization. Their values, beliefs, practices, institutions, and creative works are our ancestral inheritance. They also shaped our beliefs, values, and practices regarding warfare. Though we commonly think of the Bible as a source of religious instruction and spiritual inspiration, it is also drenched in war horror. "The two greatest works of war mythology in the West are . . . the *Iliad* and the Old Testament," Joseph Campbell observed, "[W]e have been bred to one of the most brutal war mythologies of all time."[9]

The legacy of war and its trauma is indeed historical, cultural, ancestral, and transgenerational, transmitted through Western civilization since its beginnings. Aware or not, as individuals, a nation, and a culture, we absorb it from our roots. We must see the depth and degree to which each of us and our civilizations have been shaped by war's transgenerational impact. Our veterans and families' service and wounds are neither individual pathologies nor modern conditions. Rather, they continue the world's ancient warrior traditions and forms of wounding in the present, perhaps to more destructive and universalized degrees. This traumatic pattern has been unfolding for millennia such that we have come to accept war and mass violence as normal and inevitable. This has generalized to such a degree that we now accept massive civilian suffering and death as "collateral damage," torture and long-distance assassinations by machine as justifiable, desecration of the earth as tolerable, and the entire planet as a battlefield in "the global war."

We examine early and formative roots of Western civilization to understand the degree and depth to which war, violence and trauma seem built into the human condition and have been shaping us for millennia.

WAR, VIOLENCE, AND HUMAN NATURE IN THE OLD TESTAMENT

The Old Testament chronicles an endless history of wars, murders, rapes, incest, betrayals, cataclysms, slavery, and abuse. Much violence is against the early Hebrew people,[10] who also perpetrated violence against each other and other tribes and religions. We are told that God commanded much of this even unto genocide. Moses tells his people: "The Lord your God will bring you into the land . . . and drive . . . out . . . seven nations larger than yourself . . . When God places them in your power and you defeat them, you must put them all to death." The people were ordered to make no alliances, show no mercy, not intermarry or let their children intermarry, and destroy their foes' sacred sites and religious symbols.[11]

Many incidents reported in the Bible have been corroborated by archaeological and historical research, demonstrating what a difficult, contentious, unstable, and violent world our ancestors lived in and we have inherited. Is war and violence, then, an inevitable part of our human condition? Will we always re-create it? Does God bless or condemn it? Under what conditions? The Old Testament offers a troubling, pessimistic, and ambivalent view of human nature in general and war and violence in particular.

In Genesis, Cain, the first son of the first human beings, killed his brother Abel out of jealousy and competition and was branded for life as a result. The very first murder was a fratricide. From this beginning, brother killed brother over land, power, or favor. The one who does the killing becomes different, separated from the Divine presence, banished and branded to wander homeless over the earth with "a punishment too hard to bear."[12]

By the time of Noah, humans had become so corrupt that God destroyed most life in order to purify the earth and start again. "Everything on earth that breathed died,"[13] and righteous Noah and his family were the only witnesses and survivors. Noah was a survivor of global trauma such as occurs today in war zones and environmental disasters.

Immediately upon disembarking the ark, Noah gave live sacrifice of a few remaining clean animals and birds. He planted the first vineyard and made the first wine. He got drunk, passed out, then cursed and banished his youngest son, Ham, who chanced upon him naked. Noah's curse was historically used to justify human slavery: "He will be a slave to his brothers."[14]

Did Noah break down in shock and horror such that a man chosen by God for his goodness became violent, abusive, drunk, and rejecting? We are told that God became disillusioned with humanity: "I will never again curse the ground because of man, for the imagination of man's heart is evil from his youth."[15]

The Old Testament stampedes forward offering a narrative of personal, historical, and natural traumas that seem to be the human inheritance. Our ancestors and religious role models were often twisted out of shape by their impact. Of many examples, Abraham gave his wife to another man to further his own position, and he raised a knife to slay his own son. Jacob lied to his father, stole from his brother, scorned his first wife for love of her younger sister, and played favorites among his sons. Joseph's brothers sold him into slavery and some became brutal. Moses slew an Egyptian, lost his temper with the Israelites, and disobeyed God by striking a rock for water. His general Joshua led hoards of freed slaves and their children on wars of conquest and pillage of other people and their lands, sometimes unto their complete genocidal destruction. Joseph Campbell calls Joshua "the greatest war book of all."[16] The rest of the Old Testament narrates a series of traumatic events from small to great and personal to global. In all these, we may hear the ancient warning, "the imagination of man's heart is evil . . . "

TRAUMATIZED ANCESTORS

Moses said, "Choose life." War is inherently a choice of death over life. In choosing war we must be utterly sure that we are making the last and only possible choice, after all other efforts have failed, for purely protective motives. We must do so, politics and rationalizations aside, in a way that minimizes harm and protects the innocent. Biblical wisdom repeatedly dictates this. David is advised not to kill without cause or for revenge so he "will not have to feel regret or remorse."[17] We are told that among "the seven things that the Lord hates and cannot tolerate" are the very conditions by which we often make war—"a lying tongue, hands that kill innocent people, a mind that thinks up wicked plans, feet that hurry off to do evil . . . "[18] With this heritage, how should troops who served in Viet Nam or Iraq feel about the falsehoods that spawned their wars? Or troops who came to believe that their war was immoral? Or anyone who, mistakenly or due to the rules of engagement, kills civilians? How do troops feel when the very rules created to protect them cause them to act in ways the Bible judges to be offensive?

We are taught not only to avoid wrong actions but also about righteous action during war. Abraham dates back about 4,000 years. In his participation in the war between nine kings, Abraham avoids fighting for land, power, or natural resources. But when his nephew Lot is taken captive, Abraham arms, fights, and frees him. He refuses booty but accepts for his men only those goods lost during the fighting.[19] Thus we are taught that though it may be necessary to fight for the survival or rescue of loved ones, we had better not profit from war.

Divine command ordered Abraham to sacrifice Isaac, and he banished his other son, Ishmael, to the wilderness. Abraham's treatment of his sons provides metaphors for what happens in war—traumatized by violence and sacrificed like Isaac, or rejected and exiled like Ishmael. Both sons are only saved by Divine intervention, also accurate to how a survivor feels—"not by my hand but by Thine," or by "chance and circumstance." From these original traumas we might interpret that the millennia-old history of Middle Eastern wars stems from unresolved transgenerational warfare between Isaac and Ishmael's descendants as they continue to fight over their father's inheritance.

When Isaac is the only son left to elderly Abraham, God orders him sacrificed. Here too is a metaphor for the war experience. Some families had to send, and some lost, many or all of their children to war. There are over 44,200 Vietnamese mothers from both the French and American wars who lost multiple or last-remaining family members. They are designated *Bà Me Viêt Nam Anh Hung*, "Vietnamese Heroic Mothers," and honored by the entire country. In the United States such mothers may get support from Gold Star Mothers and recognition at parades, but most often carry shattering grief alone.

Isaac is saved at the last minute, but the death of Sarah is the next Biblical event reported. More war metaphor replicated: My uncle was a medic in the Battle of the Bulge. When he was reported missing in action, my grandmother's hair turned white almost overnight. Like Sarah she died an early and painful death only a few years after he returned. And like my traumatized uncle, we hardly hear from Isaac after his sacrifice. His story has been cited by combat survivors to demonstrate that war is betrayal and sacrifice of the sons by fathers or fatherland.[20]

This story, called the *Akedah* in Hebrew, means "binding." Binding refers to both Isaac's literal binding on the altar and the symbolic binding of Abraham and Isaac to God by an oath. Through taking oaths, man and woman become husband and wife, immigrant becomes citizen, private citizen becomes public servant—and civilian becomes soldier.

Oaths bind us in irrevocable ways and oath-taking effects an identity transformation and accompanying change of social status.

Civilians taking oaths of military service become bound to serve and sacrifice no matter what is asked of them, even unto killing or being killed. Combat also binds, producing an intense intimacy between brothers- and sisters-in-arms and with foes. Survivors often take oaths to remain loyal forever to those with whom they have shared the experience of hell. They strain to honor the memories of their fallen, prove themselves worthy of their sacrifices, and fulfill last promises, such as delivering messages home.

The poet Walt Whitman was forty-two when the Civil War started. He traveled to Washington, D.C., in December 1862 to nurse his wounded brother. Moved by the suffering of all the wounded, he served as a nurse for the duration of the war: "The hurt and wounded I pacify with soothing hand, I sit by the restless all the dark night . . ."[21] Whitman remembered and dreamed of them decades afterward. "In midnight sleep of many a face of anguish, / Of the look at first of the mortally wounded . . . , / Of the dead on their backs with arms extended wide, / I dream, I dream, I dream."[22] Survivors shape their lives and suffer their nightmares as ways to not break faith with the fallen. Canadian Lt. Colonel John McRae's World War I poem, "In Flanders Fields," reads, "If you break faith with us who die / We shall not sleep . . . "

War is eternally and archetypally this binding. "In essence, war is always the sacrificial altar. The father raises the knife, and his child awaits it."[23] Did Abraham, as commentators have asked for centuries, fulfill or fail God's test? Do our troops, after the din clears, feel that the cause justified the command and its consequences? Politicians forever justify the sacrifice with rhetoric meant to ennoble it. But how do parents who send their children feel about the sacrifice? A young American, Barry, thought of fleeing to Canada rather than answering the draft for Vietnam. His mother told him, "If you do, you will never set foot in my house again." He went to a war he did not believe in. Too often veterans and the public suffer over whether their sacrifice was worth the cause and whether we passed or failed God's test. As Wilfred Owen wondered, what permanent and necessary transformation has occurred to the world that redeems the unspeakably painful violent sacrifice of a child by parents?

On his deathbed, Abraham's grandson Jacob gave a final blessing to each son, but he refused to honor or promise success to two. Of Simeon and Levi he said,

> They use their weapons to commit violence.
> I will not join in their secret talks,
> Nor will I take part in their meetings,
> For they killed people in anger
> And they crippled bulls for sport.
> A curse be on their anger, because it is so fierce,
> And on their fury, because it is so cruel.
> I will scatter them throughout the land . . .[24]

Roy was a helicopter door gunner in Viet Nam. "I tested my guns on water buffalo every chance I got," he confessed, shuddering. "Boy, did those things splatter." He killed people and animals from a distance, in revenge for his own fallen, for sport, because "I was a kid and just reacting," because "we were all high on drugs." Though his family, care providers, other vets, and the Vietnamese offered him love, understanding, and forgiveness, he never forgave himself. He had "killed people in anger" and "crippled bulls for sport." He never felt deserving of blessing; he had discovered that he was "fierce" and "cruel." He carried the curse of Jacob.

WAR TRAUMA IN THE ANCIENT GREEK WORLD

The Greeks, our other Western root culture, recorded many stories of war trauma in mythology, literature, and history. In his *Histories* Herodotus wrote of men who "shook and trembled both before and after battle." He reported that two of the 300 Spartans sent to meet the Persian invasion at Thermopylae appeared before their king with identical eye inflammations and were dismissed for recuperation. One rejoined the fight and was killed. The second returned home, lived in disgrace, became depressed, and was nicknamed The Trembler. He regained honor when he proved himself at the battle of Plataea. One more of the 300 missed the battle, carrying a message afar. He hanged himself afterward.[25]

Such stories recur today. Jeremy, a Marine who volunteered for mortuary duty in Iraq, was ill in the hospital when his unit deployed. Though Jeremy stayed stateside, he tended the bodies of fallen comrades for a year with respect, dignity, grief, and prayer. He judged himself to be less of a man and Marine because he was not at the "hot gates" with his comrades. He felt guilty and suicidal. Ancient or modern troops may sometimes miss or be removed from combat due to illnesses, injury, or psychosomatic conditions. Later they may suffer over it and, as with the absent Spartans, depression and suicide can follow.

Plutarch reported that soldiers defending Syracuse against a Roman siege were "stricken dumb with terror." Soldiers often become mute during modern wars. Mutism was common during World War I; strong electric shocks were administered at high pain levels to forcibly propel mute soldiers out of the condition.

Jonathan Shay explicated the striking parallels between troops in the ancient warfare of 3,000 years ago as recorded in Homer's epics and the Vietnam War.[26] He rightly declared that "Homer has seen things that we in psychiatry and psychology have more or less missed," especially moral trauma, which Shay calls "betrayal of what's right," and the onset and importance of the berserk state.[27]

The *Iliad* can be read as a textbook on traumatic war wounding. Achilles was the Greek army's fiercest warrior. He tried to avoid service by disguising himself as a girl when the "recruiters" came for him. He did not believe in the cause, but there was no honorable way out.

Achilles raged at incompetent and selfish commanders. He disagreed with the reasons they fought and the ways they ran the war. He hated his commander Agamemnon, who took his troops' spoils for himself, and wanted to "frag" him. Achilles was so enraged that it took Divine intervention—the goddess Athena ordering him to "slay him with words instead"—to prevent him from committing murder.

Achilles became despondent and refused to fight. His "battle buddy" Patroclus entered the contest in Achilles's armor and was killed. Achilles then ranged the battlefield slaughtering numberless enemies, torturing and killing prisoners, and committing atrocities.

Achilles went *berserk*, a word originally used in the Norse tradition for ravaging warriors possessed by savage bear and wolf spirits.[28] He lost all gentle and humanizing feelings, plunged into unredeemable grief, and fought only for revenge. He knew from Divine prophecy that if he remained in the battle, he would be killed but remembered with honor. He preferred this fate rather than a return to a placid civilian life and decrepit old age. The Greeks judged this a noble choice. Today as well, many veterans feel like they only know how to function in the combat zone—the only place life is worth living—or that the only honorable choice is to fight to the death alongside their military brothers and sisters.

The *Iliad* began, "Sing, O goddess, the rage of Achilles . . . " In Greek, the *Iliad*'s first word is *minis*, which means "rage," "wrath," or "anger" so extreme it seems to be of the gods. Jonathan Shay translates it as "indignant wrath" and declares, "*Rage* is the proper title of Homer's poem."[29]

In any armed conflict a warrior is prone to wrath because his and his comrades' lives are immediately and violently threatened. Wrath overcomes terror. It hurls against someone threatening us. "Kill or be killed" means "I kill you before you kill me." Wrath powers it. Jack was a jungle reconnaissance squad leader credited with over 200 kills. "You don't kill 'cause you want to hurt somebody," he explained. "Only sick people do that. It isn't a killing rage really. It's just a rage to save your own life . . . In the bush you don't kill from rage. You kill from fear."[30]

Wrath may save us, but eventually it can overwhelm and distort the ego and its reason—those parts of the psyche meant to regulate and channel intense emotion. British Maj. Gen. J. F. C. Fuller observed at the end of World War II—which he called a war of "unparalleled destruction" and "unrivaled inhumanity"—that "if the aim of the statesman is purely destructive, then clearly the activities of the soldier must become those of the slaughterhouse . . . If policy be mad, war can be nothing else than madness lethalized."[31] Wrath is more enflamed and troops become more distorted when a war's causes or commanders prove unjust, immoral, or questionable; its duration unceasing and unendurable; its losses disproportionate and excruciating; and the people at home uncaring, neglectful, or in opposition.

In the *Iliad* Achilles was the symptom-laden berserk warrior. His chief adversary was the Trojan prince Hector. Though equally engaged in struggle and slaughter, Hector practiced a strictly moral and selfless use of force. He was fighting to protect his wife and child, his elderly parents, and his people and city. He only fought invading enemy warriors and did not attack civilians.

Unlike his brother Paris, whose lust triggered the Trojan War, Hector was not after fame, gain, land, money, power, revenge, or any goal that renders the use of force immoral. Shannon French, when teaching at the US Naval Academy, cited Hector's character and fate to her Navy officers-in-training:

> Hector derives his code from the collective judgment of his culture and his peers . . . Achilles fought for personal reasons and was not concerned with the welfare of others . . . while Hector fought to defend Troy and her people from harm. Achilles dreamt of no future beyond the battlefield, while Hector longed for a peaceful life at home with his family. Achilles was consumed by rage, Hector driven by duty.[32]

Professor French's students insisted, "The greatest warrior would be a Hector who wins." His strict warrior's code was Hector's shield against trauma. War's tragedies arise, in part, because "Hectors" sometimes do not win and weapons do not differentiate between the good and the bad. Moral superiority is no guarantor of victory or even survival. Even when Hectors triumph, suffering is so immense that many survivors conclude that in war nobody wins.

Can a soldier construct a moral shield like Hector's under modern conditions?

I lead annual healing and reconciliation journeys to Viet Nam. Every year my group of veterans and civilians travels to the Mekong Delta to meet with Viet Cong veterans. There we meet with Nguyen Tam Ho, known as "Mr. Tiger." Mr. Tiger is ninety-two years old. He spent twenty-five years of his life at war, fighting against three generations of invaders—the Japanese, French, and Americans. He was Viet Minh, then Viet Cong—like early American Minutemen, unpaid local militia organized for defense. In spite of being a combatant for a quarter of a century, Mr. Tiger is healthy and happy, welcoming and serene. He lives on a small island nursery surrounded by three generations of his family, and he basks in the beauty of the Delta that he has labored for forty years to help restore after decades of bombs and poisons.

Ben, a helicopter door gunner during the Vietnam War, "shot everything that moved." His chopper was shot down and Ben wounded after a few months and scores of combat missions. He was then transferred to the Pacific, where he helped load the bombs that devastated the very land . . . we walked on. He has had physical complications from his wounds, diseases from Agent Orange exposure, and frequent nightmares about his crash and the deaths of his fellow crewmen.

"I don't get it," Ben blurted in the shade of palm fronds on Tiger's porch. "You were at war for twenty-five years and sleep like a baby. I was only here for four months and it's tortured me my whole life. What's the difference between us?"

"As far as I understand," Mr. Tiger answered, "there is no PTSD for the veterans in Viet Nam, no psychological wounds. This is because we were never invaders. We only fought to protect our families, homes, and country." His hands spread to embrace our group. "During the war I never thought of you as Americans," he explained. "I have always respected America. An invader is anyone who comes to your country and tries to kill your children and take your land. I was only fighting invaders."[33]

In ancient and modern times, from the Bible to the Geneva Conventions to George Bush redefining "torture" and Barack Obama justifying drone aircraft killings, political leaders have dictated moral and immoral uses of force and violence. Soldiers must carry out their orders. But they want to know "what I should do in combat, how best to conduct myself," declared General William Lennox, Jr., while superintendent at West Point. Said the general, the possible sacrifice of their lives dictates "the cause must be worth it."[34] Nick had yearned to be a great warrior in one of history's world-shaping battles. He served in the National Guard for twenty years before getting his chance. "I went to war," he declared, "to be like Hector defending the gates of Troy. But they didn't give me Troy or Gettysburg or Normandy Beach. All they gave me was that dirty, shitty little Iraq War."

To protect against trauma and achieve honor, warriors must emulate not Achilles but Hector, not Ben but Mr. Tiger. The citizenry's task is to protect devoted warriors from serving causes that betray their consciences.

WAR, TRAUMA, AND RELIGION

Worship and the search for meaning seem contradictory to war making. In fact, they are profoundly related. We cannot take others' lives, lose our citizens and loved ones, or damage the earth and destroy its people and resources without harming ourselves and everyone involved. We need guidance from moral, spiritual, and religious sources to avoid conflict or at least reduce immediate and long-term harm. But throughout history and into our present crises, religious sources themselves have often caused or promoted war and violence. When we believe that our aggression fulfills God's will, then the marriage of religion and power releases savage and overwhelming destruction.

Antagonists evoke ethical and religious dimensions to strengthen their positions and refute their foes. "Behold, O God, and judge between us and our enemies, who have forced upon us this unholy and unnatural war . . . " Thus preached Rabbi James Gutheim from his pulpit in Montgomery, Alabama, during the Civil War in support of the Confederacy and slavery. "Bless, O Father, our efforts in a cause which we conceive to be just . . . [B]less and protect the armed hosts."[35] This common position of "we are right and holy, they are wrong and evil" reinforces violence as each side tries to prove its position, including justification of slavery and genocide, through military victory. All parties replicate King David's belief: God "maintained my rule over the nations. People I did not know have now become my subjects . . . He gives me victory over my enemies; he subdues the nations under me and saves me from my foes."[36]

It can seem that the spiritual and ethical dimensions are separated as by an unbridgeable chasm from our secular, political, and religious lives. Righteous talk and violent actions often reinforce rather than restrain each other. Troops commonly express betrayal due to these contradictions in an almost formulaic way: "I thought I was going to war to _____. But when overseas I did _____ instead. I feel like a mercenary rather than a warrior. I wonder if I'm a murderer."

Some people have spent months, years, lifetimes in physical and emotional replications of our worst versions of hell. They have been plunged into quagmires of agony and suffering reminiscent of Job's—families, friends, possessions, homes, livelihood, their entire world destroyed wantonly, unjustly, unexpectedly, as if in a bad bet with Satan, while all they could do was helplessly watch.

The result? Like Job, war survivors may lie on the dung heap of life feeling betrayed by and alienated from humanity, crying out to God, unable to continue ordinary living until they receive an answer. Suffering forces them to ask key existential, moral, and spiritual questions. Is there a God? If so, how could God let wars happen and innocent people die? Is there any meaning to life? To striving against evil? Am I guilty or innocent? Did I earn this suffering? Is it my fault? Are suffering and evil part of God's plan? If so, do I even want to go on living?

Such questions challenge survivors. Tina, an Army lieutenant back from Afghanistan said, "Sometimes my comrades and I feel like we are in league with the devil." A colonel said after several deployments, "I have come to believe that the US Army can thwart even God himself." A battalion chaplain just back from Afghanistan said, "The Army was out for the kill, not out for truth or justice."

Survivors' moral and spiritual foundations may be shaken or smashed, drenched with the impact of evil and death. Instead of David's faith when he wrote Psalm 23 that in "the valley of the shadow of death I will fear no evil, for Thou art with me," they feel:

Save me, O God!
The water is up to my neck . . .
I am out in deep water
And the waves are about to drown me.
I am worn out from calling for help . . .
You know how I am insulted
How I am disgraced and dishonored . . .
Insults have broken my heart
And I am in despair . . . [37]

Whosoever survives modern war and terror may feel this troubled, in a crisis of faith, unsure if the Creator or anyone walks with them, unsure of whether they do good or evil, unable to discover trustworthy answers or companions. From ancient and modern testimony we see that warfare is so brutal and destructive that we cannot perpetrate it without producing such suffering to our personal and collective beings. It is an arena in which the soul will be put through its most demanding tests. In Afghanistan Chaplain Tyger concluded, "In combat, honesty demands that we finally come clean with ourselves and admit that answers do not exist, only questions and only human responses to human frailty."[38] About war, such honesty and truthfulness can be most difficult to discern and admit. When we do, it can come at a terrible cost because it undermines our most cherished beliefs. A GI named Peter survived the flying bullets—at the siege of Khe Sanh and in the Demilitarized Zone in Vietnam and later at the Kent State shootings in Ohio. After decades of silence he finally declared,

> Far from "doing my job honorably," I did my job because I did not have the courage to walk off the battlefield. The horror upon horror is that we willingly sacrificed so many of our own, and twenty-fold of THEM, even as our leaders doubted the cause. My awful truth is that I knew at the time that the enemy I faced deserved to win. There, I said it. THEY DESERVED TO WIN. WE FUCKED UP. And it cannot be UN-FUCKED no matter how many bands of brothers' days or Veterans' Days or Fourths of July we throw at it. What is honorable about being dishonorably used? A band of brothers? Yes, but can my band of brothers admit to being honorably dismissed from the dishonorable cause? And can we resist the easy myth that in military service heroes must emerge from less-than-heroic ventures?[39]

Regarding war, we must not impose what we wish, project, fantasize, imagine, or invent to glorify and justify it in order to protect ourselves from its pain. Regarding war, we must only declare what is true.

FOUR TRUTHS OF SOLDIERING

Chaplain General Kevin Turner is Assistant Chief of Chaplains of the US Army. He is strong and direct with a bulldog build and startling blue eyes gazing out of his clean-shaven head.

Turner, with a total of twenty-eight years in service, began his military career as an infantry private. He was a Special Forces officer for eight years, serving many deployments, including in northern Iraq in the 1990s.

Later he became a minister and chaplain. At first, he said, he had no righteous sense of calling but had had enough of combat. Ironically, "my best years in the military were the four and a half years I served as a chaplain to Special Operators from all services." Many military chaplains evolve from combatants. Chaplain Turner and I have pondered together: Does becoming a chaplain help to "balance the beast with the priest"? Is it a path to atonement?

General Turner traveled to Afghanistan in 2013 to help open two-way communication between the military and home front that is lacking. He wanted troops to know they are supported and cared about and those at home to know the challenges and needs of troops in harm's way.

We both lectured at 2012 Army Chaplain trainings.[40] From the podium Turner stared into the audience of several hundred uniformed personnel wearing several thousand ribbons and said, "All soldiers feel fear. All soldiers feel guilt and shame. All soldiers ask 'why?' And we must love them." Then he sat down.

Not only are there war and Warrior archetypes but there are also universal dimensions of soldiering and warfare that recur in all times and places of human conflict. Chaplain Turner reminded us that we cannot reduce invisible wounding to a psychological disorder but "all soldiers" in combat will experience primal conditions causing great ordeal and will thereby be challenged to the core.[41] These conditions are true of the soul and inherent to the military and war.

WAR IS A SACRED ARENA

During warfare, we human beings take over the Divine functions of granting life or administering death and of determining the destinies of peoples and nations. We make the judgments and enact the behaviors that determine "who by fire and who by water," "who shall be brought up and who shall be laid low." Taking life is the essence of war and is also in essence a moral and spiritual act. Only for the highest purposes, so we are taught, may we wield such ultimate power. Some traditional cultures even taught their warriors to explain to their victims why they had to be killed. Precisely because we become arbiters of life, death, and fate we enter religious and spiritual dimensions and are in a world of ultimate matters that Karl Marlantes calls "this wartime sacred space, this Temple of Mars."[42]

"From the moment the command for war is given," Geronimo explained about his people, "everything assumes a religious guise."[43] For the Apaches, war and its life-preserving and life-taking functions were so sacred, profound, and important to survival and honor that during conflict their entire way of life changed. Important activities, such as camping and cooking, were proscribed. All objects pertaining to war were called by sacred names, "not 'horse' but 'war horse' or 'charger'; not 'arrow' but 'missile of death.'" A warrior's code guided them. In the Apache tradition "it was no sin to kill enemies." Warriors were addressed by the honorific titles of brave or chief to which were affixed their sacred names. Young men acted as servants to elder warriors on their first four combat excursions. Part of warrior preparation was to learn the sacred language. "War," Geronimo summarized, "is a solemn religious matter."[44]

Wartime transformations of the secular into the sacred were practiced among traditional peoples around the world. They dressed differently for war, took utmost care in preparing, carried special amulets, and participated in spiritual and communal ceremonies before, during, and after conflict. They sometimes spent time in purification rituals or alone in the wilderness talking to Spirit. Holy people often accompanied them through combat. Going off to battle was of superhuman dimensions and needed spiritual support. Warriors evoked and identified with cosmic powers and tribal mythic heroes and traditions. While the "universal soldier" is one among millions in identical uniforms and mass battles, the individual warrior seeks to embody his or her cultural heroes who fight sacred causes under Divine protection and wield potent or even blessed weapons meant to serve high purpose. In this way, consciously or not, warriors believe they are serving not just their people but also the Divine. Sacred scripture, world mythology, and political belief connect the Warrior archetype to the Divine. Warriors from any side of a conflict, no matter what their foes' or history's interpretation of their cause, may see themselves as servants of the Divine and their cause as holy.

Belief, Faith, and War

Two dozen gnarled and grizzled World War II veterans filled the chairs in front of me. Some wore baseball caps displaying their units, ships, or places of service. A few held artifacts. We were discussing what war had done to their belief systems. What happens to the practice of faith and urgency of prayer during moments when death stares at us nose to nose? I quoted the adage, "There are no atheists in the foxhole."

Three of the old vets were concentration camp liberators. One stood and shouted. Another turned red. The third shook his head sadly.

"That proverb is meant to soothe all you who don't know," the standing vet blurted. "Were any of you in the camps? Did you ever see what human beings do to each other? It's worse than combat. No God would allow that! No atheists? Bullshit! The foxhole creates atheists!"

Legions of survivors have become disillusioned and lost belief in a Higher Power because of their experiences during war. If we are made in the Divine Image and that image includes war, the human shadow, and all the horrors we enact upon each other, then Who, Where, or What is God?

War, as the liberators testified, can plunge us into such unremitting darkness and despair that we no longer have any sense of the Divine and perhaps are no longer able to believe in a Higher Power or Purpose that has any concern with us. How, then, can we survive in the valley of the shadow? Poet Siegfried Sassoon confronted this condition in the trenches of World War I:

> Have we the strength to strive alone
> Who can no longer worship Christ?
> Is He a God of wood or stone,
> While those who served him writhe and moan,
> On warfare's altar sacrificed?[45]

SPIRITUAL DIMENSIONS OF TRAUMA

Sassoon's fellow poet and shell-shock patient Wilfred Owen wrote, "The sons we offered would regret they died / If we got nothing lasting in their stead." Survivors wonder, how shall we judge our service? How shall we be judged? Were the results worth and worthy of the costs?

For war's survivors, the worst dimensions of humanity and fate took everything. An Afghanistan combat vet said, "I can't care about anything that isn't about to blow up." Veterans become blind and numb to civilian existence with its small pleasures and challenges. They cannot be restored to life until, like Job, they achieve a redemptive vision that enables them to carry their experiences with meaning. Lacking these, they will live life in the ashes.

These ultimate conditions of warfare immerse us in the sacred. It is proper, for spiritual healing and restoration are necessary for war's soul wounding. Yet these are the very dimensions regarding trauma that have been most neglected. N. Duncan Sinclair was a chaplain in Viet Nam during the war, later serving as both clergy and clinician. More than twenty years ago he differentiated "horrific trauma" from trauma of lesser impact or scope.

> The most corrosive impact of horrific emotional trauma is to be found in the spiritual fabric of persons. This is where the profound damage is created . . . [and] the facet . . . so often overlooked by the mental health systems of our country. The condition of PTSD is spiritual at its deepest levels.[46]

Chaplain Sinclair emphasizes that "the person who experiences the full impact . . . has been impoverished by the loss of a series of vital spiritual attributes that are essential to living a full life." These include losses of hope, intimacy, a future, peacefulness, healing memories, spontaneity, wholeness, innocence, trust, and awe.[47]

Remember Lot's wife—all that remained of her after she viewed the destruction of her city was a pillar of salt. And Job's wife: "Curse God and die." Loss of awe completes the disconnection between individual and universe because it creates "the belief that there is nothing greater in the universe than that which inflicted the original pain."[48] No Higher Power, no benevolent directing forces in the cosmos, not love but the trauma itself becomes the highest power. Life is defined by the wounding experience while the rest of the life span shrivels in comparison. "Anyone who sees Leviathan loses courage and falls to the ground."[49]

Ayelet Berman-Cohen, an Israeli air force veteran, voices the degree to which horror is war's essence; we crave it, its wound becomes our identity, and we, war, and wound all become one:

> PTSD, the God of War itself, is dwelling within us . . .
> We are the host.
> PTSD is our hidden language.
> We hide our devotion to war, our love for it,
> And the horror that war inflicts on our inner being . . .
> We danced and killed and participated
> In wounding the heart of the world . . . and now . . .
> With fierce devotion and determination
> We capture the virtue of war,
> The way we know her, the way we love her,
> Our beloved, demanding God of War.[50]

The terror and horror of killing, death, and destruction in war are so impactful, disguised, or ignored that we need all our strength and courage to look at them with a naked glance. War is not just a sacred arena where the soul is challenged. It constitutes a genuine journey through hell. We must plunge more deeply into that hell in order to understand the wound and emerge with wisdom for healing.

CHAPTER 5

The Journey Through Hell

But once in war I came to know
I was outranked by any child
Great midnight bombers slew.

HARRY C. STALEY, *Memoirs of a Shell-Shocked Chaplain*

Jim was a Phantom F-4 fighter pilot during the Vietnam War. He judged himself to be safe, distant from fighting and killing, and "not a real vet" because he flew at extreme speeds over the battle rather than being a grunt in the muck below.

"Were you shot at? In danger of being shot down?" I asked.

"Of course." He shrugged.

"Did you fire at troops on the ground?"

"Yes, but shooting and being shot at doesn't make me a combat vet."

"How many missions did you fly?"

"Two hundred seventy-four," he answered.

"In one year?" I asked. Tears crept into my eyes as I thought of my friend so often alone and vulnerable in his cockpit.

Jim looked at me. His face turned white.

"Two hundred seventy-four! You climbed into your cockpit 274 times? How did you feel, what did you think—each time?"

"Each time I was sick to my stomach. I loved to fly but hated why I was flying. Scared every time that enemy fire might shoot my balls off. Nauseous every time I had to fire on people below. For decades I couldn't think of them as human beings. But I never thought about what it did to me until now—seeing your feelings over my situation." We were silent for a few minutes. "Even screeching in my jet above the battles, it was still just 'kill or be killed,'" Jim reflected. "I am a combat vet. I've got to own it."

This is war's bottom line. The reasons, causes, and personal and collective histories that brought these people together all disappear. All being is reduced to this pinpoint moment—killing—that defines and shapes the survivor's life forever. You must do it quickly, without a second thought, before the human being you are facing kills you. Karl Marlantes put it directly, "Warriors deal with death. They take life away from others. This is normally the role of God." He laments, "The Marine Corps taught me how to kill, but it didn't teach me how to deal with killing."[1]

WAR IS HELL

From ancient Greece comes the "Homeric Hymn to Ares," dating to about 600 BCE. Our ancestors once sang to the war god not to encourage slaughter but to "restrain the keen fury of my heart which provokes me to tread the ways of blood-curdling strife."[2] It is the hell of war, the gargantuan beast released and raging within and all around us, that drives us to fury and stamps us forever. During World War I, Wilfred Owen wrote that he and his comrades "were in one of the many mouths of Hell."[3] Another ordinary British soldier, killed at age thirty-seven and leaving behind a widow and five orphaned children, wrote home, "This life is something hellish—we never see anything but shells and hard biscuits."[4] Tyler Boudreau carried Dante's *Inferno* with him through Iraq to help guide him through combat. He said, "Hell is war. If you want to curse someone, tell them to 'go to war.'"[5]

General William Tecumseh Sherman described war's inferno on numerous occasions public and private. At the end of the Civil War he wrote:

> I confess, without shame, that I am sick and tired of fighting; its glory is all moonshine; even success the most brilliant is over dead and mangled bodies, with the anguish and lamentations of distant families appealing to me for sons, husbands, and fathers . . . It is only with

> those who have never heard a shot, never heard the shrieks and groans of the wounded and lacerated . . . that cry aloud for more blood, more vengeance, more desolation . . .[6]

Later General Sherman warned future soldiers against glorifying war and, as in the Greek hymn, urged young recruits to restrain their enthusiasm for action:

> I've been where you are now and I know just how you feel. It's entirely natural that there should beat in the breast of every one of you a hope and desire that someday you can use the skills you have acquired here. *Suppress it!* You don't know the horrible aspects of war. I've been through two wars and I know. I've seen cities and homes in ashes . . . thousands of men lying on the ground, their dead faces looking up at the skies. I tell you, war is Hell![7]

Traumatic wounding can occur from combat even in victory. A young Union soldier told his father, "It was a most bloody fight." Only seven of the eighty-five men in his company survived. It was so devastating that despite their victory—"the flag was brought through"—he remained "sad, lonely, and down-hearted."[8]

With war we human beings indeed create hell on earth. We may suffer natural conditions such as hurricanes, floods, fires, or tidal waves that cause extreme suffering and loss. But those events had no human cause. War is different. We imagine it, invent it, create it, practice it. We define other human beings as enemies, less than human, even godforsaken creatures to eradicate. We judge other lives as less worthy than our own and justify their killing. We use untold and uncountable resources to invent ways and means to kill. The threat of an "endless war on terror" is not new; it is only the modern form of the endless series humanity has been waging for millennia. World War II was "a war of remarkable mobility . . . conditioned by science and industry . . . "[9] Advanced technology has now exported war in old, new, and far more brutal forms all over the planet.

Sacred literature and mythologies teach of the hero's descent into the Underworld—the place where our worst terrors are real, the human shadow runs amok, and we are threatened with destruction every second. In Joseph Campbell's map of the universal hero's journey, this descent is the necessary, critical step after leaving comfort and familiarity behind and setting off on an adventure. It is part of the process of initiation, and its map is found in world traditions. In Christian teachings, Jesus had to encounter Satan and resist his temptations, and at the end he had to descend to Hell before climbing the cross. In both Greek and Roman mythologies, heroes who survived the Trojan War encountered long and terrible ordeals trying to return home. Many did not survive. Two of the greatest heroes, Odysseus in Greek legend and the Trojan Aeneas, had to descend to the Underworld to encounter and propitiate the dead in order to receive instructions on how to return home. Without this second descent after the turmoil of combat ceases, the warrior cannot return. Only through willingly encountering the ghosts we harbor in the dark may we hope to make peace with them and gain the path home.

Encountering the powers of the Underworld teaches and transforms us—if we survive. Combat survivors have returned from seeing and doing things foreign and forbidden to most of us. Their very acts that protect us simultaneously counteract our most cherished civilian values. Their journeys must be treated as sacred, genuine and initiatory descents to hell.

KILL OR BE KILLED

Killing another human being may be the most traumatic act a person can perform. Chaplains report that many troops consulting with them wonder whether they have killed or murdered. No matter what the justification, or how necessary or under a moral shield the killing seems, it still profoundly disorders and disturbs. Lt. Colonel Grossman writes, "The dead soldier takes his misery with him, but the man who killed him must forever live and die with him. Killing is what war is all about, and killing in combat, by its very nature, causes deep wounds of pain and guilt."[10]

We have heard that our root Western religious traditions put war—its making, consequences, victories, and defeats—in Divine hands. God is called a Lord of War throughout the Bible. Victories are given God's people when they are faithful and righteous and follow Divine commands. When they don't, their lot is defeat.

Our other Western root traditions—the Greek and the Norse—had specific deities of war and likewise put these decisions of victory or defeat for individual warriors and entire armies and nations under the gods.

The accurate translation of the Sixth Commandment is not "Thou shalt not kill" but "Thou shalt not murder." The Bible differentiates killing from murder and instructs us on when we may take another human life. We require transcendent reasons to justify the taking of life. Our reasons must be so clear and in line with higher law that the death we cause is the lesser evil than allowing that person to live. We are taught to distinguish between just and unjust killings and that sometimes killing may be necessary to protect ourselves or rid society of people who so abuse that they may be unredeemable. Thus a soldier may feel righteous or moral in killing an armed Taliban fighter, but what about the civilians he killed in the same firefight?

Troops suffer moral trauma for having killed when they should not have. Or killing the wrong people. Or killing civilians to get to the foe. Or killing foes defined by the government as an enemy but posing no threat to the homeland. Or killing these foes, then studying history and politics and realizing these were "ancient wrongs painted to be right." Or just from realizing that the other was a human being.

Veterans often complain, "Our therapists will not talk to us about the killing we have done, but only what was done to us. They treat us like victims, but we have perpetrator PTSD." A unique dimension of modern war with as yet unknown impact is that with modern technology people take lives on the other side of the world but are not in danger of being killed in return. As the pilot Jim testified, many troops engaged in distant forms of military action often feel detached from the experience of killing, their victims, and their own status as combat veterans. They may not rehumanize the foe or reconcile with their own histories until long after their service, if at all. Paul Tibbets and his crew of the *Enola Gay* held until their dying days that they had "no regrets" for dropping the atomic bomb on Hiroshima and that it never bothered them; they believed it was a proper action driven by military necessity.

Drone warfare epitomizes issues over long-distance killing. Our new technoweaponry puts troops into a military situation where ultimate conditions have been changed: technology has taken them out of the "kill or be killed situation" and put them into a "kill and go home for dinner and live with it" situation. The more technology develops to protect our "boots on the ground" while allowing us to strike distant others, the more detached from the actual combat experience and traditional warrior roles our troops become. The stranger and more unreal combat becomes, the more detached from the consequences of our actions we all become. Many combatants testify that they tolerated the killing they had to do because they were in a fair fight facing armed professionals in which they might have been killed as well. This is not the case with long-distance killing. Once again, only the method is new, not the impulse, determination, or expenditure of resources. Medea Benjamin points out after an exhaustive investigation, "Drones don't revolutionize warfare; they are, rather, a progressive evolution in making murder clean and easy."[11] We have created this challenge: can human beings kill distant strangers with impunity, then at the end of their work day go home to their families undisturbed? Chaplain Antal wrote from Afghanistan in 2013:

> One of the primary causes of my moral anguish—five months living under drones at Kandahar Airfield I thought—*I don't have thoughts of harming someone else, but I know about the Commander-in-Chief really—and he has this kill list . . . and a whole fleet of armed drones to execute on demand all over the world . . .* War hurts, and *moral pain* can be the most excruciating wound of war—the moral pain of knowing I helped cause the innocent to suffer, like when a hell-fire missile launched remotely from an unmanned drone rips through the most intimate spaces of living rooms and the most sacred grounds of schools.

IT HURTS TO KILL

One soldier returning from deployment reported, "On my way home from Afghanistan I stopped by Fort Bliss, where the military handed me a form to fill out. One question asked, 'Did you receive any injuries in Afghanistan?' I thought to myself, 'Yes, war hurts, and it hurt me.'"

The moral dimension—whether killing was right or wrong, justified or not—is not the only one we must consider. There is another basic and immediate matter.

Brian Turner was a poet before going to Iraq. He used poetry throughout his tour to witness as well as support his own journey through the sandbox. He wrote:

> It should make you strain and sweat,
> Nightmare you, strand you in a desert . . .
> . . . No matter
> what crackling pain and anger
> you carry in your fists, my friend,
> it should break your heart to kill.[12]

Beyond threat, anger, vengeance, protection, politics and policies, codes, rules of engagement, and all factors attempting to guide troops in combat, this is simple, true, and real—it hurts to kill. It should. When it does not, we must be concerned that the survivor has gone numb or is using rationalizations and dehumanization to protect the heart. Iraq veteran Kevin Powers declared simply that after battle, when the screams do not end, "Think of not caring. Call this 'relief.'"[13] Most people believe that we must be numb and dehumanize the other to kill and that we must not grieve the act. Troops commonly hide or repress their pain over killing, not feeling it, keeping it secret, or transforming it into nightmares.

Because of troops' pain at taking life, struggles to figure out who they have become, and questions about whether they are in good stead with the Divine, Army Chaplain Adams said, "I have come to understand that my task as a military chaplain is to help my soldiers create a new covenant with God. It must include their actions in ways that bring them forgiveness and solace. And it will be forever different than God's traditional covenant with civilians."

THE BEAST

Combat survivors speak of the Beast. It awakened in combat, turned them savage, propelled them into their "mad moments," and may pursue them in nightmares and anguish as they trudge through life under its shadow. The savage in us presents as an enraged beast. It is a personification of the berserk experience.[14]

Willy was a combat Marine in Viet Nam. He served as a reconnaissance squad leader deep in the jungles, and he walked point so no one else would have to. He did not count kills because it dishonored the dead, yet he excelled in warfare. Aeschylus said, "The gods fail not to mark / those who have killed many."[15] The Beast pursued this Marine. As warriors from King David to Aeschylus to Siegfried Sassoon have done, he composed his own "Ceremony of the Beast":

I hear, within me, deep soundings.
Rumbles beginning, like a great rage,
Quaking upward, intensifying,
Like the first
Flame . . .
He is come of war, his breeding ground,
Death, his lover . . .
He is come, this beast,
This killing machine . . .
And he is always with me . . .
My name is but a monument
Before his fiery passage . . .

The Beast is the primitive and savage core in us that can go berserk and rend the world. The Furies from Greek mythology are the equally primitive forces of guilt and punishment that rise up when we have done wrong. Against them there has ever been little antidote. In the Furies we hear the imprisoned, haunted, grief- and guilt-tortured soul screaming from the heart of trauma.

THE FURIES: TORTURED CONSCIENCE

In ancient Greece the Furies were "the handmaids of justice," said the philosopher Heraclitus.[16] They were portrayed as three Divine feminine spirits, righteous but brutal and relentless. From the cosmological perspective, they are primitive, godlike forces that hide in the depths of psyche and universe whose task is to assure that cosmic harmony reigns: "The sun will not overstep his measures; if he were to do so, the Furies . . . would seek him out."[17] Their task was to pursue and torture those who had done wrong. From the psychological perspective, they are personifications of a guilty conscience. Archetypally they are justice untempered by mercy. The Furies torture wrongdoers with guilt and anguish until they gain wisdom and atone or else destroy themselves. They enforce our most primitive form of justice, a simple code that children and ancients believed—blood must be spilled for spilling blood; vengeance is just.

Originally called Erinyes by the Greeks and renamed Furies by the Romans, their name derives from the Latin *furia*, which meant rage, madness, and violent passion. To be furious, possessed by these avenging spirits, was to be overwhelmed by passions and rush wildly around, to be out of one's mind. To resist the Furies is to deny a primitive morality that seems built into our natures and early codes of civilization and is still with us. Just after 9/11, a usually compassionate Navy veteran screamed, "They took out two of our buildings. Let's take out two of their countries!"

The *Oresteia*, a three-play series by Aeschylus, dramatizes transgenerational war trauma and gives a portrait of the Furies. Agamemnon, commander of the Greek forces going to Troy, kills his daughter as a sacrifice for fair winds to sail his army. He is away ten years at siege, rampage, and slaughter. While he is gone his queen consolidates power and takes another lover. On his return she murders him in revenge for their daughter. Their son Orestes returns from exile and murders his mother, a heinous crime even in revenge. The murdered mother's ghost invokes the Furies to torture Orestes.

We view eternal themes of war's wounding. A child is sacrificed when her father leaves for war. A husband goes to war, becomes savage and cruel, and kills his tender feelings. A wife finds her power while her husband is away. A wife abandoned and betrayed seeks love elsewhere. When the warrior returns, their intimacy is polluted and marriage and family destroyed. Pain, rage, grief, and guilt pass down the generations. The angry dead haunt the survivors who blame, hurt, and do violence to each other.

Untold numbers of vets are scattered across our landscape, inaccessible to loved ones, haunted, pursued by guilt, grief, and ghosts, constantly changing homes, jobs, and partners, and destroying what they built.

Orestes flees. The Furies pursue him everywhere, allowing no escape, rest, or relief. Orestes has murdered kin and "must give back for her blood . . . red blood of your body . . . " He "must pay for the pain of the murdered mother . . . "

Payment exacted by the Furies echoes the complaints and symptoms of trauma sufferers. One cost is joy. Orestes will live "without knowing where joy lies anywhere inside your heart." Another is the loss of feeling itself: he is "chewed dry by the powers of death." Yet another is relentless suffering: "you shall feed me while you live . . . " A tortured conscience will be his constant companion. This is not wrong, for in guilt the Furies are present. They are "witnesses of the truth"; they destroy "men's illusions in their pride . . . "[18]

In our day we invoke the wound as a clinical and medical condition, relegate treatment to hospitals and mental health centers, analyze it as pathology, and bombard the sufferer with medications, reframing, and positive thinking. In ancient Greece, the response to haunting trauma was utmost solemnity expressed in prayer and poetry performed through public ritual that included dramatic performances. It challenged us to live in tragic nobility and reverence. Traumatic wounding caused a Divine trance by sweeping the individual into a collision with primitive cosmic powers that are the seeds of morality. The powers awakened in war had to be invoked, worshipped, and propitiated.

The trance of the Furies is induced when we perpetrate violence for selfish, immoral, or unnatural ends and when we take the laws of the universe into our own hands. Such actions, Dr. Jonathan Shay points out, are betrayals of *themis*. The Greeks worshiped Themis. Hesiod called her "reverend" and a daughter of heaven. She was a Titan, a god-power built into the order of the cosmos, an "august form . . . which means the Right, or Divine Justice."[19] Themis sat beside the king-god Zeus on Mount Olympus, helping protect the balance of the universe. Shay renders *themis* as "what's right in all things."[20] We can understand Themis as the moral order in the universe and the Furies as her enforcers through conscience. When we betray Themis through war or other forms of violence, we awaken "outrage . . . binding blood and blighting brain . . . " in suffering that can last "till one goes / Under earth. Nor does death / Set them altogether free."[21]

War was so prevalent in the ancient world that people were "war literate" in ways we today are not. How might they have conceived of invisible war wounding? The Greek world declared that their disordered heroes had *trauma*—pierced to the core by the violence of the world and betrayal by their leadership. They were afflicted with *minis*, indignant and surpassing rage. They were "furious"—pursued by inner demons driving them into moral anguish over unjust or overwhelming violence. Their women and children were helpless victims who screamed *anathema*—cursed, wrong, against the order, against the way of life.

A soul-wounded warrior's fate cast in ancient terms: I went to war to preserve life and order as a servant of Athena, the warrior goddess of wisdom and civilization. Instead I became a servant of Ares, the berserker god, a misused weapon spreading chaos, terror, and destruction. Now I am fallen away. *Anathema!*

RELATIONS WITH DEATH

There may be nothing more strange and mysterious to human beings than death. One minute we are here, the next not. No matter our religious beliefs, we cannot know for certain what death is or what comes afterward. Warriors become familiar with death, stained by its presence and captivated by its mystique. Captain Frank Hill, XO (Executive Officer) of a battlefield surgical team in Afghanistan, reported in 2006, "Three more Americans killed here yesterday and three of their buddies . . . peppered with shrapnel . . . Busy makes the time go but adds a certain weight that leaves a mark." A month later Captain Hill reflected:

> It is a chaos, terrible and turbulent with no respite. But in the center of all the madness, there exists a momentary silence. When all the pinging alarms and buzzing beepers

> cease and the squeak of blood-soaked shoes on linoleum goes still. That instant when there is nothing to do and nothing to say. No words to fill mouths. No thought, no will, no desire. Void of any possible appropriate design to impart. Empty of every possible accessory but the truth of the moment. The inescapable, cutting, deliriously vacant truth, ever present and teasingly intangible: this man, this brother, whose name I will carry forever, died today . . . [22]

Warriors are overexposed to death while civilians are protected from almost any exposure. This too differentiates classes. Captain Hill's duty was to try and save lives, but he was drenched in the "death imprint." How much more impactful if we cause a death and become a life taker. It cannot be undone.

Nupkus Roger Shourds is the only one of the highly trained and experienced warriors cited earlier who included the encounter with death in his definition. Nupkus is a Native American warrior whose culture names warriorhood for its encounter with death and does not hide this truth from anyone. Few veterans discuss this feature with outsiders, but the purpose of war is to kill, and to be a warrior is to become a familiar with death—to deal it to others and accept it for oneself, whenever and however it may come. In many Native American tribes, warriors painted themselves and their warhorses red to signify that they had been in battle and drew blood . . . black signified their encounters with death. The Lakota, for example, painted their faces black for the dance held on their return from battle. "By going on the warpath," the medicine man Black Elk explained, "we know that we have done something bad, and we wish to hide our faces from *Wakan Tanka*."[23]

During World War I, Wilfred Owen declared what millions of warriors have experienced: "Out there, we've walked quite friendly up to death."[24] It is perhaps this encounter, the experience of oneself as target or executioner, and the unforgettable lessons that we are small, weak, vulnerable creatures only here for an instant yet able to cause untold harm, that most radically transforms warriors. Also during World War I, Siegfried Sassoon declared, "death has made me wise and bitter and strong; / And I am rich in all that I have lost."[25] From Afghanistan,

Chaplain George Tyger reflected, "When we lose friends, an emptiness remains which even the highest ideals cannot fill. The cost of these ideals is the struggle to find meaning in these losses."[26] Inherent in the warrior's encounter with death is the necessity to make meaning and gain richness in loss. This is a daunting challenge if the veteran judges the deaths he or she caused or witnessed to be illegitimate, immoral, or unnecessary. Without meaning we cannot exalt.

Marine combat veteran Larry Winters condensed this wounding from killing and the necessity for spiritual healing into a single short poem:

When a soldier kills
he must dig two graves
one in the earth for the dead
one in his soul
or he will not return.[27]

As Professor Brooke states, "The warrior's soul does not return to him from the scenes of battle until he has made peace with the souls of the enemy dead."[28] The pain and stain of killing, our inability to undo it, faces and bodies we see for the rest of our days, give the invisible wound its unique, penetrating, irresistible power.

OUR TRAUMATIZED ANCESTRAL WARRIOR-KING

We again examine our root traditions to see how these morally demanding and hellish conditions of politics and war affected our ancestors and have been passed down through the millennia. The Old Testament offers two "case studies" that began the rule of Western civilization and helped set the patterns in psyche and culture we have been replicating ever since.

Saul and David were the first two rulers of ancient Israel and are thus the ancestral kings of the Judeo-Christian lineage. They were both warrior-kings who committed atrocities, disobeyed. Divine commandments, danced on their enemies' graves, behaved selfishly and lustfully, and invoked God as a "Lord of War." They both showed the rages, unpredictability, mistrust, and betrayal of intimate relationships, emptiness of spirit, loss of meaning, instability, forsaken conditions, and desperate appeals to Divinity that characterize the invisible wound even today. We will visit David later, but now Saul helps us see the war trauma built into the very origins of our civilization.

About 1030 BCE, Saul was chosen through the "seer" Samuel when the Hebrew people insisted they wanted a king like other peoples had. God considered this a turning away, a rejection of their true King. Warning against it, God granted the request. Contention with the Divine was built into Saul's reign from the beginning.

Saul was a daunting figure, "in the prime of life . . . a foot taller than anyone else . . . and more handsome."[29] A formidable warrior, Saul defeated the Ammonites, Philistines, and Amalekites, crediting God with each victory as proof of . . . Divine favor. "The Lord saved Israel that day."[30] Saul instituted a selective draft. "Whenever he found a man who was strong and brave, he enlisted him in his army."[31]

God ordered Saul to commit genocide against the Amalekites: "completely destroy everything they have. Don't leave a thing; kill all the men, women, children, and babies, the cattle, sheep, camels, and donkeys."[32] This was because generations earlier their ancestors had opposed the Israelites escaping from Egypt—transgenerational trauma again as well as revenge as a Divine motive. Saul captured rather than slew King Agag and kept the best sheep and cattle. Rejected by God for this disobedience, he defended himself arguing he had saved the animals for sacrifice. God, Samuel answered, demands obedience no matter what the orders. Samuel then cut Agag to pieces with his sword in front of the altar.

Saul plummeted into a private hell that he imposed on his family and people. He raged when "the evil spirit entered him." David was brought to soothe him with his harp. When David played—music therapy—"the evil spirit would leave and Saul would feel better."[33] But Saul also raged against David, several times nearly killing him with his spear. He almost killed his own son Jonathan when he and David became best friends and Jonathan tried to mitigate his father's wrath. Saul slew eighty-five priests who tried to convince him of David's allegiance. He tried hunting and capturing David even after David twice spared his life.

Spiritually destitute, fearing the assembling Philistines, Saul consulted a holy woman, a medium of Endor, though he had previously banished all such women from his kingdom. She conjured Samuel's spirit, who affirmed, "The Lord has abandoned you and become your enemy . . . He has taken the kingdom away from you and given it to David . . . [because] You disobeyed and did not completely destroy" your enemy.[34] Saul collapsed. The woman comforted and fed him—tending the wound. Soon after, he fought the Philistines on Mount Gilboa. As prophesized, the Israelites lost; Saul killed himself on his sword.

Saul was prone to rages, betrayals, and atrocities. He turned against family and friends. He banished holy women and killed priests, then begged their survivors for help. His moods changed abruptly. He flashed from friendly and approachable to misinterpreting others and exploding in violent rages and then to feeling bereft and begging for relief. We hear the Biblical interpretation of the traumatic wound at least three times—"an evil spirit from God suddenly took control of Saul and he raved in his house like a madman."[35]

Saul, ancestral founding king, presents a vivid portrait of a severely traumatized warrior, dangerous to his loved ones and irrational, impulsive, and violent in his rule, destroying others and finally himself. We have seen his pattern repeated in leaders and grunts from ancient times to the present day.

How do we interpret God's hunger for vengeance and command to commit genocide? We seem to be told that vengeance is of the Divine and should be enacted with utmost brutality—although we are instructed elsewhere not to kill in vengeance. We are taught that absolute obedience to the command of authority is our prescribed way of life and to refuse an order can have consequences severe enough to destroy us. We might respect Saul for not following such a command. "I was only following orders" could have been his defense against the charge of genocide. Warriors have been morally wounded and become spiritually bereft by following immoral orders from Saul's day to ours. And like Saul they have paid dire consequences for refusing.

WAR IS A MORAL ARENA

One soldier back from Afghanistan wrote on his deployment return questionnaire, "I have a moral injury, a betrayal of what is right."

Just as war is inevitably a spiritual arena, so it is a moral arena. During warfare we unleash gargantuan forces of good and evil as created by humans. Important actions, especially impacting life and death or creation and destruction, are not value-neutral but inherently moral or immoral. Philosophies and religions worldwide have taught that doing right or wrong is of the soul and must be aligned with universal principles, serve the preservation of life, and benefit the highest good. This has been especially true of our beliefs regarding warfare. In the purist traditional interpretation, war is "an act against but one thing: whoever, whatever interferes with generating life . . . [W]hoever interferes with circulating good becomes the enemy."[36] We must only preserve and protect; all actions must have these ultimate goals; we must not "destroy that which [w]e lack the power—the knowing—for putting back together."[37]

For these reasons our choices and actions in military service will have, in Brian Turner's words, "consequences seared into the vein." The heart and soul will struggle with and suffer from them until they are resolved. Troops and veterans will judge their commanders from squad leader up to the president and to the Divine on whether or not they ordered moral service. When the service did not fulfill the reasons given—for example, the Communist threat to the United States from North Viet Nam, keeping the remote Falkland Islands from Argentina by British forces, weapons of mass destruction in Iraq—veterans will feel moral trauma over the actions they judge to be illegitimate and from leaders who put them in the situation. They are in danger of feeling, as one said, "I left our country as a warrior protecting America, but in Iraq I merely became a mercenary for corporations."

CHAPTER 6

The Invisible Wound Today

Many a man has gone crazy since this campaign begun . . .

OLIVER WENDELL HOLMES

I stood in an auditorium beside Lt. Colonel Frank Houde. Stocky and strong at seventy as when he was young, Frank served as an Air Force reconnaissance squadron commander in Viet Nam. He recalled beautiful sunsets from thousands of feet above green mountains, and flames and smoke from the bombings that ravaged them. Groomed to become a general in the Strategic Air Command, he became so disillusioned by the war that he retired as soon as possible afterward.

We were lecturing high school students. One teen asked, "Colonel, please describe PTSD from a combat veteran's point of view."

Frank has felt the aftershocks of war for forty years and into a new generation. His son was severely wounded in Iraq. He looked at the student and said, "It hurts. It's a wound. Right here." He patted his heart with his hand.

Contemporary thought equates holism with body-mind medicine and holistic healing as tending body, mind, and spirit. These formulations help restore parts of our humanity excluded from healing regimens for centuries. Yet they are incomplete. Colonel Houde patted his heart. Mr. Tiger declared that "in Viet Nam we know the wound is here," and also patted his heart. Holism must include not only body, mind, and spirit but *body, mind, heart, and spirit in community and guided by transcendent meaning.*

THE WOUND RETURNS

How do we know there is a wound when there is no blood? How does an invisible wound make itself known?

Vietnam veterans, women survivors of domestic violence and sexual abuse, and Holocaust survivors lobbied for years for public and professional recognition of their characteristic breakdowns. They had all survived life-threatening violence and over time manifested similar sets of symptoms—insomnia, nightmares, rages, hypervigilance, emotional distance, mistrust, intimacy problems, and other symptoms. The American Psychiatric Association finally entered Post-traumatic Stress Disorder into our present classification system in 1980. At one professional conference a decade later I heard a presenter exclaim, "Now we finally know what is *really* afflicting our veterans."

In Special Forces, Kevin Turner served in danger and secrecy. He had no one to rely on but himself and his small elite team. He wrote in his song "Nobody Knows:"

> It better mean something, this death and despair . . .
> This wound to my soul . . .
> Silent cries deep in the night,
> Ancient wrongs painted to be right . . . [1]

"The light had gone out," combat vet John Fisher explained. "It was all dark inside." Combat platoon leader Dick McHenry said, "I am learning more and more about how war destroys. The men directing the drone killings are suffering with PTSD now. It all comes to this—war scars the soul and a man's values. I am in pain almost daily from this, and medications do not help make this kind of pain go away."

Charles Pacello served for more than five years as an Air Force officer on the Nuclear Detonation Detection System, retiring in 2001. He was responsible, in part, for keeping American nuclear weapons prepared to make a first strike. He described what nobody could see:

> "Soul wounding" felt like a big piece of the puzzle that made all the events I experienced in the military understandable, and why I lost my moral compass and connection to the

> Divine. Life simply didn't make sense to me. I turned away from God (I actually can remember the day and where I was at when I said it), and to a life of reckless and wild wantonness. The immense guilt and shame I felt for the man I'd become was so filled with self-hatred and disgust, I would anesthetize myself even more to block out the overwhelming feeling of having ruined and destroyed my life, not to mention others' lives I had permanently altered. I took residence in the Underworld, got stuck there, and dug the pit to the very bottom. It was only through the Grace of God I was able to climb out of it.

General Douglas MacArthur knew of such wounds. "The soldier above all others prays for peace," he said, "because it is the soldier who must suffer and bear the deepest wounds and scars of war."[2]

"Boots on the ground" up through general staff testify to how deep, comprehensive, painful, and life-transforming war's soul wounds are. Some political leaders and therapists believe it is better for the public not to hear of these wounds and their stories. But survivors want leaders, helpers, and the public to know war's impact and that its wounds do not go away. Generations of veterans recite, "Only the dead have seen the end of war."[3]

THE MODERN DIAGNOSIS

The *Diagnostic and Statistical Manual* (DSM) is the "bible" of psychiatry. It classifies recognized mental illnesses and disorders and is regularly updated. The DSM named Post-traumatic Stress Disorder a modern affliction in 1980, classifying it as a stress and anxiety disorder constituting a cluster of symptoms surfacing after traumatic events beyond the scope of normal experience. Events include threats to one's own or to others' lives and would cause such responses in almost anyone.[4]

The DSM was updated in 2013. PTSD has been shifted in the DSM-5 to a new category called Trauma and Stressor-Related Disorders. Does this signal that trauma itself is finally recognized as a unique, foundational, and transformational category of experience for us as individuals, a species, and for the large family of vulnerable sentient beings around the planet? What we call PTSD has been observed in elephants, bears, wolves, geese, parrots, dogs, cats, dolphins, and whales. Animal trauma psychologist Dr. Gay Bradshaw writes,

> It is often said that human PTSD is a natural response to abnormal conditions. So is it for other animals. Symptoms that haunt human survivors of violence also haunt elephants subjected to genocide, chimpanzees tortured in biomedical experiments legally prohibited for humans, and parrots torn from their families and confined to cages and abuse. Trauma knows no species bounds. No soul is exempt no matter if they wear feathers, fins, fur, or plain skin.[5]

TRAUMATIC WAR WOUNDING IN MODERN HISTORY[6]

Every era names, diagnoses, interprets, and treats diseases and disorders by the values and beliefs of its time. Nothing is *really* its current name. Post-traumatic Stress Disorder and Operational Stress are new names for an ancient condition. The condition is neither a new discovery nor *really* PTSD. We heard the Biblical King Saul's war madness attributed to this: "The spirit of God left him and an evil spirit sent by the Lord entered him."[7]

The first systematic treatment of war's psychiatric casualties dates to ancient Rome, "where soldiers suffering battle-induced psychiatric problems were cared for in the psychiatric wards of legion hospitals."[8]

Rome followed Greece as the dominant power of Western civilization. The Romans worshipped militarism. Might, power, and wealth were noble and just ends in themselves. They elevated their war god, Mars, to second in command after the king-god Jove and emulated his fierce ideal. Military power was their political tool to create and sustain one of the largest empires in history. Their veterans periodically rested and did penance by breaking from combat duty to rebuild roads, bridges, and buildings.

No matter how successful their conquests, there were angry, tired, disillusioned, betrayed old veterans in the Roman world. Josephus recorded a case from the Jewish Wars during 66–70 CE. An "old soldier" named Tiro protested the wrongful execution of two comrades. Tiro, "in the excess of his indignation, lost his reason. He went about shouting that justice had been trampled underfoot, truth was dead, the laws of nature confounded, the world full of iniquity."[9] We hear modern veterans, homeless on the streets or in political confrontations, cry the same messages. They nod in recognition at Tiro's words. They declare that the story is always the same; it does not matter who, when, or where. Soldiers always love their comrades and rage at betrayal of the ideals they entered the military to uphold.

What we call Post-traumatic Stress Disorder was diagnosed as "nostalgia" among Swiss soldiers in 1648. Early German and French doctors called it "homesickness." The French also called it "disease of the country." The Spanish called it "to be broken." Buck Fever and Old Sergeant Syndrome were among evocative former names.

Testimony of the wound recurs throughout world history, mythology, literature, sacred writings, and survivors' tales. It has been treated by other strategies in different times and places. It has also been treated with similar strategies to what we try today and call "new"—natural and synthetic medications, food and rest out of danger and in nature, gentle talk and tending, expression through the arts, electroshock, isolation and confinement, intimidation, and accusations of cowardice.

Let us examine the wound's modern history and recurrence.

The American Civil War is considered the first modern war because of its masses of citizens and immigrants pressed into service, massive numbers of casualties, scorched-earth policy, and highly destructive new technology. Oliver Wendell Holmes, later Chief Justice of the Supreme Court, served in the Union infantry and was wounded three times, including at Antietam along with more than 17,000 others. Fearing for life and sanity on the battlefield, he wrote his parents, "Many a man has gone crazy since this campaign began from the terrible pressure on mind and body."[10]

Soldier's Heart was the term commonly used during the Civil War era for the diagnosis of Da Costa's Syndrome, first studied and reported by Jacob Mendes Da Costa. Da Costa was an assistant surgeon in the US Army and later in a Philadelphia hospital. Calling the condition "irritable heart," he documented the physiological manifestations of severe anxiety among soldiers. These included fatigue, palpitations, chest pains, and sweating—all without physical causation.

The names Da Costa's Syndrome and Soldier's Heart were often used interchangeably. Use of the former term might stress physiological conditions, the latter psychological, a distinction we seem to have lost today. The condition was often accompanied by a debilitating loss of will and called "the Effort Syndrome." As described by Captain H. P. Wright of the Canadian Army Medical Corps during World War I, "The will seems to have lost control of the brain."[11] Modern sufferers and caregivers will recognize this aspect of the wound. Like a car that won't start, nothing seems visibly wrong but the ignition just won't turn over and the car won't go. We often hear laments, "I'm frozen." "I'm stuck." "I just can't get moving." Will, motivation, drive, inspiration, and the ability to initiate are common casualties of trauma. An external power invaded and harmed. An inner propelling force surrendered or was broken. Lieutenant Pacello described it as "stuck in the Underworld." Plato explained that the will is a function of soul and drives us from within. Though today we may include it in depression, to be rendered will-less is a soul wound.

In the modern era, Russia was the first nation to restore systematic care to battlefield psychiatric casualties, using military psychiatric wards during the Russo-Japanese War of 1904–5.[12] During World War I the wound was famously called "shell shock" and during World War II "combat fatigue."[13] Soldiers recognized it in each other. In the trenches Wilfred Owen noticed "the very strange look on all the faces in the camp; an incomprehensible look . . . more terrible than terror . . . a blindfold look."[14] He wrote of men who "let their veins run cold . . . cease feeling . . . loose imagination . . . laugh among the dying . . . blood all over our soul . . . not vital overmuch."[15] He "heard the sighs of men, that have no skill to speak of their distress, no, nor the will!"[16] In the Nazi concentration camps such stricken inmates were called "zombies." At this stage of deterioration they lost all will to eat, work, talk, or survive. Their companions knew their spirits were gone and avoided them. Death came within days.

During twentieth-century wars the wound was commonly treated as an acute breakdown in the combat zone. It was believed to be limited in time and scope and sometimes blamed on character flaws, especially cowardice. Treatment was to get the afflicted combatant off the front lines and out of immediate danger, give him three square meals a day and some bed rest, then return him to his unit as quickly as possible. This was intended to reduce the loss of troops due to shock and fear, keep the front supplied, and discourage soldiers from escaping through breakdown.

Reuben Levinson was a young Army doctor in World War II. He participated in the D-day invasion and treated the wounded in small aid stations and field hospitals from Normandy Beach across Europe. His unit helped liberate the Nordhausen concentration camp. Levinson remained in the camp to treat survivors, working with thousands of emaciated skeletons barely alive among uncountable remains of the murdered. After surviving what his daughter called a "barrage more than any mind could take in," Levinson collapsed. His only treatment was two weeks of rest on a French beach. The result was unrecognized traumatic wounding characterized by workaholism, depression, emotional detachment, unavailability, and loss of faith. His lifelong condition planted loneliness, confusion, depression, and sorrow in his children.[17] This pattern of workaholism and emotional unavailability, often accompanied by alcoholism and rages, seems to be the common form of traumatic wounding that characterized countless tens of thousands of World War II veterans, causing the much-discussed "father wound" in their children.

Strategies like safe, short-term rest and quick return to the front lines sustained the war effort but did little to heal broken soldiers. They also upheld the masculine myth that only the weak or cowardly collapse during war. During World War I, the British executed 306 soldiers who broke down during combat and refused to return to the front lines.[18] During the invasion of Sicily in World War II, General George Patton slapped, kicked, threatened, and berated as cowards two American GIs who had been evacuated with shell shock. Patton declared such men guilty of "cowardice"; they "shirk their duty . . . [and] should be tried and shot."[19]

Modern war casualty rates demonstrate the danger and extent of psychological wounding. During World War I, around 80,000 shell-shock cases passed through British military hospitals. By 1916 shell-shock constituted 40 percent of their casualties, and during the entire war around 200,000 troops were discharged from service for psychological breakdown. During the first decade following the war, over 114,000 veterans applied for pensions due to shell shock.[20] The result: shell shock was "raised to the dignity of a new war disease before which doctors seemed well-nigh helpless."[21]

In World War I, US forces suffered 116,516 deaths but 158,994 psychiatric losses. In World War II, US forces had 405,399 deaths but 1,393,000 debilitating psychiatric breakdowns. In the Korean War, 33,629 troops were killed but 48,002 became psychiatric casualties.[22] In the Vietnam War, 58,212 service people, including eight women, were killed. According to Department of Veterans Affairs statistics, the diagnosis of PTSD has been rendered in at least 30 percent of those who served, with another 22 percent experiencing partial disability, creating at least 1.3 million cases.[23] In modern wars, former Intelligence Officer and military expert Professor Richard Gabriel writes, "the chances of becoming a psychiatric casualty—of being debilitated for some period of time as a result of the stresses of military life—were greater than the chances of being killed by enemy fire."[24]

The individual's experience of mass technological warfare is not equitable with the one-on-one duels between heroes recorded in myths, legends, and sacred texts or the personal and initiatory practices of warfare among traditional peoples. Ancient mass warfare, like modern wars, included siege, pillage, atrocity, rape, and the destruction of civilians, their homes, possessions, livestock, lands, entire cities, and enemy troops. Yet today, warfare has become more deadly, debilitating, and "invisible" than ever. This is due to the high numbers of available combatants around the world; the transformation of civilians into acceptable targets; and modern weapons that inevitably kill civilians, destroy infrastructure, poison the environment, annihilate millions in a blow, and can strike anywhere on the planet without even being manned. We can surmise that the greater the destructive reach of our weaponry, the greater the moral stress and burden on troops and the nation, and the more penetrating yet mysterious the invisible wound will be.

As the first modern war, the Civil War saw new practices of massive destruction rationalized as military necessity that are with us to this day. Consider a few of the innumerable examples. Regarding casualties, more men were killed at the Battle of Shiloh in 1862 than in all previous American wars, including the Revolution, the War of 1812, and the Mexican War combined.[25] At Gettysburg, it only took two hours to reach such a casualty rate.[26] Ulysses S. Grant was a highly effective general in large part because he broke with the romantic tradition equating war with nobility and glory. Instead he affirmed that war was truly about brutality and killing. The realist Grant was willing to kill and lose as many soldiers as necessary, sometimes many more than his foe, to gain victory. In fact, over the course of the war the Union army lost about twice as many soldiers killed in action as the Confederates.[27] Grant fought a war of attrition, meaning that victory came by killing as many of the enemy as quickly as possible so that they would run out of soldiers with which to fight.[28]

Damage to the infrastructure and environment was also practiced on a massive scale and presented as necessary. The largest land mine in the history of warfare was used, and the longest, heaviest naval bombardment of a civilian city occurred. Of innumerable examples, we can peek at scenes from Sherman's March to the Sea. Union officer Frank Blair recorded, "We have destroyed nearly four hundred miles of Railroad . . . and we have burned millions of dollars worth of cotton which is the only thing that enables them to maintain credit abroad . . . & actually gobbled up enough provisions to have fed Lee's army for six months."[29] The *Boston Advertiser* described Charleston, South Carolina, after Sherman: "A city of ruins, of desolation, of vacant houses, of widowed women, of rotting wharves, of deserted warehouses, of weed-wild gardens, of miles of grass-grown streets, of acres of pitiful and voiceful barrenness . . ."[30] Practices of fighting itself were reset during the Civil War that would characterize combat through World War I: ". . . a seemingly endless series of attacks against trenchworks . . . Artillery bombardments, mining, bayonet charges, sniping, and hand-to-hand fighting became the defining activities."[31]

The civilian casualty rate has risen dramatically with each new war. During World War I, civilians accounted for 10 percent of those killed, in World War II 50 percent, in Vietnam 70 percent, and in the Iraq War 90 percent.[32] This has become not only acceptable but also expected. The US Army created an Army Experience Center for children in a Philadelphia shopping mall. At a cost of $14 million, it includes high-tech equipment replicating the contemporary war zone and is meant to entice children and teens into the military. Visitors participate in computer-generated, virtual-reality Humvee drives through a combat zone. Afterward they learn that they "killed" many people during their mock drive; commonly 25 percent of their casualties were civilians. "Don't worry about it," the Army representative tells them. "That is actually a low civilian kill rate."[33]

HIDDEN TOLLS

Any people will interpret the world through the dominant views of their times. Cultural assumptions, beliefs, and prejudices are embedded in theories and practices regarding medical and health conditions. This is true of war and its aftermath. Hidden assumptions exist in military, health and mental health communities, and popular culture that influence our response to war's wounding.

A modern soldier does not serve at will, and once mustered in is a GI, "government issue," no longer a free agent and bound to follow orders no matter his or her agreement. The welfare of the individual soldier is subordinate to the goals and missions of military and political authorities stretching all the way to the president, just as it was elsewhere to kings, dictators, emperors, or chiefs. During warfare, combatants must be kept on the front lines and their numbers sustained. Maintaining troop levels no matter the psychological cost has become a special concern during current American wars dependent upon an all-volunteer military that has a limited number of available fresh troops with many experiencing multiple deployments. We no longer have a citizen army mustered as needed with most people eligible for service. Now troops are considered in the profession of arms, available for combat, and often kept in constant deployment rotation. These factors in military culture militate against recognizing the extent and severity of trauma. Rather, a professional, specialized, and competent but isolated, exhausted, and traumatized military has become the norm.[34]

These issues transcend current wars. As a culture and civilization, we have inherited basic assumptions about service. We believe that men—and now women—should be able to "take it" or, as we now say, "develop resiliency." That is, we expect them to be able to tolerate the degree and intensity of terror, rage, loss, and pain experienced during combat. We believe they must accept the killing they do to survive and complete their assigned missions. With "warrior preparedness training," we try to strengthen their characters so that combat is less psychically wounding.

But killing inevitably takes a toll. Troops, their officers, the general public, and even health practitioners may consciously or unconsciously assume cowardice and weakness (as did General Patton), unstable childhood personalities, or other negative traits to be causes of traumatic breakdown. Such judgments can further wound someone already shaken to the foundations. Dr. P., military director of a leading trauma treatment center, confided that he no longer travels in uniform because he does not want people to offer a shallow "thank you for your service" when they don't understand the suffering behind it. A combat veteran stood up during a conference I attended and scolded the audience, "Don't thank me for my service. My service was to kill human beings!" I met a recently returned young Ranger wearing a T-shirt with his places of service on the front and "If you weren't there, shut up!" in large black letters across his back.

Trauma therapists understand that a life can be thrown off its trajectory at any time by experiences of significant intensity, threat, and strangeness. Yet some therapists assume that we can generalize from the treatment of one type of trauma to all. They may equate, for example, rape victims, car accident survivors, and war veterans. Focusing on the similarity of patients' traumatic response, they may not recognize the special conditions of military culture and the experiences of one who was a sanctioned killer many times over in a combat zone. Shawn Nelson was a machine gunner who was trapped on the ground and went deaf during the 1993 Mogadishu, Somalia, battle known as Black Hawk Down. He insists,

> Returning veterans are not "primed" to engage in conventional or new age services. At best, they may "go through the motions." This is especially true for killers. Therapists do not distinguish well enough between vets who killed and "office veterans" who were not engaged in actual face-to-face killing.

Even in war there is a vast continuum of exposure to violence. It proceeds from civilians awaiting their loved ones' return to civilian victims and survivors, from noncombatant veterans stationed stateside to those behind the lines, then to personnel supporting or exposed to combat and its losses, then to those who actually did the fighting and killing, and then to how near or distant the vet was from the killing, which branch of service he or she was in, which weapons and methods were used, when and where in a conflict service occurred, and whether the troops believed in the reasons for which they were serving and slaying. There is a bottom line: veterans reserve greatest honor, respect, and concern for "boots on the ground," those up front and in gravest danger. They insist that the only heroes are their fallen. They differentiate the rest of us into veterans or civilians and those who "get it" and those who don't. To "get it" means to see through the eyes and feel with the heart of one who has been in the kill-or-be-killed situation, experienced life focused on a razor-blade moment, and been changed by this encounter forever. Veterans will walk through hell with someone who gets it because they trust that that person would remain by their side in the real hell of war.

We must apply this dictate to healers as well as military leaders. Veterans may refuse to walk "into the deepest valleys" even with the best-intentioned helpers because they do not deem the journey safe with one who does not understand the world of the military, combat, warriorhood, and the Underworld, and who does not practice deep love, compassion, and comprehension on a shared moral journey as the medicine that can bring us through.

POPULAR APPROACHES TO TRAUMA TODAY

Let us examine some of the popular approaches to the invisible wound today to see how close to the survivor's living experience they come and what they indicate about our underlying societal beliefs about war and its impact.[35]

Grouping war-induced troubles with all traumatic disorders and including them under a group stress or trauma label reveals a belief that the experience of war is not different in kind but only in intensity from civilian experience. It reduces wrath and wounding into stress, despair into depression, and soul loss into dissociation. It applies the medical model indicating that we are dealing in large part with a biologically based disorder or biochemical dysfunction that must be treated by specialists with drugs. Even the name contributes. Psychologist Paula Caplan points out that for "terms used in earlier wars . . . the language of war is used, is crystal clear. 'Post-traumatic Stress Disorder' helps with the cover-up of the fact that it is *war* that is causing this suffering."[36]

Contemporary strategy assumes that survivors have become hypersensitive and "maxed out" in their ability to absorb or manage stress. It even minimizes the seriousness and pain implied in the word *stress*, which has become so commonly used that its original meaning and power have been lost. Stress is a shortened form of *distress*, which originally meant "to draw apart" and indicated extreme anguish, agitation, pressure, compulsion, and imminent danger. The word *distress* is over 700 years old, but stress was not used in its psychological sense until the 1940s. Stress is not reducible to the everyday buzz with which the modern world bombards us; rush hour traffic and unpaid bills are not on a par with combat.

The diagnosis underscores, as recent research indicates and many treatments address, that survivors' brains and nervous systems may have been damaged or altered. This interpretation, too, is not new. During the Civil War, the wound was believed to be caused by physiological changes to the heart; during World War I, the changes were believed to be to the heart and central nervous system. In each instance, military, government, psychiatric, and health communities largely denied the emotional, psychological, and spiritual components of troop distress.

Today survivors are taught to manage and minimize everyday stressors such that symptoms are not triggered. They are retrained to compensate and correct cerebral functioning. They are medicated to provide symptom relief. They are financially compensated for damage but may have to apply, reapply, fight, and wait for years or decades for a settlement. The recipe: you have a chronic condition, avoid stimulating it, use supportive or corrective cognitive training and medical treatment including medications, acquire a disability rating, and seek benefits.

Many veterans report that during psychotherapy they were discouraged from discussing war experiences and their impact as a way of teaching them to avoid stressors, especially painful memories. Some counselors only allow the examination of childhood experiences or current reintegration challenges. Sean Nelson reported:

> I was frustrated with both individual and group therapies because neither the counselor nor the doctor wanted to let me tell or even hear my story. I saw this happen to other vet friends. We were enraged that these people didn't care. They wanted us to talk about "where you are now" or "how you feel today," not how we felt when we were killing people or seeing our friends killed. This was absurd. I wanted to get the shit off my chest, see if I could comprehend what I lived through, and purge my knotted-up feelings that I could not express at the moment when two men are aiming their guns at each other. Whatever these professionals were doing only made things worse.

Steering veterans away from discussing war can sometimes be due to the belief some therapists hold that life-shaping experiences only occur during childhood and that the adult personality cannot be significantly altered. James Hillman has called this "the developmental fallacy." It can also be due to helpers' pain, fear, or revulsion at the horrors they must witness if stories are told. Have we, like Job's comforters, reached our limits of tolerance when we tell veterans to "get over it," "move on," stories are unnecessary? Who are we protecting?

Strategies that teach the afflicted to steer away from stress triggers may help the sufferer achieve grounding and functionality. Yet they may also unwittingly deny the intensity, severity, and life-changing impact of war and reinforce societal silence about it. Not telling stories, in one vet's words, "keeps war locked in my head." Silence does not protect society. War denied will emerge, sometimes violently, through symptoms. Symptoms are the language of our soul wounds.

"Bringing the troops home" does not only mean returning them from downrange but also transitioning them back into stable and participating community members who have become something beyond their civilian identities that are no longer complex enough. Of course veterans want to rejoin their families and become employed, and loved ones want them back. Many ask, "Can you make me [or him or her] the person I was before going to war?"

This is a noble ideal and part of our nostalgia. But it equates homecoming with becoming again who we once were or adaptation to civilian life in mainstream society. Greek mythology tells of the dilemma of Achilles. The warrior was given the choice between brutal service and early death with fame and honor or a long but dull and routine civilian existence without honor. Achilles chose the first. Many vets find the return to the ordinary boring and meaningless and make their version of Achilles's choice by reenlisting for another deployment or at home refusing to participate in the ordinary. Sean Nelson said,

> I was past the point of frustration with the VA, their "meds," and detached, obfuscating denial of the true problem that combat veterans deal with. It is that veterans have had their hearts and souls torn apart from engaging in warfare under a set of false pretenses. This is/was *my* particular problem. I believe this is what lies at the core of all American veterans' issues.

War survivors rankle when their experience is reduced to stress, they are not allowed to give it witness, their experiences are equated with civilians, and they cannot get at the true issues that disturb and alienate them.

CHALLENGES OF MISDIAGNOSIS, ALCOHOL, AND MEDICATION

The invisible wound can be misdiagnosed or mistreated as one or several of its dominating symptoms. Depression and substance abuse are common. The wound can also be difficult to distinguish from psychological conditions that preceded it, including preservice trauma. Many troops in today's military are recruited from the urban and rural poor; many have had difficult, challenging, stressful, abusive, or violent earlier life histories and arrive at boot camp already traumatized. This makes military training and development more challenging and may render some more vulnerable to military-related trauma. In addition, the wound may be difficult to distinguish from accompanying wounds with similar symptoms such as Traumatic Brain Injury. Misdiagnosis can leave a veteran feeling misconstrued, disappointed, betrayed, or angry, and may discourage cooperation in a healing regimen. Sometimes veterans may themselves avoid their most painful war issues by clutching lesser diagnoses.

Vince, a combat infantryman, worked eighty hours a week and frequently exploded. He sometimes disappeared to hide out with liquor bottles in lonely motel rooms for days at a time. But he ran a business, supported his family, loved his children, and behaved well "especially after one of my lost weekends."

Vince entered therapy after he had lost his license three times for driving while intoxicated. Several times he quit rehabilitation programs. "They only want me to control my drinking," Vince told me. "But I'm not an alcoholic. That's not the problem. They won't let me talk about the war. Don't they understand that I can't stop drinking as long as the war is locked up inside me?"

Had I stressed controlling alcohol intake before tending war wounds, Vince would have left counseling just as he had left addiction programs. Instead he revealed that terrible combat memories lurked behind his drinking and he used alcohol to numb them. Soldiers using alcohol to cope with pain and terror is as old as war. From ninth-century China we hear:

> Drinking or not drinking,
> the horns summon you to mount.
> Do not laugh if I am drunk on the sandy battlefields.
> From ancient times,
> how many warriors have ever returned?[37]

Many of Custer's officers were alcoholics. Many troopers at the Little Bighorn carried liquor-filled canteens and galloped drunk and dazed into the Lakota village and slaughter.[38]

As Vince related his stories, he spontaneously and willingly connected them to his drinking. Previously his drinking increased as an expression of anger and rebellion toward helpers who refused to deal with his war.

As we emptied the war inside him, he quit running, reconciled with his family, and remained sober.[39]

Countless troops in the field and veterans afterward take countless medications for anxiety, sleep, rage, and depression. Their use of legal and illegal substances is epidemic. In this we see how disturbing to ordinary functioning the wound can be, how desperate survivors are for relief, and how dependent on medications as our response to discomfort our society has become. Some troops in the field become so medication dependent that they return home addicted.

Medications suppress symptoms but change nothing. Medications control; they do not heal. They alter the ways our bodies function; they do not change who we are. We become dependent upon the medications to sustain any changes.

Trauma symptoms may become so severe that they endanger the lives or safety of veterans or loved ones. They may become so painful they are intolerable to live with. They may become so disorienting that daily functioning becomes impossible. Under these conditions, medications may be helpful or necessary. But by themselves they do not bring transformation and growth. When we rely on medications for symptom control, then society becomes dependent on our veterans' chemical dependencies. Some vets wear T-shirts that declare, "This Combat Veteran Is Heavily Medicated for Your Protection."

Even the word *veteran* does not carry exclusive reference to the war experience. The word derives from the Latin *vetus* or *veter*, meaning "old," and refers to anyone who has seen long service in any occupation. In contrast, in Australia and New Zealand, the word *veteran* is reserved exclusively for those who have survived combat. Other former service people, an Australian trauma specialist told me, are not veterans. "They're just blokes who served in the military."

THE SECOND ANCESTRAL KING: DESPAIR AND TRANSFIGURATION

Before we leave the Underworld to examine how we restore soul in both survivors and society, we return to our roots once again to witness the entire warrior's journey. This tale contains the full mythic pattern of the warrior's journey from innocent boy to tried warrior and weary king to spiritual godchild, from destitution to victory and despair to transfiguration. Just as the wound is built into who we are as humans and as civilizations, so are mythic road maps marking the full warrior's journey.

We take comfort in King David's declaration, "The Lord is my shepherd," but our hearts tear when hearing any of his more than seventy-five psalms of soul distress. "I am weak and poor; come to me quickly, O God."40 There are so many passages of despair in the Bible that we can choose almost any. Consider David's condition before Psalm 23. In 22, he cried out, "My God, my God, why have you forsaken me?" He lamented like those who have been to hell and are unable to return:

But I am no longer a human being; I am a worm,
Despised and scorned by everyone.
All who see me make fun of me . . .
Do not stay away from me.
Trouble is near and there is no one to help . . .
My strength is gone, gone like water spilled on the ground.
All my bones are out of joint;
My heart is like melted wax . . .
You have left me for dead in the dust.

David saved himself by renewing his Divine connection through praise. But first he cried out his desperate need, the cause of all: "Rescue my soul from the sword."[41]

David was living the quiet, idyllic life of a young shepherd when he was chosen, again through Samuel, to become king. Tormented Saul needed a musician to soothe him. David entered his service to be his harpist but also because he was "brave and handsome, a good soldier, and an able speaker."[42]

Youngest of eight sons, David carried supplies to his three brothers serving in Saul's army arrayed against the Philistines. There occurred one of the world's most famous rites of passage.[43] In the Valley of Elah, young David, armed with a slingshot, was the only Israelite willing to meet the Philistine warrior giant Goliath in single combat. He defeated his foe in view of the opposing armies, the Philistines fled, and David transformed from youth into warrior and culture hero.

This Old Testament story perfectly demonstrates the initiatory tradition regarding warriorhood. David was called Divinely chosen, and anointed by a spiritual master. He volunteered as champion of his people, accepted a life-threatening ordeal, and met their foe's champion in personal and single combat before the eyes of both armies. He displayed warrior and leader traits during his trial by combat that none had seen in him before. The entire army witnessed his victory, and he rose to a place of honor and high status among his people.

We have heard of David's difficult service under Saul. David fought in Saul's army and won many victories. He fled when Saul betrayed him, twice trapping Saul and sparing his life.

As a warrior David was even more savage than Saul and committed what we would today consider atrocities. While hiding from Saul by serving the Philistines, David attacked numerous tribes long at home in the region, "killing all the men and women and taking the sheep, cattle, donkeys, camels, and even the clothes."[44]

His own kingship established, David continued his brutality. He defeated the Moabites and put two out of three helpless prisoners to death. He crippled all the defeated Syrians' horses that he did not keep for his chariots. He killed 22,000 Syrians and 18,000 Edomites. He took all the booty he could wherever he fought. Victory was again proof that the people and their leader had God's favor: "The Lord made David victorious everywhere."[45]

David took Bathsheba from her husband, Uriah, and sent him off to be killed in battle. World War I poet Siegfried Sassoon retold this story of soldiers' heroic sacrifices for leaders who betray them in his poem "Devotion to Duty."[46] After her mourning period, David married Bathsheba. Only after this are we told, "The Lord was not pleased." Not when David killed tens of thousands but when he used his power for personal betrayal and lustful gain did he curry God's displeasure. David conquered while his children committed incest, fratricide, and rebellion.

During David's forty-year kingship, he vacillated between despair and faith, grievous losses and great victories, personal heartbreak and public acclaim. Psalm 18, his Victory Song, is a preening conqueror's paean:

God trains me for battle so that I can use the strongest bow . . .
O Lord, you protect me and save me;
Your help has made me great.
You have kept me from being captured
And I have never fallen.
I pursue my enemies and defeat them;
I do not stop until I destroy them . . .
I crush them and they become like dust;
I trample on them like mud in the streets.[47]

Surviving battle with Goliath and many thousands more, abused and attacked by Saul, betraying marriages and soldiers, raising a discordant and abusing family, a great general yet tortured soul, David seemed to transform his suffering into faith, praise, and blessing. He left many prayers of pain, declarations of confidence in Divine help, and hymns of praise and thanksgiving through which he connected to divinity.[48] David's last prayer expressed a vision from God and his faith:

The God of Israel has spoken;
The protector of Israel said to me:
The king who rules in obedience to God
Is like a sun shining on a cloudless dawn . . .
And that is how God will bless my descendants,
Because he has made an eternal covenant with me . . .

But David's final words were not about God and not peaceful. He reverted to his dark, mistrustful vision of humanity, declaring that we must use war and violence to enforce our ways against those unlike us, of competing lands and beliefs.

Godless people are like thorns that are thrown away;
No one can touch them barehanded.
You must use an iron tool or a spear;
They will be burned completely.[49]

David has been called a "PTSD sufferer" but also, in contrast to Saul, a "PTSD victor."[50] His life was replete with personal, familial, and historical traumas. He was involved in betrayals, murders, treasons, infidelity, incest, and conflicts with his children unto making war son upon father. His Psalms reveal a man, warrior, and king in confusion, despair, loneliness, and spiritual collapse. They also reveal a person of deep faith who sometimes felt Divine presence and favor, in distress sought its renewal, and through life gave it praise. David's invisible wound sang through his flood of anguished poetry and sounded a relentless appeal for Divine help. He could not survive all that he felt, suffered, and carried without help from sources around him and sources beyond.

Nor can any warrior.

Now we seek those sources and the path of warrior return.

PART II

Bringing Our Warriors Home

Without your wounds where would your power be?
. . . The very angels themselves cannot persuade the
wretched and blundering children on Earth as can
one human being broken in the wheels of living.
In Love's service, only the wounded soldiers can serve.

THORNTON WILDER

CHAPTER 7

War Trauma and the Social Contract

Regard your soldiers as your children.

SUN TZU, *The Art of War*

Warriors are linchpins in any society's well-being. Offering their lives and lifetimes of service, they are taken apart, re-created, and given ordeals by their society in ways that are meant to prepare, protect, and mature.

Since time immemorial, becoming a warrior has been a rite of passage to becoming a mature adult and citizen. Military service has often been the passage from outsider or foreigner into honored and legitimate citizenship. This has certainly been true in the American experience.

Frederick Douglass escaped slavery at age twenty to become an activist for abolition and equality. During the Civil War he recruited free African-Americans and former slaves for the Union army. "He who fights the battles of America," he wrote, "may claim America as his country—and have that claim respected."[1]

Irving Greenfield was born in Hungary in 1923. His family fled as the Nazis began to consolidate power in Germany. Irv arrived in America speaking no English. Sensitive to his foreign origins, he willingly served in the Pacific during World War II "in order to finish earning my place as an American. I had to give back through military service and protect my family's new home."

Fredrick Douglass believed slaves might become free citizens of the republic that had enslaved them through military service. Two of his sons served in the Union army. All these men heeded an ancient call: risk your life by going to war for the tribe, and you may prove your worth and belong.

In the American military many minority groups serve in percentages higher than in the general population—Native Americans serving in the highest proportion of all. Has full acceptance by society resulted from minority and immigrant military service? From May to June 1943, while the United States was heavily involved in World War II, destructive race riots swept across the nation. Poet Langston Hughes asked, "How long will I have to fight / both Hitler and Jim Crow?"[2] Today our military is integrated, and its brother- and sisterhood declare that there are no differences that can break their mutually dependent bonds. But also today, less than 1 percent of eligible people serve; the country has become dependent on a volunteer force in which poor, disadvantaged, disenfranchised, and unemployed recruits crowd the ranks. All are one within the military but many are the hurting among them, and few are the Americans who join or serve them. Becoming one nation through service is a story in progress that we actually may be reversing as we shrink the military; it no longer represents a cross section of the nation, and we ask nothing of those who do not serve.

The proper relationship and implicit social contract between warriors and civilians are interchangeable concentric circles of protection and caring. Society is responsible for warriors' well-being in preparation before, support during, and tending after conflict. This includes how any society uses its warriors, takes responsibility for their actions duringm and provides for their well-being afterward. Whether and how this happens can itself account for the traumatic wound. Native American, Vietnamese, and other traditional cultures prepared their people before combat to help prevent breakdown. Nupkus Shourds reports Pend d'Orielle practices:

> During their entire lives, the people were exposed to all phases of warriorhood. Warriors were not sent to far-off boot camps to receive training. Elder warriors trained them from youth while the rest of the tribe watched and experienced this training on a daily basis. The entire tribe knew and accepted what they were training for.

> Non-warriors knew their responsibility and received their own training to welcome the warriors back.

When a society neglects its tending role, war horror becomes imprisoned in participants' psyches. There it festers until it becomes a chronic secret wound. Nupkus declares:

> This is a major problem in our society today—nonveterans are not taught what their responsibility is toward veterans who go off to fight their society's battles. This leaves the veterans to themselves when they return. Consequently they have no support or anyone to listen to their war stories that they then internalize, causing serious mental problems. We must not only help the veterans but also educate nonveterans on their responsibilities if they let our leaders continue to start wars.

In the social contract between warriors and their societies, alienation and betrayal can originate anywhere—from the warrior, loved ones, the community, the leadership, the entire society, the judgment of public opinion or history—or any combination of these. Then the social contract is broken and psychospiritual-social wounding results. This wounding can be so painful and disillusioning that it leads to the veteran's loss of the will to live and can even haunt a veteran on his deathbed.

Tomas Young was paralyzed during an ambush in Iraq. As he lay dying, he published an open letter to former president Bush and vice president Cheney:

> I have, like many other disabled veterans, suffered from the often inadequate and inept care provided by the Veterans Administration. I have, like many other disabled veterans, come to realize that our mental and physical wounds are . . . perhaps of no interest to any politician. We were used. We were betrayed. And we have been abandoned.[3]

Such pain and abandonment is the result of breaking our social contract with our vets. It is what remains in the absence of true tending upon return and in the resulting pervasive holes in our shared social circle. We could translate the acronym PTSD as *Post-traumatic Social Disorder*.

We must "see the relationship that needs to be cared for and protected in the pattern and process rather than looking separately at individuals," wrote cultural anthropologist Mary Catherine Bateson. "Where is the pathology? It's not in the individuals . . . It is a characteristic of the system."[4]

We cannot rush our warriors home to turn them loose and on their own, never listen to or learn from their stories and hearts, refuse them the guidance and audience they need when they cry in anguish or collapse in screaming symptoms of soul distress and broken connections, and neglect the long tending and inclusion owed by an honoring society to its warriors. We cannot act thus and expect them to be whole, well, and of service again.

"I know my job is to kill," declared Sergeant Ruckles, who had been a squad leader on three combat deployments in Iraq and Afghanistan. "I'm not happy about it, I hope I won't have to do it, but when I'm ordered to, I admit what I am doing and accept it as necessary." But the sergeant despaired of support from his country afterward. "Society today," he continued, "has no idea what the real purpose of soldiering is—to kill. I blame society for PTSD."

Neglect and abandonment, including difficulties procuring adequate and immediate health services, amount to society's betrayal of its veterans. "At eighteen I left the country to fight for it overseas," said a young combat veteran. "At nineteen, when I returned, America had left me."

HOMECOMING AS A SOURCE OF TRAUMA

Neglect and its consequences can last a lifetime.

I was addressing a church convocation on ministry to veterans. Someone asked, "Everyone does terrible things in war. What about those who engaged in atrocities? Do they have special religious needs?"

An elderly man bolted up in a rear pew. "I need the podium," he cried.

Ed Bloch served as a Marine in the Pacific during World War II, "the good war." He shuffled down the aisle, reached the dais, and faced the audience.

"This is my church," Ed said. "I am deacon here. We have known each other for decades. I want to say this: I committed atrocities in World War II. I killed innocent people." He scanned the somber faces in the pews. "Why has it taken over sixty years and these new wars for me to finally be able to confess this in my own church? To ask you all to hear my story? Yes, we have special needs!"[5]

Initiation through ordeal and return is meant to prove worth and earn membership and belonging. But for many in our modern era, this path has led to loneliness, abandonment, neglect, silence, and despair instead.[6]

When ultimate requirements are put on us—killing and dying—we must be spiritually and philosophically supported—not just with arms, equipment, and Christmas packages—by the country and people in whose name we act. Senator John McCain has written, "No other national endeavor requires as much unshakable resolve as war. If the nation and government lack that resolve, it is criminal to expect men in the field to carry it alone."[7] Or to return.

Resolve reveals a people's character, will, strength, and purpose. Resolve must be present not only during conflict but afterward. It must ignite citizens to serve and sacrifice to provide troop support during ordeal and return. Without it veterans can feel abused, abandoned, betrayed, or violated by the very country, people, and leaders to whom they had offered their faith, trust, and lives.

"Gunny" was a career Marine. He served his first combat tour during the Korean War and two more in Viet Nam. "Combat didn't bother me," he explained:

> I never felt bad for taking the life of an enemy soldier. We were both armed professionals. We knew why we were there and that some of us would not go home. Our jobs were to meet on the battlefield and either kill or be killed.

Gunny intuitively echoed a number of ancient warrior ways. Homer: "To meet destruction or to come through / these are the terms of war."[8] Buddhism: Anyone in battle, "even though it be in a righteous cause, must be prepared to be slain by his enemies, for that is the destiny of warriors."[9] A war song of Sitting Bull: "No chance for me to live; / Mother, you may as well mourn."[10]

Gunny believed that warriorhood was meant to bring honor and belonging. Instead, his reception at home drove him to reenlist for combat.

> I was ignored after Korea, as if I had never been to war. So I went to war again to try to win some honor and respect at home. But when I came back from Nam I was called names and spit on. And then there's this trap built into your service—you kill for your country and only afterward they tell you it was wrong. How are you supposed to live with that?

After three combat tours Gunny was ready to come home. "My trauma happened in America," he explained. "I served in one forgotten war that nobody cared about and another that everyone hated. When enemies shot at me, I could forgive them. But when my own countrymen spit on me, that broke my spirit and sent me into a tailspin."

Gunny's suffering due to dishonor and neglect is not a new condition. Ajax, the second greatest of the Greek warriors at Troy, was destroyed by lost honor among his own people. After Achilles's death the army voted to determine which warrior would be awarded his armor. Their commanders turned the vote against Ajax, and Odysseus was chosen. In the Greek world it brought high honor to win but dishonor to lose such a contest. Like many modern vets, Ajax felt unappreciated, unjustly judged, and publically disgraced. He flew into a fury. On his way to murder his commanders, the goddess Athena struck him with madness. Instead of killing comrades, Ajax slaughtered the army's flocks and herds. Seeing he had brought greater disgrace upon himself, he drew his sword and committed suicide.

This story is retold in Sophocles's play *Ajax*. Like Gunny returning for three combat tours, Ajax felt valuable only in combat but deteriorated, worthless, and shameful afterward. He lamented, "Unflinching in the shock of war . . . what a mockery I have come to, what indignity."[11]

Raging, traumatized veterans *after* combat can be even more frightening than sane men in combat. Athena asked Odysseus why he now feared Ajax. The warrior replied, "He was only a man before . . . Certainly if he were sane, I should never shrink from him."[12] One Green Beret told me, "My beast has devoured my human." A chaplain who had first been in Special Forces said, "My beast and my priest are always at war, and I never know which one will triumph."

For the ancients, the more intense the human experience, the more they imputed Divine influence or presence. Archetypes were living forces. Athena declared about Ajax, "I checked him; I threw before his eyes obsessive notions, thoughts of insane joy . . . " The chorus echoed, "Frenzy comes when the gods will."[13] They believed in spiritual causation of physical and psychological ailments. The traumatic wound was a disturbing and intense condition, its sufferers so distorted they were hardly recognizable. The gods must have caused the affliction. Poetry was needed to express its suffering and public ritual to assuage it.

Many veterans are in anguish over the ways—hostile, demeaning, neglectful, political, patriotic, or gratuitous—they were greeted upon return. They carry the traumatizing consequences of being dishonored. One young Iraq veteran was refused a VA disability rating, benefits, or help. In early 2011 he left a suicide message that declared, "Maybe they'll finally see my invisible wound when they stare at my flag-draped coffin."[14]

HONOR AND ITS LOSS

Honor is "soul food" for warriors. Honor is spiritual glue that holds the character together, protects and uplifts it. Around the world the opportunity to achieve or defend honor was and still is a principal reason for going to war.

The quest for high honor and avoidance of social shame were prime motives for warriors of traditional societies. In ancient times to achieve honor meant to be judged by comrades as able to "go into danger and fight competently."[15] It also means to be held in highest respect and esteem. Honor is inherently a social concern, a public perception, in large part defining the warrior's relationship to his or her community.

"Honor" derives from the same root as "honest"—the Latin *honos*. We attain honor and gain in reputation before our peers through maintaining honesty, dignity, integrity, and truthfulness under challenging conditions. Honor requires truth; to deny war's truths deprives its survivors of honor.

Pericles ruled Athens during the building of the Acropolis and the Peloponnesian Wars. In his 431 BCE funeral oration, he told the mourners that warriors triumphed only by "a keen feeling of honor in action." He continued, "It is only the love of honor that never grows old, and honor it is, not gain . . . that rejoices the heart of age and helplessness."[16]

Pericles meant to drench the war disabled and mourners with honor in order to give meaning to their sacrifice, assuage grief, and inspire more sacrifice. This has been humanity's formula for millennia. "From these honored dead we take increased devotion," Lincoln said at Gettysburg. Whether true of false, "We will never forget our fallen who died for our noble cause" is every national leader's formula.

As happened to Ajax and some survivors today, honor denied or betrayed, to be ordered or compelled to act dishonorably, can be so wounding that it leads the vet to madness or suicide. Lost or denied honor is one source of character breakdown.

One reason despair or collapse may be so high in veterans of the present wars is that many troops do not perceive them as honorable. Troops in Iraq reported this adage: "Strive to be honorable under dishonorable conditions." One reason some veterans fight so hard, often for decades, for disability ratings may be that they wish their wounds would be acknowledged and honored. A disability rating with benefits is sometimes the only substitute a veteran can find for lost honor.

Gunny, like Ajax, was wounded by dishonor that fueled rages, despair, loneliness, and alienation. Pericles declared over the Athenian war dead that honor, not wealth, sustains through age, illness, and loss. "I was our country's warrior so our people should have helped me," Gunny declared, "no matter what they thought about the wars. Instead I got scorn and rejection. It wasn't the killing. It was being dishonored at home—that's what wounded me." Warriors are willing to die, but not to be scorned by those for whom they would.

On Families and Communities

Gunny's story was not his alone. Nor was Ajax's. Warriors serve and are willing to die for their loved ones, their homes, and their homeland. Everything they do during war and experience afterward affects everyone in their lives from family to community to nation.

Over the course of three combat tours and repeated societal betrayal, Gunny changed. He became angry, distant, mistrustful, and morose.

This created a "walking on eggshells" home environment. His wife became everyone's care provider, protecting her veteran from life while also protecting their children from his rages.

We heard this in King Saul's story, and it is the same with Ajax. Ajax's friends and family see changes in him that he hardly realizes. They fear his irrationality, despair, and rages. Like some military spouses today, Ajax's wife keeps their son from him, "For fear that the poor little one might come in your way and be killed."[17] They fear for his life, instructing each other not to leave him alone. And their fear was well founded; Ajax flew into rages, threatened loved ones, and had meltdowns in which he believed that innocent animals were his human enemies and friends. He first killed them and finally himself.

The story of Ajax dates to the Trojan War more than 3,200 years ago. Sophocles, who retold it in his tragedy, was twice elected general and so knew war. His play dates to more than 2,400 years ago. Myth, religious teachings, history, and our warriors teach us that warriors will return "still loaded" and wives, children, friends, and neighbors will be affected and afflicted. In some remote Alaskan and Native American communities, nearly every adult male has served in combat. Violence, sexual and substance abuse, homicide, and suicide are rampant there. The community itself becomes a war zone.[18] From ancient times to the present, we see that war wounds can spread like an invisible toxin through everyone touched. For this reason Yup'ik Eskimo Harold Napolean says that PTSD "is not a physical illness, but an infection of the soul . . . because [it] attacks the core of the person, the spirit . . . and it affects even the innocent."[19]

WARRIORS IN THEIR SOCIETIES

Warriors are not meant to spread war's infection to their society. This is our tragic modern reversal of the initiatory purpose of warriorhood. The warrior's core purpose is to preserve and protect society and all that is most precious to it. Ideally it is service for life, from training before service into elderhood, and society is meant to be safer, not more endangered.

We heard the 2,600-year-old "Hymn to Ares," the Greek war god, a prayer not for battle prowess but for restraint from fury and strife. Restraint refers to society and its leadership as well as to the warrior. "No ruler should put troops in the field merely to gratify his own spleen," Sun Tzu warned 2,500 years ago.[20] Colin Powell, the only combat veteran in the Bush cabinet, was the only member to warn against invading Iraq.

If all means of restraint or peaceful resolution fail and the society is genuinely endangered, the warrior is to fight and defend, kill or be killed if necessary. Biblical law did not forbid all killing, just homicide. Killing in self-defense, as capital punishment for heinous crimes, or in war legitimized by the state was allowed. Buddhism called war "lamentable" but did not blame anyone who fought after having exhausted all means for preserving peace. "Be a little against fighting," was Sitting Bull's creed, "but when anyone shoots be ready to fight."[21] The warrior's code, as we have heard, is meant to guide proper action and protect the warrior from misusing force or becoming savage. When a warrior does other than the code dictates, or when society or history do not support or condone his or her actions, trauma may result.

Warriors' roles do not end when conflicts end. They are to serve in war's aftermath in ways that advance the core values of preservation and protection, now turned to society's restoration and benefit. Elder warriors in traditional cultures teach about war and service to everyone and tend the young, new warriors and the needy. Sitting Bull said,

> Warriors are not what you think of as warriors. The warrior is not someone who fights, because no one has the right to take another life. The warrior is one who sacrifices himself for the good of others. His task is to take care of the elderly, the defenseless, those who cannot provide for themselves, and above all, the children, the future of humanity.[22]

This warrior ideal is not quaint ancient creed but is of the essence of warriorhood. General Douglas MacArthur wrote, "The soldier, be he friend or foe, is charged with the protection of the weak and the unarmed. It is the very essence and reason of his being . . . a sacred trust."[23]

Honors do not come to warriors solely from the fight. They have social roles and tasks to fulfill throughout the life cycle. A society needs its warriors or it is weaker because key participants—links in the chain of social connection—are missing. The younger warriors are deprived of elders; the youth are deprived of teachers, mentors, and parents. They feel it. It is passed on. Thus George Washington observed, "The willingness with which our young people are likely to serve in any war, no matter how justified, shall be directly proportional to how they perceive the veterans of earlier wars were treated and appreciated by their nation."[24]

WARRIORS AND THE NATION

John F. Kennedy analyzed "the kind of faith on which democracy is based." The essential components, he said, are "trust in the wisdom of the people . . . their ultimate sense of justice . . . their ability to honor courage and respect judgment . . . and that in the long run they will act unselfishly for the good of the nation."[25]

Warriors must have such faith in themselves and receive it from the people and nation they serve. If our faith, trust, or confidence in these virtues is damaged or lost during combat or homecoming, we are spiritually traumatized, our belief systems are shattered, and only shells of human beings remain. Kennedy's words were written during the Cold War. We can ask regarding service in wars like Vietnam, Iraq, Afghanistan, our numerous forgotten wars, and uncountable secret operations around the world: Do our warriors feel that our country and their service was ultimately just? That their courage was honored? That their judgments were respected? Do they respect and trust the judgments of the political and military commanders who sent them? Do they feel that the institutions that sent them to these wars and profited off them, or the wars themselves, were ultimately for the good of the nation?

Kennedy held that the best interests of the individual and nation must ultimately be the same. Both combat survivor and visionary leader, he believed in the reciprocal social contracts between warrior, citizen, and nation and that we all must serve in some capacity: "Ask what you can do for your country."

In Kennedy's time "public life became increasingly centered upon a seemingly unending war."[26] Then it was called the Cold War, now the Global War on Terror. One source of soldiers' enduring "sorrow of war" is this: my war was not "the war to end all wars." Combat vet Ron Orem declared, "I yearn most of all for the day to arrive when our ranks thin because there are no more veterans being added to our numbers."[27] It was too terrible to be for nothing, to go on and on, to cause increasingly more suffering and death, to be endless.

When we teach people that war will go on forever, we condition them to mistrust and fear their neighbors around the world. We plant despair in those who fought because the horrors they endured will never end, are never resolved, do not lead to a better and more harmonious world that is renewed and made wiser by their sacrifices. Ares's lust is never satisfied. The wounded and their survivors wonder, "Was it worth the sacrifice?"

To restore our warriors we must restore core values that are not just American but essential to the success of any culture. Truth, trust, faith, integrity, courage, self-sacrifice—warriors are asked to give these to the utmost. They must experience the same from us in return.

THE PLAINS INDIAN MODEL

The Plains Indians provide an exemplary model of the proper relationship between the warrior and society. To the Plains Indians the buffalo was a totem a spirit, a god. It was the source of food, clothing, shelter, tools and weapons, as well as personal, sacred, and religious items—all that sustains life. Living in close proximity, in the same demanding environment and dependent on the buffalo for survival, the Plains people studied the animal's behavior, qualities, and social organization. As the people's model for living well, the buffalo gave all and the people worshipped, studied, emulated—and ate.

The people observed that the buffalo were brave, strong, and stubborn. They never gave up but always plowed forward into difficult weather or dangerous conditions. Against hunters and the elements they showed courage, endurance, and determination, and they would sacrifice themselves to protect their herd.

The people also observed how buffalo cared for each other and protected their young and vulnerable against threats and predators. During the buffalo hunt, the herd would push its calves into the center. The cows ran forming a protective ring around them. Then bulls ringed the cows, and older bulls ringed the younger bulls as well to keep them moving forward rather than turning against their aggressors. Old bulls, like old warriors, declared through action, "I am expendable. Save the young ones. I offer myself first."

When a buffalo was injured, its herd did not stampede away but gathered around their injured member to try to help and protect it. Buffalo lived not for themselves but for each other.

The structure of society and the warrior's character traits and place in the community were modeled on this buffalo behavior. When danger threatened his people, the warrior's proper place was in a protective outer circle around the village. As long as he was able, the older or more experienced the warrior was, the farther out he strove to be. Young warriors and bulls had to be restrained and trained until they were experienced and mature enough to not waste lives but provide leadership.

Inside the circle the civilians had been protected and sometimes owed the warriors their lives. Now the civilians gave thanks, honor, and duty through tending their returning warriors. They became a circle of welcome. They witnessed their stories, grieved or celebrated with them, attended to their necessary purification and healing rituals. In mainstream society the survivor becomes a misunderstood outcast. In indigenous healing "the man of the dreary edge becomes the center."[28] As among the buffalo, when a member of the tribe was injured or fallen, the rest of the tribe would surround him, offering aid and protection. After battle the concentric circles reversed—the civilians on the outside tended their warriors within. In this way both circles were renewed, the camp's interdependent social organization remained intact, warriors were restored, and civilians gave back. Everyone was cared for.

Indigenous peoples recognized and practiced this unspoken yet inherent social contract: when the people are threatened, the proper relationship of warrior to civilians is in the protective outer ring of concentric circles. When danger passes and warriors return, the circles reverse. The citizenry's task is to receive, support, tend, and initiate the warrior in gratitude and honor for the sacrifices made and protection rendered. In a healthy social order, warriors and societies exist in concentric and interchangeable circles of protection.

Just as ethical warriorhood necessitates moral service, warrior return necessitates tending by a grateful and supportive society that recognizes and utilizes the transformations warriors have undergone in life-affirming ways. Without this reciprocal social contract, warriors experience betrayal and abandonment, and civilians remain isolated, frightened, ignorant, and in moral and spiritual debt.

VIET NAM: NO TRAUMATIC BREAKDOWN

Western psychology teaches that massive violence is so traumatic that its characteristic breakdown and wounding is inevitable and universal. This is so much the case that, as we heard, the wound has been diagnosed in other animal species as well as humans. Though it is judged to be "a normal response to abnormal conditions," we see that preparation, social and spiritual support, moral and homecoming issues are central to the wound. Is it possible, then, that by attending to these issues we may reduce or even prevent invisible wounding?

During the Vietnam War, casualties and damage were astronomically higher for the Vietnamese than for Americans.[29] For example, the Vietnamese lost about three million people killed, two-thirds of whom were civilians, and over four million wounded compared with America's loss of 58,000-plus GIs killed and 300,000 wounded. And the war was there; the Vietnamese infrastructure and environment were so severely damaged that now, forty years later, that nation still labors to recover from and halt additional war wounding. In spite of this, in Viet Nam there is little of the invisible wound that causes so much suffering here.

Dr. Nguyen Sinh Phuc fought and was wounded in the People's Army in Quang Tri, called "the meat mill" because of the brutal fighting. Today he is a psychologist with years of army psychiatric hospital experience and now teaches at the University of Ha Noi. Dr. Phuc declares, "The number of PTSD cases among the veterans of the Viet Nam People's Army is very small." Dr. Phuc explains that he knows how severe traumatic breakdown can be among American veterans but has not seen any such severe cases in Viet Nam since the 1970s, just after the war.[30] Severe post-war breakdown does not occur in the same degree or fashion in Viet Nam as in the United States. How is this possible?

The Vietnamese were invaded and experienced themselves as defenders, not aggressors. A Viet Cong veteran said, "We were only defending our families and homes, so we have no psychological wounds." Vietnamese as Buddhists accept even difficult fates without protest. An elderly father in the Mekong Delta who lost all three of his sons in the war comforted me as I prayed before his family altar. "Thank you for your sympathy," he said, "but I am at peace that my sons did their duty and met their proper karma."

The Vietnamese are communal and their entire society is organized as a kinship system. Thus they carry history and wounds together and do not leave anyone to suffer alone. In America we labor around the country to create veteran talking circles with civilian witnesses. In Viet Nam veterans and civilians all over the country spontaneously gathered at village pagodas, even as the war raged on, to witness and share the returnees' stories.

The Vietnamese admit that they also became brutal; they tortured, disfigured, and used booby traps. Dr. Huu Ngoc, a Viet Minh veteran and renowned scholar, explained, "Your air war was especially brutal. We had no weapons to fight against it. We had to come up with primitive forms of psychological warfare that might terrorize your soldiers as much as you were terrorizing us with your technology." Viet Cong veteran Tam Tien said simply, "Even in a just cause combat makes everyone crazy."

Additionally, the Vietnamese are largely free of traumatic breakdown because, though they were fierce combatants, their warriors and leadership strove to remain aligned with codes of moral conduct under horrific conditions. Only defend, they believed—try to preserve life. Ho Chi Minh told soldiers departing for the front: try to capture rather than kill the Americans; they too are victims of this war and have family waiting for them at home. Mr. Tiger explained that though he fought French and American soldiers to the death when necessary, "I preferred to capture them. Unarmed, I was responsible to protect them." Mr. Tiger reportedly saved some captured American GIs from abuse, torture, or execution. The poet Nguyen Duy reported that while fighting in Quang Tri he pursued a fleeing Ranger who had almost killed him: "Chasing him was much harder / than pulling the trigger," he told himself. "Save him, it's harder . . . with all my strength / I forced him / to stop."[31]

"From the time we were in middle school," explained a North Vietnamese army veteran who survived the siege of Khe Sanh and is now a communications professor, "we were told the truth about war. Most of our parents, teachers, and elders were veterans. They had survived earlier invasions and taught us the realities of the battlefield and that many of us might come home wounded or not at all. We were prepared, protected, and loved by being told the truth. This way, even though we were marching into hell, we were able to leave happy and trusting." The professor emphasized that parents, mentors, teachers, and trainers must tell the truth about the horrors about to happen, preparing future soldiers against shock. Such lessons communicate love, respect, and concern, unite a society across the generations, and give purpose to elder warriors.

In Viet Nam, as in other kinship societies, all elder men are considered uncles, and elder women aunts are responsible for parenting the child's soul. In Native American and other traditional cultures, whether or not they are blood related, aunts and uncles are the primary confidantes and teachers of youths. Everyone needs a mentor watching over his or her well-being through the life cycle, especially as he or she becomes a warrior. In the Eastern martial arts traditions, teachers do not just train in the physical arts but are revered as spiritual masters who train their students' souls as well as bodies. Such mentoring belies our military tradition. Today we expect those in command, from drill sergeants in boot camp through general officers, to exact demanding discipline, training, and obedience through surrender of individuality, conformity to mass identity and behavior, and the use of fear with harsh discipline and punishment as motivators.

The Vietnamese experience makes us wonder how commanders and societies can achieve the greatest devotion, discipline, and endurance among their troops. The Chinese philosopher-general Sun Tzu counseled that determining which of the contending rulers "is imbued with the Moral Law" should be the first of five factors in evaluating war plans. He taught that commanders either inspire or fail their troops to the degree that they represent "the virtues of wisdom, sincerity, benevolence, courage, and strictness." He counseled, "Regard your soldiers as your children and they will follow you into the deepest valleys. Look on them as your own beloved sons, and they will stand by you even unto death."[32]

Combat troops ask themselves, would you follow this man to the end? Would you obey him without question? Would you die for him?

Decades after the war, I was driving with Jack, a Vietnam combat veteran, discussing his opinion of leadership during the war. I asked, "What would you say if we were chauffeuring your commander General Westmoreland right now?"

A haunted smile crept across Jack's mouth. He turned to the empty backseat. "'Sir,' I'd say, 'this is for my dead brothers, the Vietnamese, and the countless wrongs you did us all.'" He mimed pointing a gun at the general's head. "Then I'd pull the trigger without regret."

In Eastern and indigenous cultures, everything regarding warfare and warriorhood was about right relationships to self, society, elders, purpose, morality, and even enemies and the dead. Confucius said, "Forgive your enemy . . . be reconciled to him . . . give him assistance . . . invite God in his behalf . . . never forget kindness." Many troops complain, desist, act out, rebel, or collapse for want of these nurturing conditions. The invisible wound is their protest.

Conditions were different for Vietnamese veterans upon their homecoming. Most soldiers remained at war until it was over or they were too severely wounded to continue. Many were at war for a decade or more and wounded multiple times. "After 1975," Dr. Phuc explained, "many veterans believed that they fulfilled their duties toward their villages and beloved people. The end of the war meant they had a chance to continue schooling or live in the homeland and marry and have children."

Honor, dignity, community support, an immediate threat and attack in their own front yards, nurturing and trustworthy leaders wishing to reduce violence, a struggle whose purpose was only to liberate their homes and homeland from invaders, welcoming and tending communities upon return, the entire population sharing the wounds of war—these are all qualities American soldiers yearn and fight for, and all qualities they lack.

A successful homecoming and the hope it holds out are as important as wartime experiences. Dr. Phuc continued,

> From the social viewpoint we, the soldiers, always receive love from the people. Soldiers who survive the war and return home after, although they lost parts of their bodies, are always welcome. The government supports them.

> Most of the veterans do not ask too much although the society and people give them much love. The veterans think that the fact that they survived the war and returned home is already a priceless reward. Viet Nam had a lot of economic difficulties after 1975, but the support from the government and community for veterans is big—not in material wealth but in spirit. The veterans who are not wounded accept a new life easily.

In contrast, countless Americans who served in our politically and economically motivated wars feel broken because they betrayed the warrior's purpose and code, because the war was not unquestionably and purely defensive, because society and the government refused their tending tasks and judged and blamed veterans for their psychological problems afterward, and because both government and citizenry refuted collective responsibility. For all these reasons American troops experience that only they and not their country went to war.

Vietnamese mental-health experts have conducted research regarding these issues. Associate Professor Dr. Tran Van Cuong was director of the National Psychiatry Hospital for many years and is now deputy president of the Viet Nam Psychiatry Association. From 2001 to 2003, Professor Cuong led the psychiatry faculty in surveying the health of the Vietnamese community in eight areas of the country. Traumatic breakdown due to war was *not* found to be among the country's significant or leading health problems. Dr. Cuong's research concluded, "The results of our survey show that PTSD is not a big problem in Viet Nam as it is in the US."

Dr. Le Van Hao of the National Institute of Psychology in Ha Noi conducted research focusing on the stress experienced by soldiers with Agent Orange disabilities. During 2005, thirty years after the war's end, he interviewed twenty-seven veterans. Their average age was almost sixty-one years, average length of time at war was over eleven years, and they had an average of 3.8 children. Eighty-one percent of the veterans' children suffered Agent Orange diseases, disabilities, or deaths; Agent Orange affected the majority of their children and all the veterans. In spite of these conditions—more than a decade at war, every veteran and most of their children afflicted by disabilities and ill health—Dr. Hao and his colleagues found no evidence of combat-induced Post-traumatic Stress Disorder and none of the troublesome symptomatology plaguing American veterans.[33] From his research as well as decades of clinical experience, Dr. Hao concluded, "Since there was little or no traumatic breakdown among the most severely wounded, therefore there was even less among average ex-soldiers,"[34] and little or no traumatic breakdown in Viet Nam from combat as there is among American veterans. He observed some Vietnamese veterans did have stress symptoms, but these were due to hardships after the war and coping with Agent Orange diseases. Dr. Hao declared that the lack of combat PTSD stemmed from "a number of protective factors ranging from the just cause to a strong sense of duty and service to the country."

The absence of invisible wounding among Vietnamese veterans thus far refers to Viet Cong and North Vietnamese Regular Army veterans. Vietnamese research has not included the impact of war on soldiers in the Army of the Republic of Viet Nam (ARVN) who fought on the American side. We report on their post-war mental health from personal encounters and extensive field observation.

Tran Dinh Song was in the ARVN air force for seven and an half years and in the reeducation camps after the war for another two and a half. His brother was in the camps for over seven years. Since that time Song has been a high school teacher and travel guide, and is now my organization Soldier's Heart's representative in Viet Nam and a learned and generous cultural liaison. Song reports:

> Regarding ARVN veterans and former prisoners in re-educational camps, my feeling is that there is no PTSD among them either. Some of them still have nightmares, several have hostility, many have deep grief and bitter memories, but these psychological states are just melancholy or disappointment; *they do not develop into PTSD*. In the thiry-nine years since the war's end I have met with tens of thousands of veterans of the Republic of South Viet Nam. I never heard any symptoms of PTSD as described in American society. Family support and the

> acceptance of karma may explain the absence of PTSD among ARVN veterans who are quieter and receive less concern than NVA or VC veterans.[35]

This is not to argue that the Vietnamese are untroubled by the war and its aftermath. Madame Tien, herself a Viet Cong veteran as well as married to one, reports that her husband, who was severely wounded, sometimes wanders off by himself and sits in contemplation of old war memories. In addition, in my organization's fourteen research, healing, and reconciliation journeys to Viet Nam since 2000, when we met with hundreds of veteran and civilian survivors, we have heard many stories of deep grief and loss, often accompanied by strong crying. From our field observations and research, we suspect that the two "symptoms" Vietnamese do experience that appear similar to those suffered by American veterans are prolonged grief—as Song pointed out, melancholy and disappointment—and intrusive thoughts and memories. These are kept in abeyance from becoming chronic or disabling because of omnipresent familial and social support; national, communal, and personal rituals; and spiritual beliefs and practices. Rituals include the annual Day of Wandering Souls when all MIAs (Missing in Action) are prayed for by the entire nation, the universal practice of ancestor worship, the adoption by pagodas of the deceased who do not have any surviving family to memorialize them, the presence all over the country of monuments, memorials, and museums honoring the sacrifices and the fallen, and the awareness that the entire country suffered together.

Viet Nam is an exemplary living and contemporary example demonstrating that societies can be organized, their warriors and collective wounds tended, their philosophies and relationships wise and enduring, and their behavior moral and responsible enough even during brutal war such that even though they experience profound grief and loss, they do not collapse into the disabling version of the wound that causes our country and veterans so much suffering.

We see that the invisible wound originates and unfolds in the public social sphere as well as in the private psychological one. The invisible wound is a social disorder of any society that makes its veterans serve in dehumanizing conditions, then denies, alienates, and marginalizes them, their stories, experiences, and suffering upon return. A social disorder does indeed cause changes in the individual on all levels of functioning, but it is not just an individual psychological or medical pathology and cannot be healed through medical strategies alone.

This is not a hopeless situation. Lifelong suffering after war is not inevitable, and our veterans ache for hope. When we understand the wound as both a moral and social disorder that we have unwittingly forced our veterans to carry alone, and with models from world traditions for guidance and adaptation, we can map the path home. We will explore specific principles and practices necessary for successful homecoming modeled on wisdom gleaned from ancient and modern traditions regarding warrior care and societal reconciliation. We will see that there is a guiding philosophy and map—stages and steps to follow—and safe and meaningful ways for everyone in a veteran's family, community, and society to participate.

CHAPTER 8

The Wound: A Holistic Understanding

War is pathological, not the soldiers who experience it.

LORI HOLYFIELD

A survivor of profound nonnormative experiences passes through a psychic death and rebirth process, essentially becoming a new person, someone *other* than the one before. The initiate's experiences are penetrating enough to change us to our cores and character structures. In traditional cultures, illnesses and crises were considered initiations that brought about the death of the old self and birth of the new. The initiate returns to the home community, is recognized as the new person he or she has become, and offers the boons gained. Both traveler and community grow and prosper.

Becoming a warrior is a millennia-old traditional path of initiation into responsible and mature adulthood, citizen status, honor, and lifelong service.

The growth trajectory of initiation is easily conceived:

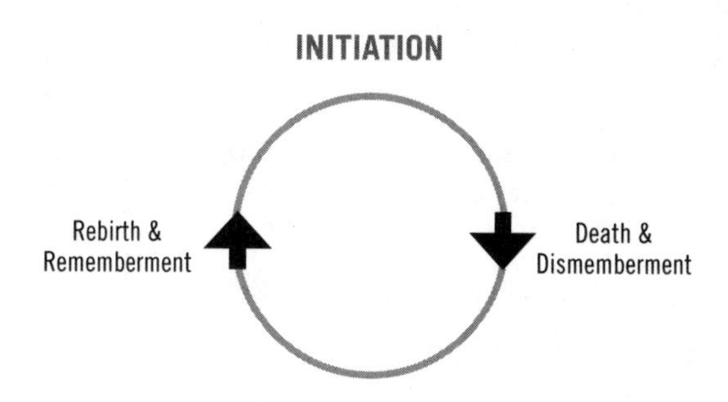

We will examine ways the warrior may be reborn or "remembered"—put back together and recognized in the new status by self and others. We have thus far considered ways a warrior may fail to return. Psychological and relationship troubles, spiritual distress, restlessness, homelessness, isolation, and suicide are all signs of an uncompleted journey. These constitute an incomplete initiation. Modern-day interpretations of war's invisible wound treat it as a pathology. Veterans may not know what is missing from their treatment, but they often complain of being treated as broken, "less than," mentally ill, or victims. A disabled Army sergeant who fought in both Iraq and Afghanistan wrote me, "I don't want pills or to feel like I'm being a clinical patient. I just need social interaction and new methods of help . . . I want to be free and me again." Commonly veterans' treatment fails to foster the positive and initiatory dimensions of the war experience. James Hillman affirms that it is only a "halfway" initiation—exposure to experience without instruction or wisdom to complete it—"initiation interrruptus."[1]

How is restoration of the soul and transformation of identity after war possible? What can it look like and how can we foster it so that "it makes us more"?

TWO PATHS HOME

If we interpret combat trauma as:

- an abnormal occasion of severe violence, stress, anxiety, threat, or danger rendering our traumatized veterans disabled civilians, and
- if the path home primarily means controlling disturbing stress symptoms and retraining the brain while reinventing a civilian identity that no longer matches who we have become or the life experiences we have had,
- then we will inevitably suffer innumerable failures of return.

This recipe, for many, guarantees disorder and breakdown into the chronic struggle we have labeled PTSD.

In contrast we can conceive that:

- warriorhood is a lifelong journey;

- warriorhood can be educated, nurtured, and tended;
- service as a warrior has been initiatory for millennia;
- ordeals can be transformative and psychospiritual-educational, provoking new growth and wisdom;
- the invisible wound is an honorable warrior's wound that has been known and tended for millennia;
- we can understand war-induced trauma and tend its sufferers in ways that restore;
- where there is breakdown there can be breakthrough; where death, rebirth; where disorder, new order and growth.

When we understand and embrace this perspective, the invisible war wound becomes proof of our humanity, an initiatory ordeal, and an opportunity for further growth and evolution.

There are two paths home for our troops and veterans. The common path too often leads to chronic disability, social invisibility, betrayal, and alienation between warriors, civilians, and society. The transformational model can lead to growth and restoration for the survivor and great boons to society. As James Hillman observed, we can either work *on* our PTSD or *with* it.[2] We either recycle the same crippling issues forever or understand our deep wound and its transformational opportunity—growing deepened souls and enlarged identities.

TWO PATHS HOME

Post-Traumatic Stress Disorder:
Civilian • GI • Veteran • Civilian

Post-Traumatic Growth:
Civilian • GI • Veteran • Spiritual Warrior • Elder

A HOLISTIC VIEW

As history unfolded, science developed, and technology increased, the names of the war-induced afflictions and our strategies for responding to them, like war itself, became increasingly less humanistic and more clinical and technical. What was once thought of as Godlike Wrath and a soul-piercing wound evolved through the millennia, finally becoming the PTSD we use today. And it is still changing.

Veterans and loved ones protest that the contemporary diagnosis is inadequate to express their condition. After Desert Storm, comedian George Carlin created a performance routine about these names. Carlin was an Air Force veteran who viewed the military as a corporate killing institution. He was purposely obstructionist during his service and was discharged in 1957. Carlin's comic routine stated that names for PTSD are increasingly medico-scientific, longer and more difficult to say, and bereft of pain. Societal honesty about veteran pain, he challenged, might lead to better benefits and treatment.

Veterans affirm that they are in pain, but the modern name of their wound indicates none. Rather, it sounds medical and scientific, guiding sufferers toward those professionals for help while excluding other sources of restoration or support. It is flat and sterile when the experience it came from was vivid and intense. It transforms war wounding into a medical condition with pathology located in the individual's mind and brain. It can steer people to think it is a disease you catch and get over or a mental illness you must adapt to and live with. It is difficult to pronounce and therefore impersonal and alienating. It has no obvious relation to the condition it indicates. Cold and without honor, it is "drained of both poetry and blame," says a vet who prefers "Soldier's Heart" as "a disorder of warriors . . . "[3]

Different in kind than any other human experience, war's invisible wound is not comprehensible from the standpoint of normative psychology. Even the most intense stress is not equivalent to the wartime experience of Godlike Wrath or Soul-Piercing Trauma. And no other experience is equivalent to the taking of life—whether we are target or executioner.

War trauma is a soul wound. The acronym could be translated *Post-traumatic Soul Distress.*

From the perspective of the soul, the wounded person is stuck in hell and awash in destruction and death. Anyone in this condition needs rebirth. Worldwide traditions teach that through the process of initiation we pass through symbolic death into rebirth. Wounded souls can be healed through initiation and guided to rebirth.

The cycle of initiation, we have seen, is dismemberment and death circling into rememberment and rebirth. Service in the war zone is a descent into the depths of the Underworld of war, psyche, and myth. We dismember—take apart both the civilian identity and that part of the world we fight in. We replace our identity with a new military one. We send the young, uninitiated, and inadequately prepared and supported to war—the descent to hell. We recycle them through "the valley of the shadow" more times than it is possible to bear. Then we swiftly bring home our troops surviving in body—with mind, heart, and soul still lingering in the war zone. The invisible wound is interrupted or incomplete initiation.

After the military and war, changes to personhood last our entire lives. Though some returnees ache for a return to the pre-war self and even set it as a goal of their therapy, life and growth are one-way streets; trauma stamps dinosaur footprints into our psyches and the pre-war self cannot be recovered. This constitutes a psychospiritual death. A new self must be constructed that includes the important stories, values, and meanings of military and war experiences. Contemporary psychological diagnoses include identity disorder. War changes who we are, but we do not pathologize the process. Iraq vet Kevin Powers voiced a healthy stance: "My identity is informed by my experience in the war, but it isn't limited to that."[4] The Chinese ideogram for crisis means both danger and opportunity. The invisible wound is an identity crisis.

In psychological, social, somatic, and spiritual identities, the war survivor has become someone else. We must help the survivor discover who he or she has become and enable the new self to thrive in ways that include the war experiences. We bring healing to an identity crisis through identity transformation and the creation of life-affirming meaning.

"The most intimate I have ever been with another human being," said the combat Marine, eyes glazed with remembering, "is when I had my hands around an enemy soldier's neck choking him to death." "I cried and begged them to go home to their families as I mowed them down," said a former machine gunner. "My trauma didn't happen from combat," declared an MP. "It happened the moment I realized that the enemy soldiers I was killing were human beings."

Combat transforms how we attach, relate to, love, or connect with others. Combat survivors' styles of relating, like everything else, are taken apart in war and reforged from the twin dynamics of battle—kill or be killed. These translate: love your comrade to the point of being willing to kill or die for him or her; kill your foe before he or she kills you. But a warrior's intimate connections do not end in the face-off. Traditional cultures teach hunters and warriors that when you take a life you are connected to it and responsible for its soul forever. Relations with the dead and death itself are key components of the wound.

Wilbert Michel, a member of the Kootenai tribe from Montana, killed his first enemy combatant in Viet Nam's Central Highlands. He reported meeting the enemy's eyes, then shooting him, and for the rest of his life remembering that face and feeling that the soldier had given him a chance to live.

As a child Wil had been taught by his elders that after an act of killing he must appease the spirit of the slain by explaining why he had to take their life. He had done this as a hunter. But as he stooped and prayed over the body of his fallen foe, his sergeant insulted him and ordered him away. He confessed to me that he had found no righteous reason for taking this life; his own survival did not pass muster as a moral reason to kill an honorable foe only defending his home. Native combatants such as Wil can suffer decades of anguish because they cannot justify wartime killing of other young men from traditional peoples much like their own. Wil only found peace over this forty-year-old act when we returned to Viet Nam together and held a ceremony for his fallen foe on their old battlefield. Finally fulfilling this spiritual responsibility brought Wil great lightness of heart and relief. Reports from his reservation declare that he is a transformed person: attentive, happy, cooperative, and engaged in community and helping restore old warrior traditions.

Psychiatry recognizes the diagnosis of attachment disorder, a characterological confusion about how we connect with others so old and deep that it is built into our psyches from early life and can distort and damage all our love relationships and social connections. War transforms the ways we love, connect, and bond so profoundly that we may seem disordered, obsessed, terrified, abusive, distant, numb, neglectful, starved, or disinterested when we try to relate.

At one of my training sessions, a civilian therapist criticized an Iraq veteran as being an abuser because he wanted daily sexual relations. The vet answered, "I don't want to hurt or disrespect anyone. But I need you to understand that after three combat tours, sex is the only way I feel human. It doesn't last, but at least I feel it while we're touching. Please don't deny me the one doorway to humanness I still have." The traumatic heart wound is so deep, repeated, and painful that it transforms the ways we love, connect, and make love. It is an intimacy and attachment wound.

Traditional warrior cultures knew trauma was a danger and prepared and protected warriors effectively. When it occurred, they recognized the condition and responded to it holistically. Indeed there were specialists, "medicine people," responsible for tending warriors. But healing and homecoming were not left to specialists alone. The entire community was involved and did not isolate, alienate, or blame their warriors.

Veterans' experiences must be made public and responsibilities transferred to the group they served. We do not practice this transfer in American society. Thus the relationship between citizens and veterans remains in disorder. This disorder is in our body politic. It can be healed to the degree that we are truly receptive to veterans, their stories, their struggles. We do not judge, blame, or scapegoat them but are open to hear and accept responsibility for war actions and wounds, including damage done in our names. We tend the veterans until they have all they need to return. Healing must include and happen in the community. The war wound is a social disorder. Heal the community of its war wounds and our veterans will heal with us.

In summary:

WHAT IS "PTSD"?

Stress and anxiety disorder
Identity crisis
Interrupted initiation
Attachment/love wound
Social disorder
Soul wound
The soul's cry of anguish

The invisible wound is in part the result of "operational stress": massive stress, anxiety, and trauma far beyond what civilians ordinarily experience. Our central nervous system and biochemistry have been impacted and altered. Our body-mind system has readapted to a life of constant danger, threat, and violence.

To express this, a new diagnostic category has been created and the wound, until 2013 called a Stress and Anxiety Disorder, is now classified as a Trauma and Stressor-Related Disorder.

It is a trauma. We have been unwillingly pierced by the violence of the world. We have looked into the eyes of destruction and death. We have been trained to kill and had our own lives threatened. We have become homeless in a devouring and dangerous universe and can never be innocent or ignorant again.

It is an identity crisis. Survivors are haunted: Who am I now after what I have seen and done? They ache: Make me who I was before! No one can.

It is interrupted initiation. The vet has experienced dismemberment and death of the old self and is stuck in the Underworld but has not reconstituted and has had no rebirth.

It is a love and attachment wound. Vets replace conventional forms of relating with ways of intimacy forged in the combat zone.

It is a social disorder occurring when society fails to support its warriors or take responsibility for their actions during any stage of their service and return.

It is a soul wound. All functions of soul are in shock, frozen, and numbed. They have been wounded, distorted, and transformed according to the ways of war.

The invisible wound is like Edvard Munch's painting *The Scream.* It is the soul's silent cry. The sun and sky, sea and sands vibrate from the scream. Only the distant unknowing civilians stroll on their ways seemingly unaffected.

When we hear the scream and grasp what the war god has done to torture the soul and create the wound, then we may envision and practice what our warriors need for their return.

CHAPTER 9

Wounding and Identity

Deliver my soul from the sword.

PSALM 22

Many soldiers, especially among the younger generation now serving, as we have heard, do not want to be labeled. They may resist diagnosis and treatment, declaring they are military professionals who have not been lessened or diminished. They want to be seen as whole people, perhaps with new challenges or limitations, but with unique warrior identities, histories, and abilities. Some prefer the Civil War–era term *Soldier's Heart* as an accurate, honorable name for their wound.

Changing what we call something changes how we respond to it. When we call the invisible wound "Post-traumatic Stress" we name an illness, syndrome, or disabling condition. We evoke medical and psychological models that locate the condition in the individual, out of control and in need of professional treatment, disability support, and medications. If it is an illness, syndrome, or stress disorder, we are helpless victims needing treatment. If it is "just stress," we must get it under control and avoid exacerbation. But if it is a wound, we must deal with a transformed identity, our need for healing, what the wound means, and how we will carry it. And society must deal with its responsibility to, for, and with the wounded.

Recently there has been significant attention to moral damage to troops participating in modern wars.[1] *Injury* is the word now frequently attached to moral wounding; we tend "moral injury." But even this term disguises the reality.

Though we benefit from its return to contemporary psychology and our understanding of war, the concept of moral injury is not new.

ANATHEMA

We met the Furies from ancient Greek mythology—personifications of our inner demons, consciences tortured from wrongdoing. The Furies pounced on the wrongdoer for unjustly harming others—causing moral injury *to* others and in the process harming his own soul.

The ancient Greeks were aware of war suffering caused to their own, the enemy, and the innocents. In his play *The Persians*, about the outnumbered Greeks' defeat of the invaders at the battle of Salamis, Aeschylus compassionately mourned the enemy dead. This was unique for his times and rare in any era. But perhaps the most compassionate tragedy in its depiction of war suffering is Euripides's play *The Trojan Women*. An elected general of Athens, Euripides wrote his play as a protest against an atrocity and massacre by the Athenians during the Peloponnesian War.

Euripides's protagonists were the surviving Trojan women who watched their city be destroyed by the invading Greeks and, after witnessing fathers, husbands, and sons slaughtered, were divided among the conquerors to be their slaves. Euripides presents every form of suffering that survivors experience and gives expression to every wound.

Themis was violated. Hekabe, the Trojan queen, suffered every one of the losses to her people. "What sorrow is there that is not mine," she lamented. "Country lost and children and husband . . . and I a slave . . . An evil fate fell on me, a lot the hardest of all."[2] Finally she cried from the core of her being, *anathema*. Anathema literally means "Cursed. Wronged. Against the theme. Against the way. Against the grain. Against the order." It is central to the invisible wound. As I wrote in my book *The Practice of Dream Healing*:

> Anathema—this is what war was and what war did. It was against the natural order of life. It caused a moral inversion, a reversal of values and purpose . . . It made us agents of death and destruction rather than creation. It was opposite the forward and growing movement of life . . . Whoever

> perpetrated war was anathema. Veterans knew it with their whole being. It was their moral trauma . . . [3]

Like Hekabe and her attendants long ago, the spouses, children, and elderly parents left behind today are war's tragic chorus. Their ultimate cry is *anathema*.

MORAL WOUNDING IN RECENT WARS

"We were not innocent," Vietnam War Chaplain William Mahedy declared. "We were participants in evil" and "moral outrage."[4] Tyler Boudreau complained that veterans are usually treated only like victims when they are simultaneously perpetrators and victims, each with its characteristic wounding.[5] To express the depth and seriousness of this moral wound, Larry Dewey referred to "breaking the Geneva Convention of the soul."[6] By treating vets like passive and injured victims, society avoids the raw realities of war, the destruction its troops perpetrate, and collective responsibility for both the destruction and the people who did it in the country's name.

We are in danger of overgeneralizing the concept of moral injury and weakening its meaning. Shortly after returning from Afghanistan, a chaplain attended a retreat meant to reconcile veterans and civilians. The mixed circle was given the exercise to share a personal story of moral injury. A combat veteran talked about killing a civilian. Then a civilian reported forgetting to pick up his child at a ball game. The chaplain called this "pseudo-empathy" during which attendees equated experiences that aren't equitable. Some veterans left the gathering feeling less rather than more understood. This exchange was yet another demonstration that, though well-intentioned, civilians "don't get it."

We commonly say that a person was "injured in an accident" but "wounded in battle." *Injury* comes from the Latin *in juris*, meaning not fair or right. It connotes damage or harm done to us as victims of circumstances or others' actions. A wound, on the other hand, connotes violence done by or to the sufferer. War causes moral wounding and moral trauma as well as "injury" because it results not from happenstance but from the violence that human beings do. When we refer to a wound, visible or not, we recognize that warriors have survived violent exchanges with others, suffer for it, and are forever different.

In the Native American tradition, wounds were not hidden while the warrior tried to appear "normal." Wounds to warriors and their warhorses were painted, decorated, and displayed. In the equine world, scars on horses are called "proud flesh." Today physically wounded warriors who receive artificial limbs are encouraged to wear their devices openly and proudly in public.

In contrast, in 2009 Defense Department officials decided that PTSD did not meet their criterion for awarding the Purple Heart, declaring the award is for wounds caused by "an outside force or agent."[7] This refusal declared that to be wounded your blood must be spilled; it must be physical and visible. It also denied that "outside agents"—people and forces trying to kill us—contribute to invisible wounding. Further, only recognizing physical injuries disguises war's true casualty figures. We only count physical wounds and deaths occurring in the war zone during active duty. If we consider long-term effects, including illnesses, disabilities, accidents, suicides, and other losses from invisible wounds and long-term poisoning, casualty rates with their needs and costs become what they really are—astronomical. The public would see that our new wars are not, as claimed, "surgically cleaner." They do not in the long term either preserve American lives or save money.[8]

Many veterans interpreted the negative Purple Heart judgment as yet another betrayal by a nation that blames them for their own suffering.

Patients are ill. Victims are injured. Society is disordered. Warriors are wounded.

Wounding Is Inevitable

Invisible wounds are as inevitable to warriors as are visible ones. As we have heard, they may occur as readily after the warrior's return as they do while in harm's way.

Senator John McCain spent five and a half years as a prisoner of war in Viet Nam. He summarized war's toll: we "ask men to suffer and die, to persevere through god-awful afflictions and heartache, to endure the dehumanizing experiences that are unavoidable in combat." But war's toll cannot be separated from a country's response. McCain continued, "for a cause that the country wouldn't support over time and that our leaders so wrongly believed could be achieved at a smaller cost."[9]

Vietnam vet turned actor and playwright Brian Delate made a movie about veterans' wounding. It focused on the relationships between a World War II father and his Vietnam vet son, and between this vet and another, who help each other through life's daily challenges. When the son heard that PTSD was once known as Soldier's Heart, he said, "That's poetic—makes me think of my dad." His girlfriend replied, "It made me think of you."[10]

Delate's movie portrays no flashbacks or explosions. Rather, his veterans carry a pervasive sadness, hypersensitivity, and inability to adjust to the ordinary. Organizing, paying attention, finding employment, paying bills, and making relationships work is just harder for them. Everything hurts. The name of Delate's movie is *Soldier's Heart*.

Combat vet Dr. John Fisher found healing through therapy, traveling the world, practicing spirituality and holistic health, surfing, writing, and returning to Viet Nam and giving free chiropractic clinics there. He declared, "We're at war, and I hurt all the time."

Our military training and practices, political and economic motivations, technological brutality, and neglectful homecoming all make wounding inevitable, extensive, and morally difficult. One Marine wondered if American children would grow up differently if they played with GI Joe and Jane dolls that had the thousand-yard stare and looked ravaged and exhausted.

In contrast, ancient and indigenous cultures recognized that psychic and spiritual wounding is inevitable and ubiquitous, if not universal. It was known and anticipated. Societies provided warrior models, roles, training, behavior, values, and practices to protect their warriors' psyches from excessive wounding—and they tended the soldiers afterward. Joseph Campbell summarizes,

> After episodes of battle, special rituals are enacted to assuage and release to the land of the spirits the ghosts of those that have been slain . . . Such ceremonies may also include the rites for toning down war mania and battle heat of those who have done the killing . . . There may

> also be special rites enacted to re-attune returning warriors to the manners of life at home.[11]

The Vietnamese educated their youth to the ways they might be wounded or killed in their wars. My staff and I have facilitated Deployment Blessing Ceremonies for soldiers leaving for Afghanistan. A few chaplains conduct spiritual preparation retreats for their units before deploying. Warriors today as in the past use relics and totems—unit coins, saint's cards, wolves' teeth, family photos—to protect themselves during battle.

We have witnessed war's wounding and character transformations in the great and the small, from King Saul and Achilles up through the present day. Since "war is hell" and veterans are people who have returned from that diabolical realm, soul wounding is not only inevitable but also proof of the warrior's humanity. After surviving hell, can we expect "normalcy"? Who could survive such experiences and not be touched, hurt, wounded, transformed?

WOUNDING AND IDENTITY

"Get wisdom, though it cost all you have," counsels Proverbs. Wounds both visible and invisible must be embraced as "the cost" of the new identity and its potential maturation and wisdom.

Consider the following responses to their wounding by Vietnam combat veterans.

Tall and endearing Carl was a forward artillery observer. He wore support braces and boots for his spine, which was damaged when his Jeep hit a mine. He exploded in road rages and struggled against alienation, nightmares, and mistrust. Carl brought his Purple Heart medal into one therapy session. The medal shows George Washington's profile and is inscribed *For Valor*.

Carl looked at the inscription and shook his head sadly, "This medal and inscription—all bullshit," he said.

"What could make it meaningful?" I asked.

"The truth," he said.

"What could we inscribe so that your medal tells the truth?"

Carl looked me in the eyes and in a firm voice declared, "It wasn't worth it." He paused, then added, "If the public read that, they might ask me what it meant and I could tell them. Without the truth, like I said, it's all bullshit."

Al, another combat veteran, worked alone, avoided people, and was twice divorced. He eventually returned to Viet Nam with me and afterward attended a Buddhist meditation retreat for veterans. After these he said, "Now I understand. PTSD is not something you have. I don't *have* PTSD. I *am* PTSD."

A survivor can be so dominated by the wound that he or she fully identifies with it: "I am my wound. I am damaged goods." Their entire identities can be sucked into the defining experiences of service and wounding. On the other hand, owning a wound means it is not something we "have," not something separate from us, but rather something we are, a condition we must fully integrate into our self-image, lifestyle, and behavior.

Continuing to feel that "it wasn't worth it," Carl spent most of his time nursing his disabled condition. Al learned that we can't take the wound away and it is not something separate from him. He would henceforth include the invisible wound as an irrevocable part of his identity. He married Minh, a Vietnamese woman he met on a return journey, adopted and supported her family, and made Viet Nam his second home. Finally Al and Minh had a baby boy, born of love and reconciliation between peoples and nations.

Invisible wounding can inhabit and dominate the psyche—an unpredictable beast in the mind and heart, an uninvited third party in relationships. When it does, we diagnose a misshapen psyche and say, "The veteran has . . . " The wound controls us to the degree that we embrace it as our identity and it crowds out the rest of our lives. Even after a single deployment or one year's tour of duty in a combat zone, vets commonly testify that their tour affected them more than the rest of life put together. In contrast, restoration is possible to the degree that we achieve "a new normal," as survivors say: working with who I am now, who I have become, what I have learned, what my new identity is, and meeting friends and family members as a different person with whom we must re-create relationships that work.

Wounding and our response to it must become an accepted, embraced, solid part of the new identity that is continuous with warriorhood and the military identity. Green Beret veteran Greg Walker explained the demands on Special Forces recruits:

> In Special Forces we say that Selection is a never-ending process. There is no end state, no final destination, and no finish line. You are always in the Selection mode regardless of what you accomplish. It is both a process and a creed that does not allow for self-limitation.

Meaningful new growth after service, Greg said, is "an experience that mirrors Selection." Warrior preparation itself can provide character traits necessary to embrace and transform wounding.

> To reach meaningful recovery and your "new normal," you have to truly demand everything of yourself that's available. When I came face to face with my own wounding and its effects in my life and the lives of those around me, it was initially devastating. However, by embracing my spiritual, emotional, mental, and physical wounds and injuries and determining even at my weakest that I would not give in or accept the defeat of my soul/spirit, I reengaged in the never-ending process of Selection.

Not only attitudes but also grindingly difficult work is necessary both to be a warrior and to transform wounds. Greg continued,

> My "new normal" was forged, tempered, and shaped by nearly six years of intense work—you have to do the flight time if you want to soar with the eagles again. It is the result of a collaborative effort of family, dear friends, incredible life coaches, and spiritual teachers. It is a prism that includes the contributions of those who entered my transition from war-fighter to healer/mentor at just the right moment where the crossroads in the Warrior's Path appears and a choice is required to go either one way or the other.

Greg evoked his warrior code:

> To continue or to turn back. To "suck it up" and drive on regardless of the challenge or to quit. As in Selection, quitting is simply not an option. The achievement of one's "new normal" is new life, new purpose, new priorities, goals, objectives. And peace that takes root deep within and ever so slowly grows upward and outward to ultimately break through the darkness and into the light of a new and better day.

New life is possible out of the detritus of war and its shattered identity.

Ironically, the very codes and values that originally shaped the recruit's military identity may be engaged to embrace, cope with, and transform wounding into a sign of honorable warriorhood.

WOUNDING AND THE COMMUNITY

Since war wounds were taken for the community and nation, they must be acknowledged, witnessed, honored, and supported there.

Army Chaplain Chris Antal attended a Soldier's Heart healing retreat before deployment. During our closing circle, civilians and veterans said to Chris, "Please take care of yourself in Afghanistan."

Lieutenant Antal looked each person in the eye. Then he answered, "I can't."

"What do you mean?" someone blurted. "You must! We want you back."

"I'm a chaplain. My duty is to take care of our soldiers. I'm also a soldier and must follow orders. You must take care of me. If you are concerned about me or how our soldiers are used, take care of us. Make certain we are used and supported correctly."

Without public involvement, reconciliation between warrior and society, and restoration of the broken social contract, the warrior may collapse. Collapse may come from the weight of carrying the collective wound and responsibility for war alone. By sharing the wounds, we return responsibility for our warriors, how they are used, and the tending of their wounds to the citizenry where it belongs.

Wounds need to be witnessed and honored. This has to occur not just in public, as in "airing out" for purification, but by the communities and nations in whose names they were taken. And the community needs to respond, to take action on behalf of its wounded in a way that addresses their needs to be seen, heard, and honored.

Understanding the war wound as something both moral and social that we have unwittingly forced our veterans to carry alone, we can shape actions and responses that say, we hear you, you are not alone, and there is a path to home and healing.

The community and its institutions can become the veteran's refuge and healing sanctuary. Communities can do much, even without professional supervision, to become veteran friendly. Here is some of what the soul wound asks us to do:

- offer immediate response to any soldier, veteran, or family member crying out in unbearable pain;
- create safe and sober gathering places for veterans in every community;
- create religious services that bring veterans spiritual cleansing and comfort;
- restore meaning, respect, and commemoration to Memorial Day and Veterans Day—close the malls and gather in houses of worship, communities, and cemeteries instead;
- create religious, educational, and therapeutic programs by which veterans can seek not just psychological help but spiritual healing, cleansing, and forgiveness;
- create veteran ministries in faith organizations that recognize veteran holidays as holy days; offer specialized liturgies and memorials, military family-support and talking circles, roundtables, potlucks, and related events;
- create safe havens that are not only shelters for homeless or addicted vets but are houses of initiation where vets receive education, therapy, cultural and rehumanization processes, and job, budget, and sobriety training;
- invite veterans into schools and community centers to educate our young about the realities of war and service;

- foster programs in libraries, community, cultural, and educational centers where veterans tell their stories to civilians and civilians honor and help veterans;
- create a Veterans Service Corps so that those who have faced life's ultimate tests can find new, meaningful ways to serve rather than collapse into disability and can give something back for the benefits they receive;
- pair elder veterans with new returnees, much as Twelve Step programs do, so that returnees never have to be alone with their nightmares and despair;
- train, prepare, and transform college campuses into "houses of initiation"; make our colleges "veteran friendly" not just in attracting vet students to their standard curricula but such that institutions have extensive and alternative programming aimed at completing veterans' homecoming and initiation processes and ensuring consistency with and relevance to their military experiences;
- create 24/7 hotlines and drop-in centers so that veterans can find immediate help when needed;
- teach veterans creative and expressive arts so that they develop tools for self-expression, public sharing, and cultural enrichment;
- create literary and artistic programming—readings, movie series, book discussion groups—through which vets offer their creative products and study them with community, and the community becomes further educated;
- evaluate veterans in the criminal justice system for the impact of military service upon criminal activities;
- create prison-based programs for the special needs of incarcerated veterans;
- create hospice programs for the special needs of terminally ill veterans and their families;
- create reconciliation programs between former foes and between veterans and civilians;
- create restoration projects so that soldiers who had to destroy or kill can once again learn that they are good people who can preserve, create, and build;

- create community-based support systems for spouses and families of troops serving overseas;
- create community-based support systems for families of newly returned veterans with preparation and training for living with traumatic wounding;
- recognize, support, and include other at-risk groups, such as grandparents and boy- and girlfriends of overseas troops and returnees;
- evaluate and re-create our military training system so that we do not dehumanize our troops or potential foes as we train and prepare them for soldiering;
- train many more health and mental health workers in veterans' psychology and teach that it is different from normative civilian psychology and they must apply different philosophies and methods in working with veterans;
- educate health and learning professionals and the public to become familiar with the ways of warriors and war so that we overcome veterans' alienation and society's denial and become war-literate.

Any community could institute such programs. By providing veterans what they need for healing and return, any community could become a model veteran-welcoming community. It would declare: We can restore the broken relationship between our society and its warriors. We can reduce the incalculable losses that result from war. We can help heal not just veterans but our society.

Dr. Glen Miller is a psychology professor who was a long-range reconnaissance (LRRP) team leader in Viet Nam. He met me at the door to the auditorium on his Pennsylvania campus where we would hold a conference on veterans in college. Before saying hello, he pointed to his suit lapel and asked, "Is this okay?" He was wearing a miniature pin of the CIB, the Combat Infantryman's Badge, earned only for significant time spent in the combat zone, the most highly honored award for ground troops. It simply declares, "I was there."

I hugged Professor Miller and said, "Of course, brother. It's your eagle feather." I reminded him that Native American warriors commonly wore eagle feathers in camp so that their communities could readily distinguish their warriors. "See me": Professor Miller was asking just this from his academic community.

Minutes later Glen rose before the packed auditorium to open the conference. He dedicated it to our new returnees, now students. Then he pointed to his CIB and told his university community, "I need you to know all of who I am. Today, with this badge, I tell you."

Glen Miller has worn his CIB pin on his lapel ever since and has founded the nonprofit Veterans Community Network for helping younger vets. He publically embraces and fulfills his social role as elder warrior.

Wandering and wounded warriors need a tribe waiting to receive, hear, and tend them. If we are that tribe, they will come home and serve the greater good.

SOLDIER'S HEART

We *treat* PTSD. We heal and restore Soldier's Heart. When we think of the invisible wound as a medical or psychological condition needing expert treatment, repair, or control, we do things to and give things for the condition. When we think of it as a communal and spiritual wound that we all share and for which we are all responsible, we love and support, listen to, engage, and restore survivors, work together with them to repair our wounded world and live together in empathy.

Soldier's Heart is a permanent wound, but we can transform its impact and how we carry it. John Fisher said,

> There is a part to a soldier's heart that doesn't go away, no matter how well the warrior is able to sleep at night. It's the part that shudders with the sound of fireworks on July Fourth, sheds tears during a war scene in a movie, feels the horror of combat when another KIA [killed in action] is announced on the news. That portion of the soldier's heart is different from the rest of the population's, except another soldier's heart. This is the brotherhood that soldiers, veterans, and warriors feel for one another. The crying is from the pain stored in that other part of the heart. Warriors will always be different.

"Soldier's Heart" affirms that warriors are brokenhearted. It honors the weight and sorrow that permanently dwell in a veteran's heart, which they must carry their entire lives. It honors that life may be more difficult for them. And it calls for an empathic and generous response from other hearts.

Mr. Tiger was right: we must restore the wounded hearts of warriors. General Turner was right: we must love them. War healing requires a spiritual approach because war is Leviathan and trauma is a deep, devastating, and enduring soul wound. It requires a restorative rather than reparative psychological approach because a moral journey must be completed, the identity must be re-created, meaning must be discovered, and spirit must be renewed. It requires a communal approach because it is a social disorder resulting from neglecting and isolating warriors and not fulfilling our social contract and because the citizens did not initiate their warriors. It requires an archetypal approach because the individual's story must be joined to the stories of the ages and to the universal and eternal patterns in these stories. Healing war wounds and restoring souls requires moving beyond conventional therapeutic practices and settings to restore the proper relationships between veterans, communities, former foes, and the spiritual dimensions of warriorhood.

RESTORING WARRIORS THROUGH THE SOLDIER'S HEART MODEL

Through more than thirty-five years of work with veterans, I had to recognize the full, complex, and transformative impact the military and war has on everyone serving and touched. Exploring the inevitable consequences to survivors and society propelled me onto a lifelong search into the myriad ways warriors and their wounds have been understood and tended through the ages. This comprehensive approach, true to warriors' experiences and to the wisdom of other cultures and ages, determines we need a philosophy and practice for veteran restoration based on love, compassion, empathy, restoration, spirituality, archetypal wisdom, and community involvement, all aimed at restoring the soul and healing society's broken contract.

In 2006, in response to "the scream" of veterans and their loved ones across the nation, and in the absence of other comprehensive spiritually and community-based approaches to tending our veterans, my wife and partner, Kate Dahlstedt, and I founded a nonprofit organization. What is missing are exactly these dimensions of holistic care—the heart, soul, spirit, community, and purpose—that are harmed in war, at the source of the wound, and most neglected by the modern world and its practices. To honor our veterans carrying invisible wounds and the ancient tradition of war healing that we serve, we named our organization "Soldier's Heart."

The mission of our Soldier's Heart organization is to restore warriors and their communities. Our recipe is "spirituality in community." Our motto is, "Caring means sharing the burden." Our comprehensive model maps the full warrior's journey and addresses the emotional, moral, and spiritual wounds of veterans, their families, and communities. We offer restoration and homecoming not by treating disorders but by guiding survivors to develop new and honorable warrior identities supported by community by restoring their spirits, and by provoking new Post-traumatic Growth and service. Having spent decades exploring ancient and cross-cultural warrior traditions that reveal the necessary steps for successful warrior return, the Soldier's Heart Model facilitates and applies them in meaningful contemporary practice to promote, train, and guide military, professional, academic, and community-based efforts to heal the effects of war. We prepare families and communities to support and heal veterans—both those returning from current wars and those who fought in past wars. We are creating a network of community-based services and organizations, a "warrior's web," to facilitate successful reintegration of veterans across the nation. In addition to intensive retreats and pilgrimages for veterans during which we teach, practice, and apply our model of the Transformational Journey, our staff educates the military, medical, mental health, and academic institutions, faith organizations, professionals, and communities on how to create holistic services for vets and their families that effectively respond to their special and unique needs.

We seek to create a comprehensive model that individuals, agencies, institutions, communities, and even nations can apply to the healing of their warriors, citizens, and war wounds. We wish the roots of peace to pierce deeply into our violence-polluted world. These roots cannot thrive until we attend to war healing. War healing is peacemaking.

What are veterans asking from their communities and society? To be seen as they are, for who they are, for what they gave, for their struggles now, and to be loved and honored for their unchanging essence of devotion and sacrifice. Tran Quang Quy, a North Vietnamese Army veteran, wrote in "Gift":

It's me here . . .
The boy from the old days, the returning soldier
Carrying the rain on my shoulder . . .
Without glory . . .
It's me here
Please don't stay distant and please don't look at me that way
Even if I bear a wound on my body
I am whole with an unchanging heart . . . [12]

We must think not only in terms of Post-traumatic *Growth.* PTSD can also be translated as *Post-traumatic Spiritual Development.*

Post-traumatic Soul Distress +
Post-traumatic Social Disorder
Necessitate
Post-traumatic Spiritual Development

CHAPTER 10

The Transformational Journey

I must become better—
better than if I were killed in the war.

ANTOINE DE SAINT-EXUPERY

The map of the warrior's journey reveals a path home for the warrior and wisdom for the community on how to guide, receive, and hold the returned warrior. What do we know thus far?

The extensive warrior medicine of ancient, sacred, and indigenous cultures and mythologies around the world, including our Western root Hebraic and Hellenic traditions, reveal maps for the warrior's complete journey. They include and give special attention to the return. Though different cultures used different specific rituals and practices, core principles were universally represented and repeated across distant times and places.

We reaffirm fundamental truths about warfare and warriorhood. From these we understand the nature of the invisible wound to warriors and how to respond in ways that provide soul restoration.

We Hold These Truths About War

- War is archetypal and demonic. It is a force existing in and beyond us that is overwhelming in its power, intensity, possessiveness, and impact. It has been experienced as a god or attributed to God.
- War is always and unspeakably horrible. War wounds everyone and everything it touches.

- War wounds will be deep, complex, and costly in every way. They will affect and change every part of us—bodies, minds, hearts and souls, our spirits, relationships, communities, nations, values, and meaning.
- Invisible war wounds occur to body, mind, heart, soul, spirit, culture, and earth. They continue wounding as they pass through the generations and history. They are as real as visible wounds and can sometimes be even more debilitating.
- Societies and their survivors will inevitably be wounded from war. The wounds may manifest in different expressions, forms, symptoms, and post-service roles depending on how a particular society prepares for, practices, and responds afterward to its veterans.
- Our contemporary version of war wounding is due to all the conditions by which we prepare for and make war, especially the usually ignored moral, cultural, and psychospiritual conditions, along with neglect and betrayal of troops upon homecoming.
- Though destruction and death were far more prevalent among the Vietnamese than Americans in that war, there is almost no PTSD among Vietnamese survivors. Their wounding should not be labeled or treated as Americans are. The experience of Viet Nam is evidence that our version and degree of invisible wounding can be significantly mitigated by social, cultural, and spiritual factors.

Understanding these fundamental truths about war, we set:

Growth Goals for Wounded Warriors

- The invisible wound that today we call PTSD is not a failure of character or a mental illness. It has been known as long as there have been warriors. It is an honorable and inevitable wound. It is proof of your humanity. It is a portal for transformation and a school for wisdom.
- It is possible to grow beyond the invisible wound and change the way you carry it.
- Restoration and transformation mean saying "yes" to a moral, spiritual, and communal journey of growth, healing, and restorative service.

- You can follow the path of a spiritual warrior. You can grow an identity big enough (Post-traumatic Growth, Post-traumatic Spiritual Development) to carry this wound, discover its blessings, and give it meaning.
- Your wound will never go away and you will be different forever, but you can transform so that the wound is integrated into your whole self. It becomes your honorable story. Its disturbing symptoms fade and are replaced by wisdom, compassion, and lifelong service.

We hold compatible goals for survivors' caregivers and communities.

Goals for Clinicians, Educators, Care Providers, and Communities Serving Veterans

- The spiritual or elder warrior's journey is a psychospiritual reality that constitutes a road map through life. You can nurture the development of this identity in survivors.
- Traditional societies provided "medicine chiefs of warriors," the original chaplains, and specialists in spiritual war healing and its nurturance in warriors, their units, and communities. The study of this role can provide missing identity and guidance for care providers serving wounded warriors today.
- There are necessary return principles and practices after war for all survivors. These are modeled by world warrior and sacred traditions and can be practiced in meaningful contemporary ways. We can shape healing interventions and programs to deliver them in ways consistent with survivors' and society's beliefs.
- There is a proper reciprocal social contract between warriors and civilians. During threat, warriors provide an outer circle of protection. Upon veteran homecoming, civilians in their turn serve as the outer circle of protection and caregiving. Civilians must engage in order to heal this broken social contract, mature through exposure to warriors, and complete a homecoming and reconciliation that includes us all, reuniting the war-sundered citizenry.

THE WARRIOR'S JOURNEY: THE SOLDIER'S HEART MODEL

We see by now that the Warrior is a foundational archetype built into our spiritual, psychological, cultural, historical, and social lives. In dealing with its warriors, any society is dealing with the Warrior archetype's contemporary manifestations of identity, social, historical, political, and economic roles and functions; psychological stage of development; and spiritual status. Every society should be concerned with healthy, honorable, and creative warrior development.

Popular culture has re-created the traditional concept of "warpath." Mainstream society applies the word to combat rather than the warrior's entire way of life. This eliminates its psychospiritual and life-mapping functions and considers "warriors" to be those who have been in combat regardless of wounding. Meanwhile, our nation regularly reverts to war as a political and economic tool whether or not the country is immediately and directly threatened. It has transformed veterans from storied individuals into patriotic totems. It has remained on a war economy since World War II in order to increase national wealth and power. It has eliminated universal service. It has substituted a profession of arms whose troops have been used for political and economic ends by American leadership under pressure from corporations with greatly increased willingness, frequency, violence, and secrecy in recent decades. It uses war and violence as forms of socialization and mass entertainment, including in the rearing of children. In all these ways the nation remains on the warpath.

Being away from home and homeland and in combat is a most challenging, difficult, and transformative part of the journey, yet we must focus on the lifelong journey supporting its unique and irrevocable identity. To the warrior even the negative, betraying, or morally questionable dimensions of military experience can provide opportunities for growth and reintegration into a positive identity. To be on the warrior's path includes the spiritual and social conditions of warriorhood, the private and public identities of individual warriors, the relationship between warriors and their societies. Our modern culture tends to treat warriorhood today as either the rare and specialized identity of one who follows the profession of arms or an honorable interruption of the common civilian life journey that often makes it more difficult. Traditional cultures mapped this path and it was available to almost every adult male as well as to some women.

The mythologist Joseph Campbell mapped the "hero's journey." It is a universalized road map drawn from Campbell's exhaustive studies of world mythological, religious, and spiritual traditions. Though there are many individual and cultural variations in how journeys unfold, the underlying pattern is identical across cultures, religions, and civilizations.

Campbell mapped three stages of the hero's journey: departure, initiation, and return. Real and imaginary culture heroes and their adventures—General Eisenhower versus John Wayne, the historical versus the mythic Davy Crockett—exemplify and model the stages of this journey. Initiates depart from the conventional, go through trials and ordeals, struggle and are transformed, and return with wisdom and boons necessary to the well-being of society. Through this journey they transform into culture heroes. The journey's purpose is not in what it provides the individual, though that is much, but rather to preserve, grow, develop, and evolve the culture through the hero's newly acquired maturity and wisdom.

Every one of us may replicate the journey. Our souls yearn to travel this path. If we do not, we remain immature, deficient, lonely, and longing for inexpressible inner experience. When we do, we develop the inner Warrior archetype whether or not we serve in the military.

The map of the hero's journey as taught by Joseph Campbell is:

THE HERO'S JOURNEY (Joseph Campbell)

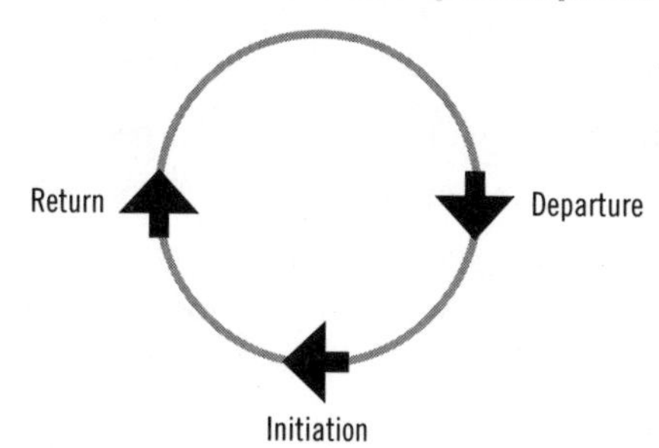

Archetypes unfold in psyche and life as the individual replicates the hero's journey through all its stages. All stages must be traversed or something is missing. We may be withered, weak, or deficient. We may be aggressive, selfish, defiant, and demanding. The soul must make the journey in some form or it does not mature. By making the journey, the individual evolves into a "hero," not someone to be worshipped but someone who has mastered extraordinary trials and gives back.

The warrior is a servant of the culture. The Warrior archetype unfolds in psyche and life by replicating the warrior hero's journey through all its stages. The psyche must do this or something is missing; its inner warrior may be withered, weak, or deficient; it may be aggressive, selfish, defiant, and demanding. Later development will be skewed if it is built on earlier wounding.

Campbell finds many substages or steps of the hero's journey and specific soul tasks that must be performed to complete the journey.[1] In order to help us see the warrior's journey clearly, consider this expansion of Campbell's model.

THE HERO'S JOURNEY (Expanded—Tick)

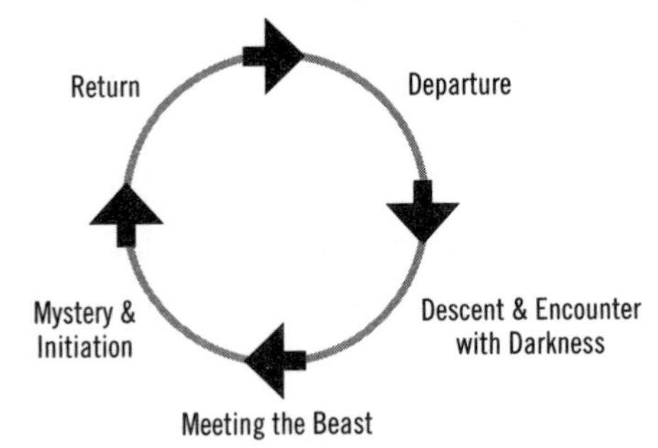

Departure includes departure from civilian society and immersion in the new, unfamiliar, demanding military culture, where the individual's identity is deconstructed and he or she is trained for service. It includes entry into another world where taking or losing life is always only a pin's thickness away.

All troops are trained in killing, and taking another human life is the greatest trauma we can experience. It is necessary but not sufficient to be concerned about our troops "in harm's way" as if combat zone duty were only about the dangers to their lives. These are indeed many and terrible. But troops also destroy, maim, or kill. Those harmed may be enemy combatants. Many will be innocent civilians used as pawns, targets, or shields and be slaughtered in far greater numbers than their warriors. "In harm's way" must include the kill-or-be-killed situation in which our troops together with all allies, foes, and innocent bystanders are trapped. It must remind us that, as one Afghanistan Marine said, "the business of war is to kill." Harm's way will still be there for targets and pilots even when drones do our long-distance killing. Destruction and death will be rampant and infect us even as we reduce the number of American physical casualties.

Descent includes learning what perhaps we should never know, "things too great for me," said Job. Descent is immersion in a world of danger, threat, fear, pain, loss, and encounters with the fiercest forces in humanity. The ferocity includes the love of brother and sister, devotion to duty and cause, willingness to sacrifice and endure, and all that we associate with glory, honor, and courage. During the descent the warrior may discover his or her inner beast, experience the "mad moment," go berserk—or resist it in self and others. Whatever happens in the lowest pit of hell is transformative and initiatory, as stamped forever on the psyche as is the image of the World Trade Center being hit.

Descent is not only horrible. It is also charged and blessed. Veterans testify that life was never so intense, immediate, penetrating, vivid, and addictive than during combat. There is awe and beauty in the powers that also destroy. And there is the famed brother- and sisterhood that develops among people who share life-threatening risks and deprivations which becomes the strongest bond of their lives.

Mastery and initiation occur after ordeal and include how we carry the experience, whether we can find or create meaning for it, whether we carry it or it breaks us, how it reshapes our identities. In Greek mythology, Odysseus was away at the Trojan War for a decade, and it took him another decade to travel home. The way up and out is as long, deep, and complex as the way in and down.

We finally return as culture heroes not for the purpose of being celebrated in uncritical patriotic displays but to give wisdom, protection, teaching, service, and guidance to society. Or we do not return. Campbell stresses what we have heard from veterans—return is the most difficult part of the journey. We have changed, but others have not. We cannot return to who we were, but others want us to. We now know and have done things others do not and have not. We have nowhere to bring them, no tools for expressing them or audiences who want to hear them. The invisible wound is the psyche stuck in the nadir of the hero's journey. Restoring the warrior's soul consists of nurturing a self reborn into a new spiritual warrior's identity.

Overlay these fundamental cycles of human development—archetypal maturation, the death-rebirth initiation, and stages of the hero's journey—on the Warrior's Path and we have the map of the warrior's journey. We call this the Soldier's Heart Transformational Model. We strive to include every aspect of the warrior's journey before, during, and after deployments and service.

SOLDIER'S HEART TRANSFORMATIONAL MODEL

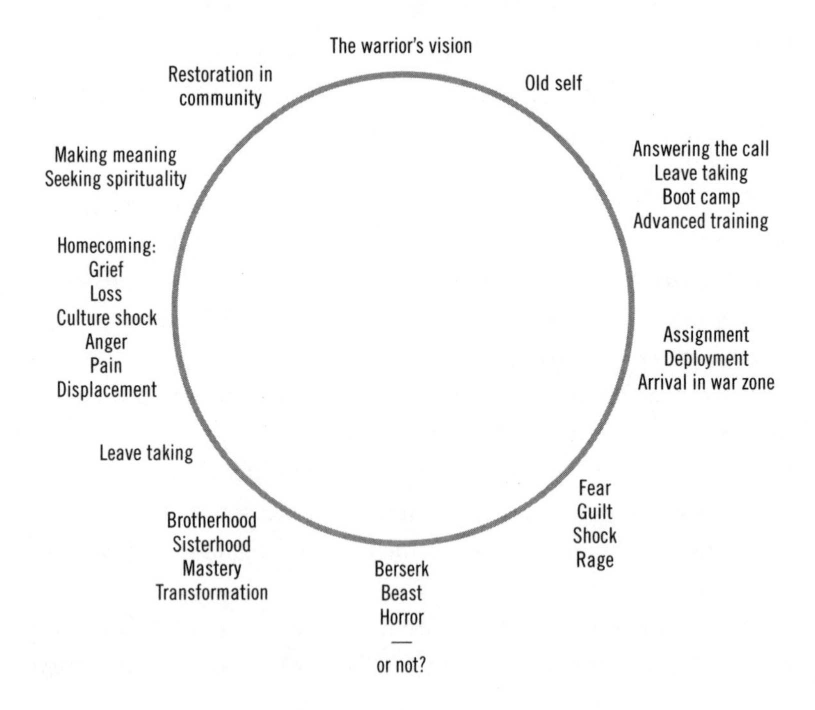

Troops and veterans can guide their own progress along the warrior's journey. Helpers and caregivers can review in detail and with associated emotions exactly what unfolded during each phase of the journey, how it was built on the previous phase, and how it shaped the coming steps. Supporters and loved ones can understand their warrior's unique identity and lifestyle and can map the journey—where they either shared it or were on different routes, where loved ones fell or thrived.

Developmental tasks must be completed at each step. Nothing is neutral. The person entering the military may be strong or weak, mature or immature, resilient or traumatized, an "Army brat" or with no previous exposure. In our current poor economic climate, an increasing number of undereducated young people from troubled backgrounds join the military for jobs, security, discipline, belonging. Many enter already carrying a psychic rucksack full of challenges. During our discussion of warrior spirituality, a command psychiatrist at Walter Reed Army Hospital said,

> Many of us here have studied our Homer and Shakespeare. We know what you're talking about. But how do we teach today's recruits who don't even know how to say "please" or "thank you"? They enter the military already traumatized and without even basic socialization. We've become a remedial institution. How can we raise warriors?"

A recruit may have had an emotional or a stoic leave-taking from community to military: one crowded among family and friends, another praying, another partying, another on a bus alone. How we leave imprints us and shapes what is to come. Strengths and weaknesses develop. Blessings and wounds are taken in every stage of the journey. Veterans may need to review and re-create some or all of the steps along their lifelong warrior's map. They often discover it started long before they went into the military, perhaps even before birth.

When veterans become aware of the spiritual warrior model and are shown its map, they commonly experience recognition, relief, gratitude, and hope. Many exclaim, "Now I understand the journey I have been trying to make my entire life without knowing it." Seeing that the journey is still in progress and that it offers the growth goal of spiritual warriorhood, they commonly respond, "I finally hear a call to warriorhood that I can answer."

All these steps must ultimately be taken in community. The stories must be told. The community must participate as sacred witness to the entire journey, as a vessel to bless the warrior on leaving, provide support while away, and receive and tend upon return. Since the wound is also fundamentally a result of the broken social contract—"social disorder"—it can be restored and healed through the community's participation. As they become aware of this unspoken broken social contract, communities commonly seek ways to take responsibility for what was done in their names and take meaningful actions to support veterans.

One bullet-eyed Iraq vet glared at Sally, a gray-haired Hospice social worker who attended a healing retreat just to listen and support. "I don't get it," the returnee said. "You don't have any family or friends in service. You're old. You've been through enough in your life and you work with dying people. You don't have to expose yourself to this awful shit from my brothers and me. Why are you here?"

Sally gently met the vet's bouncing eyes and answered, "Because you are my warriors."

CHAPTER 11

Lessons from the Chiefs of Old

My Father has given me this nation;
In protecting them I have a hard time.

SITTING BULL, 1865 Eagle Vision Song

In 1868, to unify the people and strengthen resistance against white encroachment, the Teton Lakota nation for the first time chose a single head chief. On being elected, Sitting Bull composed a song for his initiation ceremony that called the tribes to witness. He evoked "the chiefs of old," calling attention to the chief's responsibility as spiritual leader. But the elder chiefs and warriors were "gone"; they were being killed off. That was one meaning.

Sitting Bull and his people worshipped and emulated the spirit, archetype, and ideal of the warrior chief. "The chiefs of old" were the great chiefs of the past who had lived exemplary lives and after death became ancestors and guardians in the spirit world. Many cultures have had a version of this belief; the original meaning of "hero" was one who had achieved beyond human limits and so was elevated and could be appealed to in the spirit world. In US history, Washington, Lincoln, and Martin Luther King, Jr., as obvious examples, achieved such mythic stature but without the attribution of afterlife influence. Sitting Bull was to be the living link in a continuous tradition. All his life he sought to personify this ideal. As head chief he would strive to emulate the "chiefs of old" under the most challenging conditions. His people's survival was dependent on him, and the ancestors were watching.

Our traditional peoples commonly had many chiefs rather than one national head. Among some tribes, the Iroquois for example, a council of wise women elders—clan mothers—presided over the chiefs, approving or vetoing their decisions. Chiefs served different functions or led different factions or subgroups of the community. Individual warriors often had freedom of choice as to which chief and orders they followed, and alliances shifted frequently. This protected the community from abuse because absolute power was not invested in any one person. Sometimes elder women had to approve decisions, and each warrior had personal responsibility for his choices and actions. Traditional cultures strove to keep the warrior's will and service united by ensuring that the warrior (and sometimes his mother!) agreed to all that he might have to perform.

Of the numerous offices and roles Sitting Bull held, he considered the most important to be medicine chief of the Hunkpapa Warrior Society. As a medicine man, shaman, teacher, healer, and leader he was responsible for the spiritual health, healing, and well-being of the tribe's warriors. Sitting Bull was a master and facilitator not just of battle skills but also of warrior rituals, ceremonies, stories, songs, dances, practices, and traditions. He believed, as did another "father of his country," George Washington, that if warriors are well, the people will be well. If the warriors fall, we all fall.

WARRIOR MEDICINE, SOUL MEDICINE

Medicine comes from the Latin *medicus*. Medicine is "that which heals"; warrior medicine is that which heals warriors. To the degree that war's invisible wound is to the soul, we must practice soul medicine for warriors.

Soul medicine teaches, strengthens, guides, and heals. It reawakens, reenergizes, and purifies the soul. It restores the soul's right and proper relationships to the rest of our lives—our bodies, minds, and hearts; our histories, families, communities, and nation; our work, purpose, and goodness. This always involves our archetypal natures and inheritance. The images, stories, patterns that repeat in all human beings throughout time—our dreams and moments of utmost connection or intensity—all express who and what in essence we are. They are our paths of access to the soul. We practice soul medicine by delving deeply into these images, patterns, stories, and emotions to discover the sacred myths and eternal histories that we replicate in our individual lives. We realize our souls are on a life journey and map it. We take up practices and studies—ways of thinking, behaving, creating, and counseling—that support and guide the journey, allow us to express it and steer it toward what is true and good. We consciously and willingly wrestle with our fates to affirm destinies and with our wounds to create meaning.

Soul medicine for warriors is archetypal. It awakens the individual to the inner Warrior archetype and teaches its recurring themes and stories. It guides the veteran to draw on the strongest powers and traditions in order to endure and succeed. It helps the individual claim his or her place in history. It helps give meaning to what was absurd and shape a transpersonal vision out of horror. It supports the warrior in achieving continuity between military and civilian service and fitting personal history into the worldwide spiritual warrior tradition. It helps the survivor create a new identity and way of life as an elder warrior.

"Medicine chiefs of warriors" guide the steps, practices, and rituals we use to strengthen, reawaken, and purify the warrior. During service they help maintain morality and morale during combat, as in ancient times priests accompanied Israelites and Roman legions into battle, as George Washington wanted to achieve by founding the Army chaplaincy.

Some beliefs, values, and practices seem innate to certain individuals, as if they were born to be warriors or chiefs. Some military leaders exhibit superior soldiering and leadership such that they inspire and reinvigorate soldiers and restore intangible spiritual qualities right on the battlefield. These leaders carry what traditional cultures called "warrior medicine" and may awaken it in their troops.

During the Korean War, Lt. General Matthew Ridgway replaced Douglas MacArthur as commander. MacArthur had pushed the North Koreans almost to the Chinese border when, against his expectations, Chinese troops poured over and routed the US/UN forces. The US Eighth Army was depressed, demoralized, inefficient, and defeatist. It had lost its will, belief, and confidence. In confusion, it retreated in panic. General Ridgway took over. His deep mythic and spiritual sense of his role in history and about the warrior tradition informed his leadership.

He believed that he and the men he commanded were the direct descendants of those who had gone before them, dating back to Valley Forge. It was as if George Washington and the men who fought with him were always looking over his shoulder. Ridgway sometimes talked in an almost mystical way of those who had fought in the Revolution or the Civil War, and of the need for his men to be worthy of the hardships they suffered.[1]

Before the battle of Marathon, one warrior had a vision of Pan assuring him that he, the god, would be with the Greeks in battle, causing "panic" in the enemy. Other warriors battling the Persians reported seeing Hercules and Theseus on the battlefield fighting with and inspiring them. In frozen Korea, General Ridgway likewise believed that warrior ancestors were watching. On the field he was careful and conscious of how he dressed, talked, acted, and appeared with all soldiers from command to front line troops in order to shape the myth.

Ridgway affirmed the value of every soldier's life: "All lives on a battlefield are equal and a dead rifleman is as great a loss in the eyes of God as a dead general."[2] Yet like Ulysses S. Grant he was a realist. He nicknamed his first major offensive Operation Killer and believed his war must be fought as a "meat grinder." He also believed we should be truthful with the citizenry about war. "I did not understand why it was objectionable to acknowledge that war was concerned with killing the enemy," he wrote. "I am opposed by nature to any effort to 'sell' war to people as an only mildly unpleasant business that requires very little in the way of blood."[3]

With this foundation—mystical, mythical, historical, realistic, continuous, personal, honest—Ridgway was a highly motivated, efficient, courageous, strategic, and demanding commander. The Army respected and followed him; morale and confidence were restored. In just two months he led it from chaotic flight to a successful pushback and stalemate. General Ridgway healed and restored an army's broken spirit.

INDIGENOUS PERSPECTIVES ON COMBAT TRAUMA

Interpretations of human phenomena are not necessarily correct or true but rather are concepts and practices arising from the cultural matrix of which they are a part. Women, the mentally challenged, and religious or ethnic minorities, to use glaring examples, have been considered to be superior or to have special powers in some cultures, to be equals in others, and to be inferiors or even property, subhuman, or disposable in others. In a materialistic, consumerist, scientific, practical, and empirical era and society such as ours, war's invisible wound is commonly interpreted as psychobiological and cognitive.

The modern interpretation of military service and its invisible wounding is culturally derived and determined and in accord with modern dominant values and beliefs. It is not necessarily correct, true, or consistent with the experiences of survivors or of history—and certainly not the only interpretation of war wounding and restoration. James Hillman suspects that Post-traumatic Stress Disorder is an American rather than universal response to war trauma.[4] Sri Lankan trauma psychiatrist Ruwan Jayatunge worries about "the Americanization of mental illness." The Western influence of drugs, illness categories, and theories of mind blunt our awareness of cultural differences and may even "shape the expression of illnesses in other cultures."[5] Roger Brooke agrees, especially regarding veterans: "It is our own culture that has socially constructed this universal as a psychiatric condition, burdening the individual veteran with all the negative consequences that implies."[6]

Interpretations direct interventions. In contrast to our modern situation, traditional and indigenous peoples had extensive spiritually and communally based warrior medicine, practices, and lineages. They lived immersed in and part of nature and its processes, conceived of themselves not as independent agents but as members of interdependent communities, and stood in wonder before a living cosmos. They considered soul and spirit to be life forces that were essential to preserve and protect those most endangered by warfare and violence. Their guidance of warriors through the life cycle, interpretations and treatments of trauma, and orchestration of the return journey were spiritual, communal, nature-based, and practical. And their guidance was extensive, specific, and designed to bring spirit back into their warriors' souls.

Let us explore some traditional interpretations of combat trauma that illustrate soul wounding and give direction for restoration.

The Hopi people call trauma *tsawana*, meaning "a state of mind that is in terror." The Hopi name the condition directly; the mind and heart are frozen in the terror of traumatic experience as if it were happening in an eternal present.

Since the traumatic wound is this terror, healing our war wounds is *Qa tutsawanavu*, "living in a way not intimidated by terror." The warrior learns once again to live as King David when he rediscovered faith: "I will fear no evil . . . " Warriors learn to act with courage, as Hemingway said with "grace under pressure," or Col. Henderson, "with . . . the willingness to act in the face of fear." The warriors' spirits grow larger than their fears, confident they can master the ordeal and not be crippled by terror.

A Hopi woman soldier, Lori Piestewa (White Bear Girl), was the first Native American to die in recent wars and believed to be the first Native American servicewoman killed in foreign wars. The daughter of a Vietnam veteran and granddaughter of a World War I vet, she was following both her people's and the American warrior lineage. In fact, there is a long tradition of Hopi women taking part in raids and defending villages.[7] Caught in the same attack in Iraq during which Jessica Lynch was captured, Lori drove her truck, trying to get her battle buddies out of danger. She died without firing her weapon. Her friends and family "increasingly opposed the war and were pleased that Lori did not harm anyone, 'the Hopi way,'" her father proudly said.[8]

The Lakota called trauma *nagi napayape*, meaning, "the spirits leave him." Trauma was that condition in which the spirits left the person so that the body feels like an empty shell. The worst cases of shock come not only from physical processes but also from seeing such horrors that the soul flees the body. Many warriors report such experiences. Art, a machine gunner at the siege of Khe Sanh, reported his soul's flight during a firefight in vivid detail.[9]

When the source of disorder is spirit loss, then healing can occur through restoration of spirit aided by community. Many cultures, Lakota and Vietnamese among them, practice community rituals for calling the souls and spirits back. In the Vietnamese countryside, a traditional belief holds that illness comes from one or more of the seven souls leaving the body.[10] Healing can occur when the village people gather to call the lost soul back or a shaman journeys to seek it. Reverend Jackson, who had served as a chaplain in Viet Nam, returned with us thirty-seven years later. He asked our group to surround him on his old battlefield where "my heart went dead." Together Americans and Vietnamese called for his soul to return. It was a clear, quiet, and sun-drenched day. As we cried out together, lightning suddenly flashed and exploded on the mountaintop opposite.

Sri Lanka is an island nation south of India that was brutalized by a civil war from 1983 to 2009. Sri Lanka reports extensive traumatic suffering among its military and civilian populations. According to psychiatrist Dr. Ruwan M. Jayatunge, Sri Lanka has had much historical trauma from both natural and human disasters and cultural and religious traditions that provide protection against and tools to deal with it. Sri Lankan written history dates back over 2,500 years. As written in the *Mahavamsa*, the history of Sri Lanka and one of the world's oldest chronologies, the Battle of Vijithapura fought in 205 BCE was massively destructive and deadly. The triumphant King Dutthagamani became severely depressed soon after the battle.

The Portuguese first invaded Sri Lanka in 1505. For the next 300 years the native population fought against the Portuguese, Dutch, and British. King Seethawaka Rajasinghe entered the wars in 1560 at age sixteen. A courageous and effective warrior, he fought many battles and witnessed much suffering. He finally defeated the better-equipped and trained invaders, saving his country from becoming a colony. But after years of combat the king "was exhausted and unquestionably suffered from battle fatigue. In later years he displayed outbursts of anger, irritability, deep mistrust, alienation, emotional numbing, and various other PTSD-related symptoms . . . [The] King . . . is believed to have suffered from combat-related trauma."[11]

Dr. Jayatunge concludes that combat trauma has been known and manifested through several thousand years of Sri Lankan cultural history, was recorded in their literature as long ago as Homer and the Bible, demonstrably occurred in ancient as well as modern times, and though tragic also helped their people develop endurance and resilience through cultural and religious practices.

The Xhosa people of South Africa believe that a warrior leaves part of his soul on the battlefield with the souls of the fallen. The warrior cannot reclaim his own soul without making peace with the dead of both sides.

The Xhosa call combat trauma *kanene* ("k-u-n-e-*nn*-y"). Roger Brooke explains, "It is the warrior's insight into the depth and burden that follows him—like your shadow that always follows you and reminds you of what you have done." Healing occurs through direct community-based response to this burden. It entails being forgiven by both the living and the dead, including the enemy dead.

The Xhosa healing ceremony called *Ukubula* ("Oo-koo-*boo*-la") is a confessional telling of what you have done before the community. The community's role is to "tolerate the pain of listening, no matter how difficult. The community carries the burden and pain of what happened, and the warrior is forgiven and healed from private suffering." Professor Brooke points out that the Truth and Reconciliation Commission hearings in South Africa that helped the country heal from apartheid were national practices of ukubula.[12] Ukubula highlights the critical role the community plays in listening and witnessing horrors without judgment and welcoming the trauma survivor back into community after confessional cleansing.

Also in southern Africa are the Shangaan, a Nguni people who are tribal cousins of the Xhosa and Zulu. They populate the areas in what are now Mozambique and the eastern border of South Africa. The Shangaan maintain extensive rituals for post-war trauma that affirms the intimate relationship between the slain, the slayer and surviving family members, all of whom become involved in community restoration. Among the Shangann, Dr. Brooke says:

> A man who kills another, even in war, must build a hut with the name of the dead. He must keep it maintained for the dead's spirit. His own daughter is then "married" to the deceased man. She must look after the hut as she matures. If she falls in love or wants to marry, then she and her father must ask permission from the dead enemy for her to be allowed to marry.[13]

Shangann practices demonstrate the lifelong intimacy that occurs as a result of taking a life, an intimacy many contemporary veterans feel but are at a loss to complete.[14] Their practices also express, Brooke observes, "a truth we see in our families every day. Daughters are imprisoned by their father's wounds, unable to live their own lives until their fathers have been released by the spirits of the dead." We heard this same lesson from Greece in Agamemnon's sacrifice of his daughter in exchange for winds to sail his fleet to Troy.

In another corner of the planet are the Maori, who settled New Zealand about 800 years ago and practice one of the oldest, fiercest, most successful warrior traditions.

Maori spirituality and lives are shaped around their relationship with the Divine, the Creation, their tribes—*iwis*—and each other. Increasing *mana* or spiritual power, protecting *tapu* or sacred being, and service and devotion to the community are at the core of Maori culture.

For the Maori, primary to any healing is the healing of relationship based on a sense of sacred being, *tapu*. When there is violence, a wound, or a crime, *tapu* becomes negative and must be set aright. Maori restoration rituals focus on healing relationships that have been harmed in order to cleanse and restore *tapu*.

Warfare was a way of life for the Maori. They believed that *mana*—spiritual power, prestige, or influence—was given by the ancestors or attained through combat and that combat was sacred to the ancestors. They fought for *mana*, expressing a widespread ancient belief that the powers of a slain warrior could enter the victor.

The United Kingdom invaded New Zealand in 1845 and fought the Maori until 1872. Though the British have significantly influenced Maori culture and there is internal violence due to their troubled social status and warrior traditions, the Maori retain much pride, honor, and influence because they were never defeated.

One aspect of Maori culture that has gained worldwide attention is the *haka*, their traditional war dance. *Haka* is a group dance with intense foot stomping and body movements accompanied by rhythmic shouting. *Haka* can be performed by women and children, as well, and can be used for many purposes: entertainment, to welcome dignitaries, before sporting events, to honor important events or achievements, and for funerals. War *haka* were specifically meant to intimidate enemies by showing warriors' prowess and fierceness. Made famous by the New Zealand rugby league, *haka* are used for many purposes today. Each branch of the military service and every army unit has its own *haka*, performed by all members of the units no matter their ethnic backgrounds. *Haka* have thus been integrated from the Maori into mainstream and military New Zealand cultures and are used at military funerals as unit rituals for bidding farewell to fallen comrades.[15]

Korea holds an ancient belief also applied with special attention in the military. It has similarities to *tapu* as a core spiritual property and individual and collective karma following us through life, shaping our fates.

In Korea, the word *han*, from the ancient Chinese, means the injustice that must be set right in the world. Those emotions arising from life's injustices—resentment, sorrow, regret—originate from disturbed *han*. Most Korean people, especially the elderly, have long believed that retaining *han* will cause various traumatic wounds and disorders.

Jae-sung Chung was a first lieutenant in the Republic of Korea Army. He served as liaison officer attached to US Army headquarters in Viet Nam from 1970 to 1971.[16] Jae explains, "To maintain sound health, individuals must be free from such *han* as worry, anger, resentment, sorrow, or regret. This applies to everyone, including the men and women in uniform." Although people face different challenges, Koreans recognize that each person must be able to get rid of accumulated *han*. In the Korean military, soldiers are periodically educated about *han* by commanding officers and chaplains. On weekends ROK soldiers in military camps commonly attend church or temple to receive character guidance education by chaplains or Buddhist monks along with the respective religious service. In addition, soldiers are taught about *han* by their commanding officers through Troop Information and Education (TI&E).

Belief in and care of *han* is common in the South Korean military. Jae believes that "the majority of soldiers will resolutely manage their spiritual attitude of *han*." The military itself tries to set *han* right. Within the military, Christian chaplains and Buddhist monks do their best to heal *han*.

During the Vietnam War, as a nearby Asian nation Korea felt a genuine and immediate threat. Thus Korean veterans felt more appreciated, justified in service, and welcomed home than did American veterans. On the other hand, war inevitably disturbs *han*. In order to cleanse his *han* after service, Jae has used self-reflection, meditation, and contemplation.

The spiritual principle declares that what was made wrong must be put right. Traditional cultures considered not just individuals but the cosmic order out of balance until the souls of the living and dead were reconciled and until wounded psychospiritual and cultural patterns and relationships were reconciled and restored.

These ancient beliefs have been carried into modern conflicts and used for resolving them after bloodshed, as in South Africa after apartheid. Soldier's Heart cofounder, Kate Dahlstedt, presented another example:

> In Papua New Guinea a brutal civil war occurred from 1975 to 1998. It was set off by destructive environmental practices during 1960s Australian copper mining. It was then enflamed when local people rose up and the government manipulated the native population to resist the uprising. As a result, families, friends, and clans were set against each other and 15,000 to 20,000 people died.

A cease-fire was declared in 1998. There was so much grief, loss, and remorse from the extreme violence and bloodshed among traditional families and friends that "the only way to rebuild and establish unity was through a reconciliation ceremony." The local people spent three years discussing "the crisis" and how to reconcile. They finally came together on the island's northwest coast for a ceremony that included preparing special foods, wearing sacred garb, sharing losses, and decorating the community with flowers to chase away negativity and attract sweetness.

The ritual consisted of dancing with arrows to symbolize the old conflict, then passing betel nuts as a gesture of peace. The people then passed a pig for roasting between former foes, joined hands, and together touched a peace stone. They then lowered it into the ground, throwing their broken weapons over it. To these people, this ritual was irrevocable.

Individuals who had killed returned the reclaimed and purified bones of the slain to their families in carefully constructed coffins. Slayers publically apologized to families who had lost members, offered compensatory gifts, exchanged betel nuts again, and together buried the coffin in its final grave. The ritual thus is a rite of passage for both individuals and community, giving meaning to the harm caused, lifting heartache, providing restitution, creating new personal and collective identities, and "rebalancing the universal scales."[17]

From North America, Nupkus Roger Shourds gives us a portrait of the warrior tradition as practiced by his Pend d'Oreille people:

> When warriors went out the first time they sang Canvas Dance songs the night they were leaving and then all the warriors would leave during the night. They prayed and painted before going to protect themselves and their horses. New apprentice warriors were given tasks by the leader, such as going for water for the proven warriors. The leader noted if they performed their tasks with honor. If the novices performed well, the leader would tell about them when the warriors returned, sang the Victory Song, and reentered camp where the entire population gathered to hear the stories.
>
> The leaders would tell how each warrior performed in battle, how many marks could be put on their coup sticks, and how many eagle feathers they earned. Each warrior would plant his ceremonial stick or spear in the ground as his hand grasped the upright spear. Then he recounted the details of each deed, stating who he had killed, wounded, or counted coup on. He spoke slowly and plainly, wore only moccasins, breechcloth, necklace, armlets, and headband. His body was painted yellow except the right leg below the calf, which was painted red, because of what he had done during the battle.
>
> As each warrior recounted his deeds, sounds from the drum and cries from the crowd followed. The drum beat one, two, three, or four times, depending on the importance of each warlike deed. If the action was great, the drum beat four times. If small, then the drum would be hit only once. At each pause, drumbeats and war cries were given as emphasis or applause. In the center of the arena was a pole in the ground with pegs sticking out like nails. While a warrior told of his deeds, members of his family hung blankets, shawls, necklaces, moccasins, or beaded bags on the center pole. Money was gathered, tied

> in a scarf, and hung on the pole. The gifts were distributed to the poor after he completed his story. The entire tribe sat and listened to all the stories until they were finished. Then the returned warriors would start special war dances until they could dance no more.
>
> Our culture honored our warriors right after they returned and listened to each and every warrior tell their war stories. This fact along with the survival reasons we fought and killed assisted in eliminating any PTSD.[18]

WARRIOR MEDICINE AND MILITARY CHAPLAINCY

A survey of traditional cultures reveals the ancient and universal nature of war trauma. Their peoples experienced violent trauma as wounding to the souls and spirits of warriors, aggressors, victims, and their entire communities. They responded to their wounded warriors with intensive practices guided by medicine chiefs, surrounded and supported by communities, and designed to directly redress the spiritual harm suffered. It was achieved through public ritual that sometimes included former foes and their communities. War wounding and restoration belonged to everybody.

"Spiritual fitness" is one of the pillars of soldiering meant to keep troops strong, resilient, moral, and effective. Military tradition, religious ethics, and modern regulations declare that spiritual fitness is the responsibility of our chaplain corps.

Military chaplaincy dates far back in history. Homer and the Bible tell us that in ancient Greece and the Middle East, priests ministered to troops on the field and after. In the English tradition, the first chaplains were priests aboard eighth-century navy vessels. The first with land troops appeared in the thirteenth century.

During the French and Indian Wars, some colonies provided chaplains. George Washington lobbied Virginia's governor for two years to provide a chaplain for his regiment—unsuccessfully. During the Revolution, a chaplain served on American battlefields from the first shot fired. Reverend William Emerson, grandfather of Ralph Waldo Emerson, ministered to Minutemen at Lexington and Concord. Washington afterward appointed him Army chaplain. He was with troops at Fort Ticonderoga and died in service.

On July 29, 1776, early in the Revolution, Washington issued a General Order instituting the Army's chaplaincy. Noting that the Continental Congress agreed to provide a chaplain to each regiment, he ordered commanding officers "to procure Chaplains accordingly; persons of good Characters and exemplary lives—To see that all inferior officers and soldiers pay them a suitable respect and attend carefully upon religious exercises." As a young officer in the French and Indian Wars, Washington had been in brutal battles. In his first, his troops were massacred; in his second, they were slaughtered and surrendered. "For the rest of his life, Washington remembered the scenes of the dead and the screams of the wounded as they were being scalped."[19] He personally knew that soldiers needed spiritual guidance and strength in order to endure deprivation and combat and remain moral. His Order declared, "The blessing and protection of Heaven are at all times necessary but especially so in times of public distress and danger."[20]

Chaplains serve *Pro Deo et Patria*, "For God and Country," bringing the lessons of their home religions and military traditions into service. Many troops find life- and soul-saving support in their religions of origin and from their chaplains. They confide in chaplains during times of distress, especially now that chaplains are the only members of the modern American military retaining complete confidentiality. Their attendance to troops' religious, moral, and personal concerns is critical and often exemplary.

But something is missing.

Dave is a career chaplain who has served six deployments. Many times he was the last chaplain to interview a service member as he or she passed through their Balkan or Middle East bases on their ways to remote assignments. "All I could do to honor them was to remember them," Dave said sadly. He took out a pile of pocket notebooks, opened them to show his tiny handwriting, and said, "There they are, every one of over 6,000 troops I met with as they were leaving to meet their destinies. Their names, hometowns, a few facts to remember. I have no idea how many survived or if I did them any good. I tried. I may have been their last connection to God or home before they went into battle."

Dave lives with a broken heart, a soldier's heart. He carries grief for his troops and is burdened because he is unsure whether he made any difference as they marched into the valley of death. "I didn't know what else to do," he sobbed.

Our military chaplains feel called by the Divine, are highly trained by both their religious denominations and the military, and are adept at providing religious leadership and other modern chaplaincy functions. Many are skilled clinical pastoral counselors. Some chaplains enter ministry after combat service. Others have no previous experience with, exposure to, or studies in military or warrior traditions.

Yet without training or experience in worldwide traditions that have evolved over millennia specifically for the preparation, protection, and restoration of the warrior's souls, chaplains feel hard-pressed to explain invisible wounding to colleagues or offer its balms to troops in terms that make modern sense. In short, we do not have but we need a contemporary "warrior medicine" or "veteran psychology" with teachings and practices designed specifically for warrior restoration.

The closest equivalent we have to "medicine chief of warriors" in our modern military is the chaplain. But our chaplains have not been raised, trained, or initiated into traditions of warrior medicine. Chaplains are often discounted by colleagues and not valued on soldier-care teams. Many are burned out due to the overload of troops needing them. Our modern medicine chiefs, responsible for our warriors' spiritual care, are themselves in crisis and under duress.

WARRIOR MEDICINE TODAY

Chaplains and clergy strain to fulfill their charge to strengthen and restore the spirits of uninitiated, dispirited, alienated troops broken in war. They pray, listen, talk. They organize gatherings, conduct religious services, trainings, memorials, and funerals. They counsel families and sit with the wounded. There is terrible exhaustion, much traumatic wounding, and even a few suicides among them.[21]

We can use traditional beliefs in the warrior spirit and legacy and traditional teachings to study, practice, and develop warrior medicine in ways meaningful to contemporary service people. The role of medicine chief of warriors can be a model for today.

Chris Antal used Sitting Bull as a model for warrior spirituality as he prepared for service as a chaplain in Afghanistan. His father was a medical doctor who had served in the Vietnam War, so "warrior medicine" was in his lineage. At his ordination Antal received a special blessing from an elder carrier of one of Sitting Bull's sacred pipes. In the presence of the congregation, Antal recited Sitting Bull's words, "My tribe, behold me . . . " He says,

> This ritual helped me develop my own self-understanding and establish my role and identity as a warrior medicine chief, which was not nurtured or developed at seminary or the Army Chaplain School. Grounded in this identity, I provided restorative and transformational ministry to my soldiers throughout the deployment cycle.

Chaplain Colonel Scott Sterling has been a chaplain for twenty-two years, with three years of prior enlisted time as a medic before college and seminary. He deployed twice to Iraq: in 2003 at the start of the war and again in 2006 for fifteen months in Kirkuk. For Chaplain Sterling:

> As an Army Chaplain, reconciling the role of "warrior" with my identity as a follower of the Prince of Peace was a challenge. I felt no conflict with providing ministry to soldiers, even accompanying them into combat, albeit without bearing arms. The legitimacy of any particular war—or of war in general—is irrelevant to the soldiers who find themselves in the crucible of battle, just trying to stay alive and go home. But even though I wear the same uniform and live basically the same life as any soldier, as a spiritual leader I could not consider myself a *warrior* in the same sense that other soldiers do. That is, until I was introduced to Sitting Bull and the concept of being a medicine chief *to* warriors. Sitting Bull not only helped me to redefine my role towards soldiers but also to embrace the identity of warrior itself in a new way. It is a way that affirms both my hatred of war and violence as well as my love of God, country, and soldiers. With Sitting Bull's definition of warrior in hand, and as I embraced the role of medicine chief to warriors, I was given new inspiration

> to delve deeper into the souls of my soldiers, to speak to the universal and timeless truths about warriors, to explore their stories and experiences, and to support the unique spiritual journeys I encountered with each of them.

It is not through less but more study of war that we may help bring about war healing. We need to immerse not just in the American but also in the world experience of warriorhood through every means and culture possible. The ancient and worldwide tradition of warrior medicine—principles and practices uniquely used to heal warriors—has been largely lost or preserved in small pockets of traditional peoples and searching veterans. To religious and military training we must provide that third tine of initiation—warrior medicine itself—to complete the trident of warrior care.

CHAPTER 12

Religion and Spirituality for War Healing

Where there is hatred let me sow love . . .

PEACE PRAYER OF ST. FRANCIS

War, which is inherently about destroying and killing, is the ultimate irreligious act. We break divine commandments and appropriate divine responsibilities, taking life when we cannot give it back. When in hell and becoming its servant, we most need spiritual and religious teachings for support and practice to guide our actions, to protect and heal our souls, and to bring peace to victims and reconcile with the dead.

Worldwide spiritual and religious traditions provide such guidance. Some were formulated specifically for protection against the inevitable spiritual devastation caused by war. We have examined some indigenous traditions and could study others and the mainstream religions—Buddhist, Hindu, even atheist and humanist—for such guidance. Since the Bible is the root tradition and sacred book with which many of us are most familiar, we examine its teachings as a model for restoring warrior medicine and finding guidance on how to bring warriors home.

THE STORY OF A PRAYER

He lived a flamboyant adolescent life and feuded with his parents and their wishes. Like most youths, he wanted to experience the great adventures of his times. At age twenty, he became a soldier, spent one terrible year in combat and a second as a prisoner of war.

Ransomed and home, like many returnees this man continued his wild lifestyle. Not fitting back into society, he again acted like many others and reenlisted. During this second combat tour, he had a spiritual breakdown and vision that sent him home.

The veteran rejected his old worldly ways, donned pauper's robes, and became a penitent. He devoted himself to aiding the poor, infirm, and most needy and to rebuilding abandoned holy sites. He confronted authority figures to live up to their ideals and composed prayers praising Creation.

One of the world's most beloved prayers is widely attributed to him. But this prayer first appeared around 1915 during World War I. Found scrawled on a the back of a St. Francis holy card thrust into a Normal Almanac, it was distributed to troops of all nations during the Great War. It begins, *Lord, make me an instrument of your peace. Where there is hatred let me sow love; Where there is injury, pardon.*

Wearing rags, confronting authority, refusing to conform, rejecting the worldly, serving the neediest—Francis sounds like so many disenfranchised veterans of today or any age. Did St. Francis have the wound that today would be labeled PTSD? Did the soldier who penned his prayer?

"The Peace Prayer of St. Francis" comes to us from two soldiers, one hardly known for his military career, the second an unknown soldier of seven centuries later. Both transcended the horror we call war, *guerre, guerra*—all derived from archaic words for "strife"—to deliver a redemptive vision. How can we guide war's sufferers to vision and service as modeled by the soldier who became a saint?

WAR HEALING IN THE BIBLE

We find guidance we can apply to surviving war in the binding of Isaac, in Jonah's descent into the belly of the fish, in Saul's and David's invisible wounds and David's psalms of anguish, in the prophets' lamentations during military occupations and exiles, and in many other tales. We may interpret war as a liminal time during which we are out of life's ordinary flow and in transpersonal dimensions. During such times we are challenged, suffer, and may kill or die. We may also come to know something of the nature of life and our fragile place in its scheme. We are more endangered but may also be more accessible to revelation. From our time in the valley of the shadow, in prison, on the ash heap, we may ironically come close to the All and develop a vision that is restorative, prophetic, and devoted to preserving life.

Our ancestors lived in highly organized and institutionalized religious societies whose kings were simultaneously high priest, military commander-in-chief, and civic ruler. They were surrounded by competing religious warrior cultures and frequently in brutal combat. They were often oppressed, often oppressing others. Of necessity they had to know all they could not just about the practice of warfare but about warrior protection and restoration.

The Bible records how frequently our early ancestors were at war, how costly these wars were, and how "evil spirits sent by the Lord" could ravage survivors' lives. It also contained prohibitions against the wrongful use of violence, as in Abraham's refusal of booty or Jacob's curse on excessive violence. Sprinkled throughout the Old Testament—sometimes concentrated in Mosaic law or implied in the Wisdom books—are soul-protecting advice, instruction, or admonition for proper behavior regarding warfare and its aftermath.

Moses the Lawgiver delivered the Ten Commandments to the Hebrew people from divine revelation. Later he derived the laws from the Commandments and traditional Hebrew practice that were believed to fulfill divine will and enable the people to live pure lives. Some laws had to do with practices before, during, or after warfare or related matters such as exposure to death and proper moral behavior such that we do not misuse violence.

The Old Testament's Book of Numbers gives the account of the Hebrews wandering in the Sinai for forty years after leaving Egyptian slavery. The tribes encountered much opposition and sometimes had to fight for survival, safe passage, or water. As their numbers increased, rules and practices arose by which they organized and protected their camps for military and survival needs. Biblical text claims direct transmission from Divinity to Lawgiver for some of these practices.

We are taught that we must purify after sinning, touching a corpse, or direct exposure to the dying. For this our ancestors dictated the Red

Cow Ceremony, a weeklong purification ceremony that used ashes, burning herbs, and sacred water and that entailed the sacrifice of a rare and never-yoked red heifer.[1]

After an epidemic reduced the population, the leaders were commanded to take a census. It was taken not by counting all people, but "all men twenty years or older who are fit for military service."[2] In those days of a much shorter life span, twenty years old was the age of maturity for military service. Family heads were considered those men fit to serve as warriors.

Our ancestors recognized unique challenges to military officers. Since officers were responsible for the lives under their command as well as their own, upon return from battle they offered special sacrifices and payments for their own and their troops' survival.[3]

The taking of life was a profound act. It so soiled the soul of the killer and community that ritual purification was called for after any act of killing. Our ancestors taught that murder defiles the land, and except by the death of the murderer there is no way to purify it.[4] In the Eastern Orthodox Church, St. Basil the Great taught that killing in war was not murder, but returning soldiers should abstain from Communion for three years because their hands were not clean.[5]

What about those who believe they may have wrongly killed innocent people? Is our high military and veteran suicide rate prompted in part by the pain and despair of people who believe they have wrongly killed and that only by their deaths can the community be purified?

Everyone engaged in the taking of life was supposed to remain pure during service. The camp had to be kept ritually clean, referring to sexual and lavatory behavior as well as higher order matters. Soldiers were admonished, "Do not do anything indecent that would cause the Lord to turn his back on you."[6]

No matter how hard or often our chaplains and troops pray, how do we reconcile this teaching with the use of pornography; medical, recreational, legal, and illegal drugs; alcohol; prostitution; and military sexual abuse that is rampant among the military at home, abroad, and throughout history?

The ancients were concerned about protecting their youths and families. They wished to ensure tribal longevity and also protect those who served from regret for a life never lived. Consequently newly married men were excluded from service for one year.[7] Men were also excluded who had built a house but not yet dedicated it, planted a vineyard but not yet harvested its grapes, or were engaged but not yet married. In each case, "otherwise someone else might . . . " Those who were afraid or had lost their nerve were also excluded lest they harm the army's morale.[8] Priests were required to examine troops to determine their fitness under these conditions and to ensure they would not harm morale or fighting spirit. In this way the ancient Israelites "introduced the first practical method of military psychiatric screening."[9]

"Regret for what I will never be able to do," for "the home, family, profession I will never have" are uncounted casualties of war. Further, many in our modern military serve tasks without the guidance once provided by their codes. Sue was a senior medical officer who never deployed but trained medics to ship to Iraq. Because she had no guidelines, she struggled to justify who to ship or hold back. She has lived with guilt since the war, as if she were the Fate who cut the life cord. Had she had humane guidelines, she would not carry this burden for her decisions about "who shall serve and who shall not."

War during Biblical times was so commonplace, destructive, and geographically nearby that Deuteronomy contains an entire chapter presenting rules for practicing humane warfare. Deuteronomy 20, akin to a 3,500-year-old Geneva Convention, tells us to rely on faith rather than superior arms or numbers in battle; to allow cities the chance to surrender before attacking; to not kill women, children, or livestock; and to not destroy an enemy's fruit trees or ecology: "the trees are not your enemies."[10]

Contemplating these rules, how do modern troops feel who harm and kill civilians; who poison, bomb, and destroy ecosystems; who attack without first giving a foe the chance to surrender; or who discover that the foe who has been fighting so fiercely against our superior weaponry is also motivated by deep faith and belief?

Psalms and Proverbs provide additional tenets about the moral use of violence and force and divine attitudes toward human behaviors that lead to war. We are admonished that we must not kill without just cause. For example, though King David sometimes killed unjustly, he wished never to wrongly harm an enemy and thought such a wrong deserved punishment. He sang in Psalm 7, "O Lord, my God, if I have . . . without cause done violence to my enemy . . . then let them cut me down and kill me and leave me lifeless on the ground!"[11]

How do troops feel who learn afterward that the violence they have done in their country's names was greedy; self-serving; for resources, wealth, power, or control; or "without cause" rather than truly for self-defense?

Proverbs tells of "the seven things the Lord hates and cannot tolerate." Among them are a "lying tongue, hands that kill innocent people . . . wicked plans . . . doing evil."

In Iraq there were no weapons of mass destruction and hundreds of thousands of innocents were killed, yet plans were laid for war in secret and before America was attacked. How do our troops judge our country? Themselves? What about their fulfillment of the warrior's code built into our common roots?

Troops and their chaplains struggle with these issues daily. Chaplain Scott Sterling reported counseling a Catholic priest who agreed to enter the chaplaincy only after being assured he would not be deployed to Iraq, a war he protested, but then was ordered downrange. Colonel Sterling reported:

> He [the priest] was ready to quit and go home because he could not see himself going to this war that he knew was unjust. I told him about my own opposition but how I reconciled myself to going. I told him simply that soldiers are forced to go and fight and kill, and that they need chaplains to be present with them as they take part in this terrible business. It is irrelevant how we feel about any particular war; our relevance comes in providing soldiers with the opportunities they need to explore and practice their faith in the midst of hell. It comes with providing them with the rites, rituals, and spiritual connections necessary to survive, spiritually and emotionally. Father left our meeting in peace and was able to deploy and serve his soldiers without considering the political rightness or wrongness of the war they were fighting. He, like I, remained opposed to the war but able to be present.

THE GI AS JOB

Chaplain William Mahedy, who served in Vietnam, wrote, "For anyone who takes [war] seriously in a religious sense, Job's question is the only one worth asking, and the experience of Christ abandoned on the cross is all that is personally relevant. All other religious considerations 'don't mean nothin'.'"[12]

The book of Job is one of the best texts we have of the individual's spiritual journey occasioned by severe trauma. Every tragic loss, his afflictions, the failure of human help, the inadequacy of answers, and Job's ultimate vision and transformation provide guidance and a role model for the warrior's fate and journey.

First, trauma invaded a quiet, reverential life. Job was good and innocent, but disasters came as a bet between God and Satan, good and evil. Like an ordinary soldier, Job was a small and helpless pawn in the collision of cosmic powers.

Troops often feel like they have encountered or embodied evil. Through Satan's agency, Job experienced loss after loss—farm, herds, children, and home—from natural and human violence. His wife despaired and abandoned him when he did not "curse God and die." Like so many survivors, Job suffered the destruction of all that had once given him identity, meaning, and security.

After trauma and its infection of the family came collapse. Job was "afflicted with loathsome sores" all over his body: mustard gas, Agent Orange, Gulf War syndrome, depleted uranium, napalm, white phosphorus and IED burns, limb losses, Traumatic Brain Injury, rape. He was reduced to despair on the ash heap. Like other survivors he was unable to move on, laid in lonely suffering, and cried to God and protested his innocence. Job's long anguish on the ash heap is in theological terms "the dark night of the soul," in existential terms "nausea" and "the sickness unto death," in modern psychological terms "Post-traumatic Stress Disorder."

During collapse, the afflicted and abandoned soul feels cursed. Job did not abandon or blame God, but life lost its taste: "Curse the day I was born." He was in despair and refusal—despair at finding relief or answer, refusal to accept his suffering. Believing that God must be just and his fate unjust, Job did not consent to live in such a universe. Like homeless vets blotting themselves out of existence, he did not want to say, "Yes," to such a destiny or world.

Like vets living in small apartments and motel rooms, endlessly waiting for hospital appointments or someone to help, Job suffered alone until his friends, the Comforters, arrived. Finally somebody might get it! For the first week his friends did the right thing; they just sat and listened in silence as he voiced his anguish.

But the friends could not tolerate Job's pain for long. They too believed we live in a just universe ruled by a good and fair deity. Friends gave canned responses and accusatory interpretations: "God doesn't cause the innocent to suffer; it is punishment for your sins"; "Get on with life"; "Just let it go"; "Your stories are too painful to listen to"; "Take it to the VA."

Poet Archibald MacLeish wrote a verse drama entitled *J.B.*, a modern retelling of the story of Job.[13] During the World War II era, his J.B. lost children, wealth, home, and wife. And the Comforters came. MacLeish's comforters are those who give today's answers. A psychiatrist, a priest, and a politician voiced their justifications for why J.B.'s suffering was his own or history's fault and he should have no complaint.

For veterans, restoration fails to come from psychiatry's reliance on medications that cannot quell spiritual anguish and moral pain. It fails to come from reparative psychology that blames our adult struggles on childhood wounding, tries to reshape cognitive patterning, or teaches adjustment. It fails to come from religion's stock answers with assumptions of original sin and justifiable suffering. It fails to come from politics in which, no matter the system, individual experience and integrity are swept under in the tides of history. It fails to come from politicians who use the military only for grand adventures and veterans for patriotic displays. One old Israeli warrior said, "Politicians abandon the wounded in the field. That's not me."[14] The Comforters, ancient or modern, fail to restore.

Job paid a high price—everything precious in life except life itself. His pain became his medicine. As the Sufi poet Rumi said, "The cure for the pain is in the pain. / Dance, when you're broken open." Job embraced his suffering as a quest and was relentless in his demand for a response.

Job was finally answered "out of the Whirlwind." He was shown the magnitude and complexity of life, its grand design, its multitude of forms, the raw Creative Force that spun galaxies. He saw how small and fragile he was, how easily snuffed out, yet important enough for the universe to pause and respond.

Given the choice between prison and the military, Jimi Hendrix enlisted in the Army in May 1961 and spent a rebellious thirteen-month hitch before being honorably discharged for "unsuitability." His first album introduced a phrase that became a battle cry for the Vietnam generation, "Are You Experienced?" The British poet William Blake considered experience the flip side of innocence. Loss of innocence is inevitable during warfare and part of its trauma. It is also part of both maturation and the initiatory journey. The challenge is to transform its loss into vision.

Good but innocent, given multiple and intolerable losses, shown a universe of such power and magnitude that he shrank to utmost humility, Job was "experienced." He had seen that divine justice and human innocence paradoxically exist together in a universe in which he was simultaneously a beloved child and dust.

Job affirmed his destiny, including his losses, ordeals and mortal fragility in a cosmos in which he was only a mote. He bowed his head before Creator, Creation, and inscrutable fate that we may not understand, explain, deserve, or control, but that somehow derives from the interweaving of all things.

With this vision Job was restored. His despair lifted. Friends and family returned. He could carry his losses with honor, dignity, and affirmation. He took his place again in the flow of life and re-created what he lost. Job emerged from the valley of the shadow, the dark night, the ash heap. He had tried to challenge the Infinite, "but now my eyes see thee."

Combatants have seen the Whirlwind. Into what kind of relationship with Being and Divinity did their time in the ashes plunge them? Have they heard the Whirlwind speak? What did it say to their souls?

Hat is a North Vietnamese Army veteran who lost scores of family and friends, his humble home, and all his belongings when American warplanes bombed his remote northern village. He lost scores more in combat where he was wounded and disabled. After the war his wife was struck and killed by a car.

"I'm just a simple farmer, but I have learned this," Hat told our visiting veterans' group as we sat before his creaky wall covered with faded photos of his many fallen. "As life flows on and on everything disappears except love."

Ryan Smithson joined the Army Reserve immediately out of high school. By age nineteen he deployed to Iraq. At first young, innocent, and idealistic with blond hair and glowing eyes, Ryan had his version of Job's vision in the combat zone.

> Flying down a desert road . . . I watch humanity's evil in the form of children begging for food. Sitting in a dump truck . . . I see evil littering the sky with pieces of children . . . As I salvage parts . . . or stand at taps for a funeral or stand in front of the fence at Ground Zero, I cannot help it.

Like Job, Ryan saw and was humbled:

> I am human. I am evil. But I am also beautiful. I can do great things, but I can also do evil things . . . I see people die . . . and I understand that it's something caused by the hand of another human being . . . [A]t face value it's terrifying and horribly ugly . . . But underneath . . . magnificent and perfect . . . this place that is beyond. This place where things are more than they seem but cost less than they're worth . . . In war, in my foxhole, my epiphany is when I realize there is something out there bigger than myself.[15]

Job transformed from demanding victim to humble visionary, "comforted that I am dust." Job—and Ryan and Hat—traveled from PTSD to Soldier's Heart.

A NOTE ON THE NEW TESTAMENT

Violent trauma, its wounding, and our responses are in New Testament stories and tradition as well. For example, in Jesus's descent into hell before rising, in Lazarus's return from the dead, in the man of unclean spirits, and in Saul of Tarsus who oppressed Jesus's followers "beyond measure" before his conversion on the road to Damascus,[16] we find portrayed the wounding and aftermath of violence and death and the hope of spiritual rebirth. From the Just War argument of St. Augustine, civilization inherited the belief that war can be necessary, righteous, and the best choice under certain conditions.[17]

Perhaps the radiance that can most touch us in considering the New Testament's relation to war is not in how it has been ill-used to inflame violence, but what the image of the suffering Christ has meant to untold numbers of soldiers. I never forget Vince, veteran of sustained and deadly combat, who swore the only reason he survived was because of the saint's card his World War II vet father had given him on departure, which he kept in his uniform heart pocket during firefights. And during World War I, Siegfried Sassoon wrote poems such as "Golgotha," "Christ and the Soldier," and "Vicarious Christ." How could such suffering as combatants endured not find identification with "The Redeemer"?

I turned in the black ditch, loathing the storm:
A rocket fizzed and burned . . .
And lit the face of what had been a form
Floundering in murk. He stood before me there:
I say that he was Christ . . .
No thorny crown, only a woolen cap
He wore, an English soldier. . .
He faced me, reeling in his weariness,
Shouldering his load of planks so hard to bear.
I say that he was Christ . . .[18]

And contemplate Lazarus. Who descends into the grave to recover our living dead? Who touches them such that they return? Reverend Jodi McCullah and social worker Don McCasland, both veterans, demonstrate great courage and love working with their veterans trapped in the Underworld. They named their Tennessee-based veteran-healing program Lazarus Rising.

CHAPTER 13

The Path of Warrior Return

With my compassion, which I put around you like a shield,
I shall make right these abominable wrongs.

EURIPIDES, *Iphigenia at Aulis*

Before reaching his village, the warrior was met on a high hill by a priest whom he called "Grandfather." Grandfather told him to strip off his uniform for it carried war. Standing naked in the sun, the warrior was purified with smoke from burning herbs, grain meal, water. Then Grandfather dressed him in new, clean clothes and decorated him with paints, amulets, and totems. He was told to look long at his village below. He had gone to war to protect these people and see!—the people were well. He was led singing and dancing down a curving grain-strewn path to the village. Its people were lined up, answering him with their own calls and waves. He was led through the crowds to a tent in their center. As he entered, Grandfather said, "You have always known there is a Warrior's Path through life. You have just begun the return leg of this journey. Your elders and people rejoice that you are safe and with us again. Now we will spend much time together taking you down this path of warrior return."

Some warriors dance and sing upon returning, some drink heavily, some hide in dark rooms. Some have their uniforms burned, others give them honorific display, others hide them in the basement. Some tell stories to counselors or loved ones, some only when drunk, many never. Some purify through confession, prayer, exercise, or steam baths, others write poetry or music, others feel stained and polluted and cannot get clean.

When we do not tend our warrior's wounds, or when we treat them as pathologies, we and they have no clear path for a successful return journey. Seeking what is universal in world warrior care reveals principles and practices given warriors over the eons to create and mark that path of return.

World warrior traditions reveal six steps in the return journey that appear universal although, of course, specific practices and rituals vary between cultures. The steps of return occur through sacred and communal rituals meant to carry combat survivors through intensive processes that address the moral, emotional, social, and spiritual dimensions of their invisible wounds.[1]

We must not think or communicate that we are rehabilitating broken people, helping anxious people cope, curing diseased people, or repairing disordered brains or minds. Rather, on the warrior's return journey we co-create and co-participate in educational, moral, and spiritual practices in the context of a caring community. The process enlightens and initiates everyone involved.

THE NECESSARY STEPS OF WARRIOR RETURN

1. Isolation and Tending

Immediately upon return from the combat zone, emotionally polluted warriors are isolated from the community and their needs tended by elder warriors and holy people.

Our ancestors were profoundly concerned about pollution of the body and soul, especially after violence and contact with death. Unlike our homecoming practices today that rush troops back as quickly as possible, our ancestors had requirements for restoring purity after battle and protecting both warrior and family members from war-induced pollution or abuse. Moses ordered that all who had killed or touched a corpse must remain outside camp for one week, and on the third and seventh days they should purify themselves and everything they wear and carry.[2] His high priest Eleazer required that all who returned from battle must purify in fire everything that will not burn, such as bronze weapons, and everything else by water. They must wash their clothes on the seventh day. Only then were warriors ritually clean and allowed to reenter camp.[3]

Many Native American tribes differed in prescribing lengths of time but practiced isolation of new warriors. Some tribes met their returnees on the outskirts of camp and purified and prayed before allowing them back in. The O'odham people required "a four-day cleansing, because they will have done stuff that is unnatural."[4] Others danced them along a sacred path strewn with herbs. Sometimes warriors went on vision quests alone in the wilderness in order to rest and put themselves right with the sacred. Some tribes kept a special warrior's hut in the middle of camp for new returnees. During their isolation period these returnees were not allowed back into the family dwelling, not permitted sex, sometimes not even allowed to feed themselves, but were fed and tended by elders and holy people. In some early pagan civilizations, returning warriors visited temples of various deities, including the goddess of love, for isolation, purification, sacrifice, gratitude, and artistic and rehumanization practices before returning home.

Isolation and tending were meant to ensure that battle poisons—the energies, emotions, and behaviors acquired during training, then used and petrified in the combat zone—did not spill over into homes and communities. We know how much higher are incidents of domestic violence, hypersexuality, crime, substance abuse, accidents, and suicides among returnees—inevitable spillovers after combat without tending. Traditional cultures that practiced isolation expected some returning warriors to be inflamed, in pain, dislocated, and in need of transition after battle. They essentially prescribed an acute period of collapse, rest, and withdrawal.

Today some National Guard units offer their troops a return retreat before going home; some require attendance at such retreats periodically for several months. The United Church of Christ has been giving their military chaplains annual retreats. In December 2013 the Unitarian Universalist Association gave all their military chaplains and chaplain assistants their first return retreat. The association repeated the practice in 2014. Retreat coleader Kate Dahlstedt reported:

> We spent much time sharing chaplains' stories of their struggles to carry the pain of the troops under their care. They all expressed personal anguish about the

> meaninglessness of the current wars and their helplessness in mitigating their impact on our troops. They were all relieved to be at a gathering where they could safely discard their professional military personae and share personal experiences honestly and with support from one another and caring civilian leadership. Many expressed renewed inspiration and motivation.

These are gentle contemporary forms of isolation and tending after return.

By expecting the invisible wound and prescribing this acute period of collapse with support, we could as a society reduce the numbers and severity of traumatic cases because we would replace neglect upon return with the proper circle of tending, thereby erasing a significant dimension of the betrayal wound. We would tend invisible wounds just as we do the ones that bleed—as soon as possible rather than letting them fester and become chronic. Such modern practices would be expensive in the short run, but they would involve the citizenry, eliminate great suffering, and save billions of dollars in long-term disability care and costs.

2. Acceptance of Warrior Destiny

Returnees remain separated until they can say a sincere and authentic "Yes!" to their destinies as warriors. This second step constitutes both inner and public acceptance of one's destiny no matter how difficult, and it affirms that he or she is on a lifelong path.

In some cultures, elders and holy people put questions to new young warriors in isolation: "Did you wish to be a warrior for your people? Do you accept its many hardships?" Negation may be directed at foes; commanders; nation; causes; the deaths of friends, foes, or innocents; neglect upon return; or a host of other targets. The invisible wound may sometimes be the psyche crying "No!" to its fate.

Attending elders and holy people listened deeply for their warriors' "Yes." That essential affirmation shifts something in the psyche. We move from victims to actors, from innocent to seasoned, naïve to wise. We agree deep inside to accept and work with our lots rather than live a life of angry protest or denial. Only when warriors found and declared this deep affirmation did they leave isolation.

Some warriors tell stories of growing up in a military family or with military lineage: "Someone from every generation of my family has served since we arrived in this country generations ago. I was raised to serve. How could I break the line?" John Fisher comes from a family in which members from nine consecutive generations, from the Revolution through Iraq, have served. We traveled to the Gettysburg battlefield together. We stood on the site where at age sixteen his great-grandfather and that boy-soldier's father, Colonel Fisher, the unit commander and John's great-great-grandfather, had both fought. We saw Colonel Fisher's name on a monument. "When I walked up the path of Little Round Top," John said, "my heart was burdened with the experiences of my ancestors. My great-grandfather and his father had both battled there, and instantly their stories merged with mine from Vietnam." Though opposed to his own war for which he had been drafted, this visit affirmed, "warriorhood is in my DNA." John was "carrying his ancestors' spirits" as part of his lineage and destiny, and he felt responsible in a new way for himself, their memories, the family legacy, and all warriors. He continued over the next several years to visit sites throughout the nation where his ancestors had served. He was practicing "healing from our roots" one ancestor at a time.[5]

Some veterans may speak of being fascinated by warrior stories, movies, books, comics, or mythologies their entire lives. They may feel like the military was the only home they ever had. In spite of hardships, many warriors have already said, "Yes," to their journeys; they will say, "Yes," with their wounds, and will say a ready "Yes" again.

For others, "I didn't want to but . . . " jail, unemployment, no support for children, homelessness, deportation, no job or money for college, better than exile . . . Service may have been occasioned by legal, economic, personal, or other reasons that are experienced as force or coercion: "no choice." They may have experienced too many losses to sustain or seen or done too much wrong. The cause may have proven false or the neglect afterward too much to bear. These veterans may have more difficulty saying "Yes."

"Grant me the serenity to accept the things I cannot change": the Serenity Prayer also applies to warriors. We cannot change what happened in the military and combat zones. We can affirm it as our story and reshape how we carry it.

3. Purification and Cleansing

Warrior cultures had intensive means for purifying and cleansing the returnee of the toxins accumulated during combat.

Irish mythology affirms this necessity of returnee purification. The warrior-hero Cú Chulainn served as guardian of tribal lands. He penetrated enemy territory and slew warriors who had slain his countrymen. He returned "still prey to the violent ecstasy which did not distinguish friend from enemy." Fearing that his wrath would be turned against his own people, the king ordered naked women to go out and meet him. Then his people grabbed him and plunged him into three vats of cold water. The first burst, the second boiled, the third warmed. These practices calmed him enough so that he could be admitted into the household without danger.[6]

Native American tribes had sweat lodges and vision quests. Some African tribes buried warriors up to their necks in the earth so the poisons would leach out. Moses dictated isolation accompanied by purification with fire and water after battle. Purification practices from our mainstream religions, such as confession, baptism, and the Jewish Day of Atonement can be adapted to warriors' needs. Traditional cultures have used all the essential elements—earth, air, fire, water—for purification. Sweat lodges, for example, use all the elements, baptism uses water, Yom Kippur includes fasting and group confession. At Soldier's Heart retreats, we commonly hold a purification fire ceremony. Attendees toss letters or mementoes or sticks symbolic of something intangible they seek to release into the fire with a verbal or silent vow. Simple in execution, the "letting go" that results can be transformative.

National purification practices are also possible. In 2004, I was in Austria presenting at a conference on "War and Human Memory." Mental health colleagues there reported national findings that their people suffer a generalized depression observed across several generations. Investigation through psychotherapy and mental health research traces its sources back to World War II collaboration with the Nazis. In 2004, Austria practiced national purification and reconciliation from this collaboration more than sixty years after. Schoolchildren in Austria "adopted" one of the 80,000 Austrian Holocaust victims, learning their names, life stories, and fates. At year's end the schoolchildren wrote letters to their adoptees. Thousands of letters were tied to helium balloons. In memory of the victims, 80,000 white memorial balloons were released into the air from the Heldenplatz in Vienna, the very place where Hitler announced the annexation of Austria in 1938.[7]

Austria also maintains an Austrian Holocaust Memorial Service, founded in 1992. As a substitute for military conscription, young Austrians can work in Holocaust memorial institutions in twenty-three different countries, including several European countries, the United States, and Israel.

Austria practices long-term transgenerational efforts at national education about their historical trauma of three generations ago. This amounts to an affirmation of national destiny, purification, storytelling, reconciliation, and collective responsibility for its healing.

4. Storytelling and Confession

Another year, I attended an international trauma conference where a psychologist from Germany expressed her anguish: "I do not know a single fact about my family's history from 1933 to 1945. As children we were forbidden to talk about it and severely punished if we asked any questions." The result? "I know my family must have terrible secrets that it continues to hide. Even though I was born after the war, this has made me ashamed, depressed, and insomniac my entire life. I am frightened to find out the truth and frightened not to."

Warriors, their families, and communities confess through storytelling. Stories release emotion, reveal secrets, educate, organize our lives into coherent narratives, point toward meaning. In the story we transform from victims to heroes and heroines. Stories transform events from personal history into community mythology. Individual warrior's stories become their culture's warrior mythology.

Though some behavioral health specialists argue that storytelling is not necessary and techniques exist for symptom treatment without it, storytelling is a necessary step in restoration and homecoming and is practiced in warrior cultures around the world. Who are we, individually or collectively, without our stories? Who are we without a history? We are not who we claim to be and are affected and poisoned by our disguises if we do not embrace our full and truthful histories. Not telling stories renders truth a casualty and our identities a mask.

We hear the cry "Never forget" from many survivors of war. Jewish people declare it over the Holocaust and make great memorial and educational efforts. Vietnam veterans declare it about their service and homecoming and pour out support for Iraq and Afghanistan returnees. Germany today requires all schoolchildren to visit at least one concentration camp during their school years, and Holocaust Studies is part of the high school history curriculum. South Africa achieved significant national reconciliation through their Truth and Reconciliation Commission, during which perpetrators of apartheid told their stories and admitted their crimes before their victims and the nation. All these represent national healing and reconciliation through storytelling.

Stories restore the truth to individuals and cultures. Without stories, we do not know. Without publically told stories, war can become locked inside and drive us crazy. Confession is an ancient form of religious purification in which one representative of the Divine witnesses as a wrongdoer relates his or her stories. The telling empties the heart and soul. The witness endures the pain in service to the sufferer. Secrets are released and no longer work as inner poison causing distressing emotions and symptoms. The dark stain on the soul lifts and evaporates.

5. Restitution in the Community

After war, the broken social contract must be healed and restored and the damage done to the world addressed. Restitution requires steps by both returnees and communities. The community carries the burden and pain, and the warrior is forgiven and healed from private suffering. Rituals we heard from New Guinea and South Africa model this process.

There are two stages of restitution. One belongs to the warrior who must pass "beyond forgiveness" to practice atonement—restoring and re-creating where he or she destroyed, remaking the shattered world and reconstituting humanity as one. As I wrote in "Atonement Practices after War":

> The root of atonement is *oneness*, "to become one with." In essence, atonement entails not just awakening or exchanging feelings of empathy, friendship, or forgiveness, but *performing acts of repair that bring what was separated, divided, or broken back into union.*

> Restoring what was broken, uniting what was divided, re-creating oneness within and between peoples and nations from the shattered bits of their worlds that are left after war's carnage has passed—these are the agonizing but essential goals of healing and repair that are available through atonement.[8]

The Marshall Plan after World War II can be considered a massive restitution practice benefiting and repairing the world and turning former foes into friends. Land and water reclamation and reforestation projects after the wars in Viet Nam, Iraq, and Afghanistan constitute restitution. Often philanthropic organizations, many veteran led, like Veterans for Peace, conduct these projects in the name of our country or of veterans who served and contributed to the damage. Australia has practiced significant restitution for their participation in the Vietnam War by building bridges and reforesting entire regions destroyed by Agent Orange.

The Vietnamese affirm the power of making amends and the peace such actions can bring. Buddhism teaches, "Donation is the best consolation," suggesting that by giving back what we took, by creating where we destroyed, we can heal. Further, they teach the lesson based on the laws of karma—that if we feel badly about actions we have taken in the past, we need not suffer or collapse into disability or despair. Rather, Vietnamese monks with beaming eyes and smiles tell American veterans on our return journeys, "If you feel badly, then open your hearts and do good. Change your karma through compassionate action. Love everyone."[9]

The community must take a step for restitution as well. Warriors have become separated from community. They are likely to feel unworthy, undeserving, unwanted, or unwilling to be a part of it as long as they carry responsibility for war actions as theirs alone or feel mistrustful of civilians.

Since warriors serve under their society's mandate, many traditional societies practice a ritual whereby responsibility for damage, destruction, and death during war is transferred from the warrior to the society served. It is as if civilians said to their warriors, "You acted in my name, for my benefit and protection. I absolve you of responsibility for any wrong or immoral actions you performed and take that responsibility upon myself. I will carry your story as my own." At her Pennsylvania community college, psychology professor Anne Marie Donahue tells her veteran students, who wonder why she tends them so well: "You pulled the trigger but I bought the bullets and sent you there." When words and actions express this transfer of responsibility, we lift heavy burdens off our survivors. When warriors receive and believe this message, they reenter the social circle, and civilians take their rightful place beside their warriors. We become one people again. What war and history sundered is restored.

> And when the one who repairs is the same as the one who first harmed, then moral trauma is reversed, the identity is re-created, and the soul heals. In such cases, symptoms very often evaporate; veterans once tortured by nightmares sleep in peace again. Thus, acts of atonement simultaneously repair and restore the outer world as they heal the inner. War shatters worlds; atonement reconstitutes them—within and without.[10]

6. Initiation

John Fisher has traversed the warrior's journey "there and back again." He declared, "A veteran does not become a warrior simply by going to war. A veteran becomes a warrior when he or she has been set right with life."[11] At the completion of the restoration process, the new warrior undergoes an initiation ritual. The warrior may be given a new name, new clothing, honors, or awards. Totems are displayed and paraded before peers. Service histories may be repeated so they become community history. Invocations of the divine, memorials to the fallen, individual or group creeds or vows may be recited. Songs are sung. Poor members of the community are gifted. A new warrior is born, and both warriors and the village are safer, wiser, and well.

We recognize as elder warriors not just those who have served in the combat zone and earned their "eagle feather," their Combat Infantryman's Badge. They are "experienced" and deserve honor. But elder warriors are more. They are those who have formally or informally, in retreat, in community, or piecemeal, traveled the full restorative journey and completed the evolution of their identities into spiritual warriors who serve for life and for the betterment, protection, and wisdom of all.

NECESSITIES OF WARRIOR RETURN

Isolation and tending
Affirmation of destiny
Purification and cleansing
Storytelling
Restitution in community
Initiation

APPLYING THE SOLDIER'S HEART MODEL IN RETREAT SETTINGS

The stations of warrior return sometimes unfold spontaneously in the lives and dreams of veterans, demonstrating that they are innate psychic needs. They can be applied slowly over time, guided by caregivers and followed as a prescriptive program for warrior restoration and return.

My organization, Soldier's Heart, has designed and conducts intensive healing retreats lasting from one day to one week during which we guide participants, with civilian community members in witness and support, through exercises that replicate every step of the return journey. Co-created with Soldier's Heart cofounder, Kate Dahlstedt, this is one way they may be conducted. Kate describes these retreats in detail:

> Healing intensives include male and female troops and veterans, family members or survivors, helping professionals, chaplains and clergy, students, and other interested community members . . .
>
> Every retreat is unique in some ways depending on the participants, their particular needs, the resources of the venue, the group dynamic as a whole, and the unexpected. We attempt to be as flexible as needed for the most positive outcome. However, we have a general format, proven to be effective over time.

We begin by calling out to our higher selves and creating an altar made up of military memorabilia and other special objects. Participants introduce themselves by telling the group the meaning behind what they are placing on the altar. Telling each other such personal information . . . brings a group of mostly strangers together in a special way, creating our retreat "community." We then break for the evening, allowing the words and images to mingle with our dreams.

The next morning we begin with a guided meditation, taking participants to their own inner "safe place" that they can return to if need be. In this way, combined with building the altar the night before, we create a safe and sacred container to hold the healing work we are about to embark on.

Our next task is to come together in a circle, all holding hands or a section of rope that symbolizes our unity as a group and a nation . . . We then slowly, one by one, peel off those who went to war and send them away from the circle to surround us in a way that represents their place of service and distance from home. Vets who served but stayed stateside stand just outside the circle, separate but not overseas.

As holes form in our circle, everyone begins to feel a powerful sense of loss. Those who went off to war share their feelings of fear, anger, isolation, guilt, envy, and grief. They were slogging it out in the jungle . . . or the desert, while many others were home getting on with life, fearing for loved ones in the military, or protesting.

Many of the country's most prominent factions are represented in our groups. Everyone has an opportunity to share how he or she feels as we reenact our own histories regarding war. The important ingredient is the act of storytelling in a sacred environment that invites our hearts to open and implies that we all have a piece of the larger "story." We are all culpable and we are all injured . . . Like it or not, in the truest sense, we are all in this together, veterans and civilians alike. Until we acknowledge this reality and reach out to each other, we will not heal as a nation.

To finish our ceremony and bring our veterans back, the civilians form two lines as a pathway and then drum, rattle, and sing as one civilian brings each veteran, one at a time, back in between us all. We shout their names and welcome each one of them home. We then proceed to lunch where each of the veterans are waited on by a civilian of their choice.

After lunch we discuss the meaning of destiny, and each veteran speaks to the group about his or her own destiny and place in history. They each then share at length the nature of their struggles since their return. In the evening, we make a purification fire with words of gratitude for our coming together and with a vow to keep our hearts open. We each feed the fire with kindling as we vow to let go of something we no longer need to carry—bitterness, despair, victimhood. Some people throw military memorabilia, old or newly written letters, photographs, awards they wish to disclaim, into the flames. More stories seep out as we gaze into the fire under the night sky, purging ourselves by sharing our wounds with the rest of the group. An intimacy and trust has formed between us as we share tears and laughter.

We devote our next full day to storytelling. All veterans take turns holding the "truth stick," symbolizing the right to talk without interruption. Each tells the group about a military experience that has been weighing on their souls. Telling their stories to this community that has bonded in love, trust, and unconditional acceptance opens the way for returnees to understand, unload, and forgive themselves and feel at home, often for the first time. We finish the day with a community forgiveness ceremony and vow to carry each other's stories. Our Soldier's Heart motto is, "Caring means sharing the burden." This is how healing happens.

Our last morning together is a time for Warriorhood Vows. After a sacred service that includes a memorial for the fallen and a blessing ceremony, the veterans each speak vows of the things they will do as acts of restoration and restitution to counteract the destruction they participated in. Veterans and civilians gaze into each other's eyes for final affirmation and gratitude. We take our places together in our reconstituted social circle in which everyone now knows and honors everyone else's sacrifices, roles, places, values. The circle is finally complete, and everyone is changed.[12]

CHAPTER 14

Spiritual Comfort and Healing for the War-Wounded

Many a soldier's loving arms about this neck
have cross'd and rested . . .

WALT WHITMAN, "The Wound Dresser"

Every few months, at the beginning of a veterans' retreat, I unwrap an old relic that is in my keeping.[1] It once belonged to a renowned Native American warrior. I relate some of this warrior's trials and triumphs. I speak of his love of peace and his people. I tell of the honorific status of warrior in his culture and what his example teaches us today.

All the while the relic travels hand to gnarled hand between old and new combat veterans, noncombatants and civilians. Even before we speak of our own sorrows and sufferings, with stories and the relic we feel ourselves in the presence of "chiefs of old." We conjure the spiritual warrior to guide and oversee our gathering so that we can know, tend, and nourish the wounded warrior within.

I place the relic on our altar. Each participant introduces him- or herself and places their personal relic beside it. We join our stories to the universal story of war. We create a composite portrait of how war affected our generations, our country, and us. And we develop vision to perceive a spiritual Warrior archetype within, behind, and beyond all our wounded manifestations.

I sometimes choose different relics appropriate to the audience: my father's World War II service Bible, a chaplain's hand-carved crucifix carried through several deployments, a pottery shard from ancient Sparta. Kate Dahlstedt, who runs women veterans' retreats, uses a statue of Athena or her mother's World War II nurse cadet medallion to help conjure the feminine Warrior archetype. Such practices create an atmosphere in which participants reexperience our lost numinous world as it relates to warriorhood. Instead of reporting to politicians or clinicians, our veterans report to their "Higher Power," an authority they can respect—the Warrior Self, their ego ideal, the warrior's sacred identity that has been sought and emulated for millennia.

In the presence of their beloved fallen and their victims, in their ache to serve a divine cause, before the witness and support of a loving community that now shares their bloodied visions and before their own Ideal, our veterans take a transformative step. They step out of an old identity as disabled veteran and into a new one as honorable returned warrior.

All through our retreat, participants feel the spirit of the warrior who carried the relic watching them. They finally stand before that spirit—and their own inner warriors—and vow to live a life of growth and service with honor all their days.

Stepping into the archetype transforms the way we carry our wounds. Our wild beasts become our protective allies and guiding spirits.

We wrap the relic. Our souls wander no more.

SPIRITUAL PRINCIPLES FOR RESTORATION

As we are well aware by now, key spiritual principles and practices were once rendered to warriors before, during, and after service. In some countries and traditions, they are provided today. Without them—disaster, heartbreak, uncountable tragedies. Karl Marlantes warns,

> Asking young warriors to take on [God's role of taking life] without adequate psychological and spiritual preparation can lead to damaging consequences . . . killing and the infliction of pain in excess . . . If warriors are returned home having had better psychological and spiritual

> preparation, they will integrate into civilian life faster, and they and their families will suffer less.[2]

Marlantes's words are true about both preparation and homecoming. The principles of psychospiritual restoration must be brought to bear before and after in order to strengthen and tend souls against the wounds of war.

Let us consider these principles that throughout time have served to guide, heal, and restore people with wounded souls.

To restore the soul, the inner life, the essence of who we are, to heal moral trauma, to make peace with society, the world and the dead, war survivors need the following.

Catharsis

Warriors and veterans throughout history have reported on the intensity of emotional experience during combat. Sometimes the berserk or possessed state takes over. Often the warrior feels rage and hatred near at hand but numbness and distance from other feelings. "Hatred was my best weapon," a Viet Cong veteran whose entire family was killed by American bombs confessed. Often there is not a second to pause and breathe, feel and grieve, but the immediate demands of combat, mission, or survival push us relentlessly on. Our hearts go numb. We can cry and feel nothing. We do not feel what we experience.

The heart does not cordon off the combat zone but fully engages everywhere else. It cannot say it will not feel sad or angry but will feel all other emotions. Rather, like a dam blocking a river, the numbness that sets in during combat can grow and strengthen as unfelt life accumulates behind it.

Aristotle described catharsis as the purging of negative emotions, especially pity and fear. Psychotherapy since Freud has understood catharsis to be the intense release of negative emotions and energies accumulated from earlier painful life experiences. No matter how frightening civilians may find the intensity of veterans' emotions, they must be purged.

The Warrior's Dance

Earlier we met Terry, a Ranger captain commanding a company in Viet Nam's Central Highlands. His unit was sent into enemy territory to lure troops out "so we could pound them with air and artillery fire. We were just bait."

Extremely loyal and devoted to his men, Terry has felt lifelong anguish that their lives were used up this way. He went numb, had a stormy life, and suffered the symptoms associated with the wound. He did much therapeutic work and could talk about his experiences but reported that he had not felt anything in years. His chest was an icebox.

During some retreats we hold a "warrior's dance." In traditional cultures expressive arts such as dancing, drumming, chanting, and singing were used extensively. Warrior's dances conjured helping spirits, practiced their movements, mimicked battle, celebrated victory or survival, and transformed the intense movements and emotions of combat into the graceful movements of dance. During our war dance we invite veterans to enter our circle and move and dance in any ways necessary to parade with honor, release memories and emotions, display actions, or reenact stories.

Inside the circle of drumming witnesses, veterans strutted, marched, two-stepped, sulked, paraded, howled, laid on the ground squirming, took fighting postures, faced off like challenging alpha males in a pack and growled and snarled, or faced off like foes and turned battle movements into dyadic dancing.

I danced with the vets. Terry and I faced off as the drumming got louder. We became two monkeys screeching over the same water hole, wrestlers throwing each other, lovers embracing, planets trying not to collide, strangers measuring each other's power and worth. We danced to exhaustion. Then he collapsed into my arms and sobbed.

I held him. The group gathered and laid on hands. I put one hand on his chest and the other behind his back, cupping his wounded and long-silent heart. He cried, howled, whimpered, and shook his head. His cheeks flooded with long-suppressed grief over the abuse and loss of his men and his faith.

Finally he stopped, wiped his face, and looked around with gleaming eyes. Then he began laughing. He laughed as long as he had cried, explosive joy following the release of decades of emotional toxic waste.

Since that retreat Terry has attended others, returned to Viet Nam, completed a master's degree, reconciled with alienated family members, and become an avid poet, public speaker, and veteran advocate. And he loudly, joyously feels.

Forgiveness

Roy, helicopter door gunner, recently heard from an old comrade. His battle buddy thought that he would like pictures of the two of them and "the hell we raised." He sent photos of mangled bodies and shredded parts not just of enemy soldiers but of women, children, and livestock they had killed. Roy threw the photo at me. "See!" he shouted. "This is what I did. This was supposed to go to my grave. I'm unforgiveable."

Forgiveness entails an utmost giving, a giving up, giving over, surrendering to, and accepting war's inevitable tragedies, dilemmas, and losses and our complicity. Difficult aspects of forgiveness include accepting that others still accept and respect us, that our humanity is flawed and prone to mistakes, and that ultimately we must forgive ourselves. We try to look through God's eyes and wonder what the verdict would be if our case came before the Heavenly Tribunal. When others offer forgiveness, understanding, or compassion for war-zone horrors, veterans who judge themselves as unforgiveable may reject the love and remain isolated.

Hugh Scanlen was another helicopter door gunner in Viet Nam. He grieves unnecessary killing and especially one incident he had carried in secret shame for four decades. As Hugh reported it: "I had killed, photographed bodies, and even laughed about those deaths at the time."

Hugh's friends knew that his service bothered him. Hugh said, "A friend told me, 'God forgives you.' 'That's great,' I replied, 'but how do I forgive myself?' The conversation came to an abrupt halt."

Hugh attended several healing retreats. He slowly gained confidence that he would not be judged or rejected. He mentored younger returnees and realized that by telling his story of his death photography that had caused him a decades-long cloud of shame, he could help lift that cloud off his younger brothers in arms. Hugh said:

> Being with other veterans and confessing my actions, admitting the guilt that remained for years, eased my wounded soul. When I told my story, I was accepted by the veterans listening, warts and all. I wasn't the monster I thought I was. They saw me as just another human being struggling with what I had done and seen in war. Not at all unlike themselves.

As our Jewish, Christian, and indigenous traditions teach, confession is a necessary component so that we cleanse before the community, discover our common humanness, and can be forgiven.

Many veterans return to Viet Nam in order to ask forgiveness of the Vietnamese people. The common response they receive from veteran counterparts, civilian survivors, officials, and young Vietnamese born after the war is, "You did your duty as a good soldier. There is nothing to forgive." From the Eastern perspective, duty to one's country is proper moral conduct and the guilty parties are not the soldiers who had to follow orders but only the leaders who gave them. While some Americans felt even angrier at its evidence of their betrayal, the Vietnamese appreciated Robert McNamara's book *In Retrospect* because they finally heard one American official calling the war a tragedy, feeling remorse, owning his misjudgments and culpability, and trying to "set the record straight."

Forgiveness is one area of spiritual concern about which military chaplains who teach of a loving, forgiving God feel prepared. Through counseling and prayer, they help wounded troops seek forgiveness from the Divine and assure them that they are recipients of divine love even when they do not feel it.

The Jewish Yom Kippur holiday, the annual Day of Atonement, teaches that God can only forgive wrongs against God but human beings must seek forgiveness directly from those wronged. Roy returned to Viet Nam twice, apologized to farmers whose remote villages he had helped bomb, and purchased livestock to help restore what he destroyed. Forgiveness is married to atonement. We ask forgiveness, act to restore, and so transform the faces we see in the mirrors.

Reconciliation

To reconcile literally means "to bring together again" and connotes rebuilding friendship after conflict. When we meet former enemies or those who represent them and share stories, we transform them into sisters and brothers who survived the same hell. Reconciliation fulfills the Biblical teaching: "To please the Lord make your enemies into friends."[3]

Traditionally warriors from competing sides often held each other in high honor, knew their enemies, and, though they fought to the death, would not dishonor the other. Some Native American tribes kept an "enemy tepee" so that foes could come into their camp, rest, and be at full strength before challenging their opponents. In the Mekong Delta of Viet Nam, old Mr. Tiger said, "I never thought I was fighting Americans. I have always respected your country. All we did was fight invaders. That is why we do not suffer your psychological wounds." Across the green river, when we arrived for our first visit with him, Viet Cong veteran Tam Tien pulled up his shirt to show us his many scars. "You almost killed me," he said with a belly laugh. "How funny! If you had, we could not have lived to this distant day to become friends." Tam had every American tell his war story "in case we met before under different circumstances." Shared survival and hardships transcend old fears and boundaries. As we bid farewell, Tam said, "From now on American and Vietnamese veterans must be the lips and tongue of the same mouth telling the world the same story."

Hugh Scanlen met Tam Tien when we brought him to the United States to attend an international conference on peace and war. Said Hugh, "Mr. Tien, shot by a door gunner, and me, a door gunner wounded by a man in black pajamas, made friends in Ohio of all places. He will remain in my heart for the rest of my life."

John F. Kennedy, another combat survivor, said, "We did not judge a man's bravery under fire by examining the banner under which he fought."[4]

During his Civil War service as a Union army nurse, Walt Whitman tended the wounded and dead of both sides. He reported:

> For my enemy is dead, a man as Divine as myself is dead,
> I look where he lies, white-faced and still
> in the coffin—I draw near,
> Bend down and touch lightly with my lips
> the white face in the coffin.[5]

His poem is entitled "Reconciliation."

Lost faith and the need for reconciliation can be as strong a need in veteran families as in vets themselves. We have heard Leila Levinson's story. A World War II Army surgeon who crossed Europe with our forces, Leila's father lost his faith and became difficult and distant. He remained so his entire life and it poisoned the family. Only after his death was Leila able to discover that he had helped liberate concentration camps and tend survivors. This secret history impelled Leila to search the country, ultimately interviewing fifty-one surviving camp liberators.

Leila heard of horrors worse than combat. Fifty of the liberators reported struggling their entire lives, keeping their stories secret, suffering serious distress. Only one liberator, Calvin Massey, was able to keep his heart open in the camps. At first he "just cried and walked and cried." Finally he just hugged survivors. Of the liberators Leila interviewed, Massey was the only one who had not kept emotionally distant from the inmates or gone numb, the only one who reached out as one human being among others. Leila concluded:

> Calvin Massey had the extraordinary fortune of opening himself to compassion upon seeing camp survivors, the only viable response. He had avoided urges for vengeance or paralysis and had chosen the only action capable of engaging the spirit. The compassion he expressed to the survivors—the hugs—became the defining moment of his life, opening him to his grief as well as providing him with a past he could claim.[6]

Exploring liberators' struggles enabled Leila, after her father's death, to understand, feel compassion for, and reconcile with his memory. She made pilgrimage to Europe to follow in her father's footsteps and stood and prayed in the remains of the camp that had so distorted their lives.

Alienation between family members and its long-term damage is one of our biggest collective war wounds. We heard about Christal Presley's troubles growing up with a veteran father. Christal finally embarked on a courageous project. No matter what fears or blocks, resistance, or denial she felt or faced, she would talk with her father about his war and their shared past every day for thirty days in a row. Christal chose the simplest, most essential of human tools—talking—for medicine, and the love and courage it takes to really talk. It worked. Finally Christal, literally and symbolically, in America and on her own reconciliation journey to Viet Nam, walked in her father's footsteps.[7]

Reconciliation also refers to our relations with our country and each other. Veterans and civilians, warriors and protestors need reconciliation.

In Kent, Ohio, a protestor whose best friend was killed next to him during the 1970 campus shootings and a National Guardsman who pulled his trigger each privately and in anguish said to me, "There are no groups, communities, or support for people like me. Who can I turn to? Who will listen to a story like mine?" And veterans, feeling alienated due to their neglectful and insensitive homecoming, ache for reconciliation with the nation and its health-care system. Combat veteran Ray Cocks demands, "Do you want to label problems, or reconcile?"

Rehumanization

In a rec room on one of our military bases, I watched a gaggle of soldiers crowded around a wall-size screen playing life-size combat simulation games. They were in uniform. The screen image made it look like they were in a Humvee. The figures they "killed" looked like people. They laughed and clapped, pointed and shouted, "Hadji!" "Towelhead!" "Bad guy!"

Military training now teaches recruits to shoot not at bull's-eyes but at targets that look like people. This works to dehumanize the people our troops will have to fight in order to reduce their inhibition against killing.

At his trial for crimes against humanity, Nazi war criminal Adolf Eichmann testified that he had to make an inner schizoid-like break, suppress his humanity, and choose duty in order to follow orders that contributed to genocide. To perform as a bureaucrat who helped kill millions, he had to kill the human part of himself.

If I dehumanize another, something in me goes cold. I detach. I need to not know, not feel, not question. The other becomes a thing or a threat to be extinguished. I am not aware that in the other faith and patriotism might be strong, family waiting, their character good, their actions consistent with values. I imagine a cruel, immoral, despicable creature and see this caricature rather than a human being opposing me. As I dehumanize the other, I damage and dehumanize myself. I bring this dehumanization home and may treat my family in similarly cold and distant ways, unable to feel compassion for my hurtful actions toward them.

We can learn the foe's history, lifestyles, and language. We can investigate their reasons for fighting. We can learn about their religions and cultures. We can hear their stories, witness their losses, understand the causes, war, history, and politics from their points of view. This makes them—and us—human again. We can do this during a war or after. Educating ourselves about potential foes before conflict might teach us instead to seek cooperative solutions.

Steven Ross is African-American and a photographer. When he was deployed to Iraq, he took his cameras with him. Whenever he could, Steve dressed in local costume and went into the marketplaces and villages. Dark-skinned, he blended in. He got to know people and took hundreds of photos of ordinary Iraqi men, women, and children bargaining, eating, farming, playing around damaged military hardware, and napping. He shot neither the fire nor the carnage. "It was my way of keeping them human in the midst of war," Steve explained, "and of keeping myself human with them."[8]

Reintegration

Nostos is an ancient Greek word meaning "to return home"; *algos* means pain. These two Greek roots form the word *nostalgia*, which literally means the pain of not being able to return home. It connotes the point at which homesickness can become so severe it causes derangement. The invisible wound was called "nostalgia" and "homesickness" among the Swiss, Germans, and French in the seventeenth and eighteenth centuries and into the American Civil War. The epidemic homelessness among veterans and their struggles for reintegration today indicate their nostalgia, their rupture with all that they once belonged to, their pain at not being able to come home.

Art Myers returned with me to Viet Nam thirty-seven years after the war, along with his wife, Linda, and his VA counselor. Art had been a military policeman in Da Nang and remembered every detail of every second of the Tet offensive, the first day he killed. Because he had harmed and had lost belief in the war's righteousness, the Myerses wanted to help rebuild. They donated a single-family, weatherproof home, known in Viet Nam as a Compassion House, to the family of a disabled Vietnamese veteran. The Myerses prayed before the family altar. Art made a speech. When they learned that the family's children scavenged in garbage dumps to survive, the Myerses pledged to support them through high school. The village adopted Art. His old identity as traumatized veteran shrank as he became older brother, uncle, grandfather, and village benefactor. At the end of his speech, Art declared, "After the war I was never able to come home in America. I felt like my country didn't want me. But now I finally have a home again—in Viet Nam!"

The next Christmas, instead of giving each other gifts, the Myerses' extended family pooled their money and built a second Compassion House in "our village."[9]

The Myerses' story of atonement and reconciliation led to reintegration in a new identity in the country where our veteran fought.

As important and honorable as the Myerses' achievement is, we want reintegration for troops in their own homes and country. Since the wound is a social disorder, veterans are not the problem. Reintegration is a challenge because society has not shown interest, taken time, made space, opened hearts, listened to stories, allowed grieving, admitted responsibility, shared burdens, adjusted expectations, or provided opportunities aligned with military experience. The path to reintegration is for families, communities, and our society to reverse these issues. These could constitute a "welcome home" that would work.

Restoration and Restitution

Restoration means to bring back to a former condition; restitution connotes not only repairing and rebuilding but also giving back something taken or making good for losses caused. Both restoration and restitution are components of atonement.

Combatants participated in destroying the world. Through atonement practices they make it one again. They may also live with grief, guilt, nostalgia, and confusion that stem from taking and destroying. To restore both their psyches and the world, they and their families can help give back what they took. Restoration practices are aligned with spiritual and religious teachings from both East and West.

Originally "an eye for an eye" did not indicate revenge or cruel punishment. It originally meant that the punishment should match the crime—money, property, even a life taken should be returned and restored. It also meant that the spiritual response to actions that destroy property or life is giving back what we took; this is the essence of restorative justice.

Bill Saa's family was caught up in the brutal Liberian Civil War. His brother was tortured to death. Since that war's end, the country has been growing toward reconciliation. Bill searched for his brother's torturer, not seeking punishment but to invite him to become his missing brother. Bill reported from Monrovia:

> I have met with him and acknowledged that I know he killed my brother. He first melted with sweat and had a very troubled face. I made him understand that it is not only about him; it is also about me finding a way to cope with a wartime incident that has already happened. I understand that in war these things happen and many others did such deeds. I made him to understand that I feel the vacuum of my brother's death and that he is the right person to fill that, to acknowledge what happened, and to find ways to live together again. At this moment, tears rolled down his face remorsefully and he bowed with a sense of true regret for what happened, asking for forgiveness, committing himself to do anything possible so that he can be seen as regretful about what he did. This is still going on. I have not requested anything more of him than to understand that the other side has a true forgiveness of heart. It is left to him to see what that means for him and his own peace. We had a drink together as a sign of reconciliation. I am planning for him to join me next year at the annual commemoration of my brother's death so that we visit the site of the killing together and show our alliance with him.

Bill concluded with this revelation: "The initiative begins with me, not the one who killed. This is important because many who see themselves as victims find it difficult to take this step." In the midst of African carnage Bill Saa wanted reconciliation with his brother's killer to be a model for others. Forgiveness transcends the torture that poisons the heart.

Nupkus Roger Shourds, accompanied by his wife, returned with me to Chu Lai where he fought. He met the family of a soldier his unit had killed. The family brought Nupkus home as their honored guest. Since he had "met" their grandfather and "returned his spirit to us," the Vietnamese family invited Roger to become their adopted grandfather.

Bill and Roger now say they have families where they once had enemies. *A Course in Miracles* declares, "The holiest spot on earth is where an ancient hatred becomes a present love."

Acts of restitution transform the survivor's identity from destroyer to preserver. Our veterans are welcomed back to countries where they fought, now as life givers and grandparents, aunts, and uncles from America. Family relations are restored, missing relatives are given back, veterans move from isolation to inclusion, hearts are soothed and consoled through giving and the loving response. The prophecy of Isaiah is fulfilled:

> And they that shall be of thee
> Shall build the old waste places.
> Thou shalt raise up the foundations
> Of many generations.
> And thou shalt be called
> The repairer of the breach,
> The restorer of paths to dwell in.[10]

Through restoring the world we transform our identities, restore our own souls, rebuild our families and the communities we harmed, and become elders.

Service

In 1989, Mitchell was stationed on the USS *Iowa*. An explosion blew up the five-story gun turret on his ship. He was a first responder. "Forty-seven of my brothers gone in a minute," he lamented. He received no attention for his trauma or later transition. Discharged after four years of service, Mitch declared, "The Navy said, 'Goodbye, here's your plane ticket. Go get a job.'"

We hear much from veterans about the lack of transition home and the difficulty of finding work, action, or forms of belonging consistent with their military experiences that contribute to society. But veterans' identities, transformed by training and service, need continued evolution. This evolution may not occur in meaningless, inactive disability or boring, routine jobs but can in new forms of service and identities as elders and guardians.

Some municipalities have instituted programs that offer veterans ways to serve that are consistent with their warrior skills. Some colleges in Washington State, for example, offer a veteran conservation corps. Veterans serve in disproportionately high numbers as first responders in police, fire, emergency medical, and conservation forces. In Viet Nam's still heavily mined Quang Tri province, I met a career military man known during the Balkan Wars as Sergeant Savage and a young Iraq vet. Both men had been demolitions experts in the military and had despaired of finding civilian service matching their experience. Then they joined a nonprofit organization that clears unexploded ordnance. They dig up and defuse old bombs. They train a team of two dozen young Vietnamese workers in bomb detection and clearance. They help educate the local population, especially schoolchildren, to the dangers buried in their earth. They now save lives and reclaim arable lands.

Hugh Scanlen found work as a veteran service officer for his county and as a mentor for younger veterans at healing retreats nationally. Hugh declared,

> Those of us who have served in past military conflicts have an obligation to continue that service by being there now for our younger veterans. It's not about telling them our experiences but rather listening to theirs. Even though the generations may be distant, there is an automatic bond among those who have worn the uniform. The best mentoring lets them know they are not alone and not crazy. There is nothing more rewarding than seeing the light come back on in the eyes of a young soldier who knows he has found the trailhead to a more peaceful life.

More than twenty years after the *Iowa* explosion, Mitchell moved back onto the USS *Iowa* moored in Los Angeles to help restore it as a museum. He lived on the ship for fourteen months, not only rebuilding a historical landmark but also restoring the death chamber into a living memorial to his lost mates.

Witness in Community

Witness has always been a sacred role. Veterans witnessing other veterans gives purpose to their survival. It gives vets an audience of like souls who have shared horrific experiences and their aftermath. It demonstrates to survivors that they are not crazy. Families witnessing their veterans complete missing pieces of family history, learn the true trajectory of their loved ones' lives, clear up long-standing mysteries about why they are the way they are, inherit a legacy they should be proud to carry, and provide their vet a safe, loving container. Civilians witnessing veterans restores the broken social contract. It matures and educates civilians and teaches veterans that civilians really do care; they just don't know what to do. It can mobilize civilians into activism on behalf of our troops or country for righteous actions to be done in their names. Stories that emerge during witnessing restore "the first casualty—truth" and transform witnesses into carriers of collective truth.

Dr. John Becknell specializes in working with, training, and developing rural first responder teams across the country and overseas. He studied spiritual and community restoration after tragedy and trauma in responders and witnesses and the needs of and challenges to witnesses. He found:

> The experience of listening to veterans' first-person narratives of war is one that challenges prevailing cultural attitudes, social practices, and personal views about self, others, war, and interhuman connections. This experience is a transformational journey.[11]

Becknell found numerous obstacles that block civilians from listening to veterans in our "war-illiterate nation." Listening to war is just not done; there are few opportunities; it is painful and intense; it demands a lot of time; civilians believe veterans need professionals or VFW posts. John Zemler, a wounded Special Forces veteran and now professor of religion, rejects what he calls "drive-by caring." "If you ask a veteran how he is," Zemler declared, "be prepared to spend an hour listening to the answer." Reverend John Schleup, an Army veteran, has created a ministry to veterans in his Tallmadge, Ohio, church based on listening.

At "Warriors Journey Home," veterans and civilians gather so that veterans can simply talk to a caring community about war, its aftermath, and present struggles. Reverend Schleup calls civilian witnesses "people of strong heart."

When civilians really listen, withhold judgment, and allow themselves to be moved by veteran stories, they too are transformed. Witnesses struggle over the political and historical truths behind the wars, become active participants in war's aftermath, help carry its suffering and bring it home, awaken to their responsibility for our nation's actions, and become more aware of their own traumatic wounds.

Meaning

Combatants said in both Viet Nam and Iraq, "It don't mean nothin'." Some troops in Afghanistan sang Country Joe McDonald's old Vietnam War protest song, "I-Feel-Like-I'm-Fixin'-to-Die Rag" this way:

> And it's one, two, three, what are we fighting for?
> Don't ask me, I don't give a damn.
> Next stop is Afghanistan . . .

"It don't mean nothin'" and "I don't give a damn" are statements of despair in which our experiences, including killing and dying, are rendered meaningless by the causes over which they occurred. They are ironic understatements of "I care so much and it hurts so deeply that I cannot let myself feel it."

Meaning resides not in seeking civilian goals and satisfactions, but in authentic warrior values and service. We cannot deal with death or offer our own lives in a vacuum or to an absurdity. Time in the valley of the shadow, the deaths of our friends and all others have to mean something; in order to emerge we must render them meaningful.

Veterans find meaning in service to each other and their younger returning counterparts. They find meaning in memorializing their fallen. They find meaning in offering life-giving service or becoming politically active to try to ensure that the military is used correctly. Ultimately they help awaken the population, moving from "I don't give a damn" to the creation of meaning out of the history that destroyed it.

Blessing

Through all these spiritual qualities, meaning is restored and purpose given to the experiences of hell and survival. Finally wounds are blessed and become sources of honor and wisdom.

War is so destructive that warriors need and deserve blessings through their entire military experience. Blessing ceremonies are needed before leaving and after homecoming. Warriors should be constantly supported by holy people and by sacred wisdom to help them act righteously, endure trials in hell, and stay on a moral path. Emerging from the combat zone, the warrior, who is covered in invisible pollution, needs to be blessed.

Some of the most meaningful blessings come from our survivors. They transform their time in the valley into sacred wisdom that can steer them and all of us through our darkest times.

Hugh Scanlen wrote this veteran's prayer at our first Soldier's Heart retreat in January 2007. With wisdom gained from his time in hell and decades of work to heal other vets and himself, Hugh blesses us all. We have used his prayer for blessing our warriors ever since.

VETERAN'S PRAYER
by Hugh Scanlen

O God, as I begin my walk out of the darkness
and turmoil of conflict,
give me the strength to find a lasting and gentle existence.
Give me the desire to treat all living creatures with respect.
Help me to do no harm for the remaining days of my life.
May I accept who I am now—
not who I have been in the past.
Help me to remember and to dim—
not forget—the tragic past.
Take my experiences and teach me to use them
to understand others
wherever I go. To ban fear, hate,
and violence from my thinking.
Let me understand how one person can make

the world a better place.
Show me the reasons I am still here and what I am to do.
Give me the strength to face the time I have left here
to reconnect with humanity. To feel and give love.
O God, make me whole again.
Amen.

CHAPTER 15

Redemption of the Wounded Warrior

Wisdom does more good than weapons.

ECCLESIASTES 9:18

An Afghanistan Marine substituted the peace sign for the eagle on his logo. "I enlisted to defend my country against terrorist attacks," he said, "not to make corporations rich on my brothers' blood."

An officer with multiple combat deployments, achieving the rank of general, put a bumper sticker on his car that reads, "I am already against the next war."

The fulfillment or betrayal of the spiritual Warrior archetype determines the degree of our heart pain, soul wounding, and societal alienation.

After decades of therapeutic work with combat veterans, Larry Dewey determined that "redemption" is the best way to conceive of veteran restoration.[1] To redeem means "to buy back." It refers to being delivered, rescued, saved, or pledged to higher service. In Christianity it refers more specifically to being delivered from sin through atonement or Jesus's sacrifice. Necessary is some form of repayment. Veterans must "buy back" the wounded archetype.

Because warriors serve at the behest of the nation, their redemption must happen in context of a "tribe." When warriors "buy back their souls," they return to their bodies, minds, and hearts—their lives. But the task is not theirs alone; that constitutes betrayal. Society must "buy back" its warriors. The well-being of warriors and their societies are inseparable. Many of our veterans remain homeless in spirit, if not on the streets, because they believe their homeland took what was most precious—their souls—but has neither brought nor bought them back. Communities must redeem their warriors, and lost honor must be restored in public eyes.

PROTECTING AND REDEEMING THE SOUL DURING COMBAT

Nietzsche called Zarathustra, his idealized philosopher, "a destroyer without wrath." A warrior in the combat zone can have strong moral alignment, a tight hold on his inner warrior, a commitment to remain true to its highest values so that he or she resists dehumanization, fights with purpose but no hatred, and serves in ways that protect the soul and the lives of innocents. By acting morally, protecting innocent lives, and doing good under conditions that might drive anyone to easy violence, warriors redeem their souls at the very moment when they might be lost.

Tommy Laughlin was an Army buck sergeant serving in Viet Nam's fiercely contested central coastal region. Tommy volunteered for Vietnam service believing he was protecting American ideals and values. He argued with his squad over the protest movement, holding that protestors were exercising the freedom of speech he wished to defend.

At least three times Tommy halted excess violence and needless deaths and protected innocent lives.

Tommy's squad had been through another difficult firefight. Yet again they had had to fight a fierce and elusive enemy. His men were angry and frustrated. They collected enemy bodies, assaulted them with insults, and brought out cameras to take photos of themselves posing with the corpses.

Tommy was appalled but paralyzed. He wanted to stop his squad from an atrocity and honor the dead. But his squad might turn on him, never trust him, even frag or abandon him in a fight.

Tommy burst into the taunting circle. He stared at his squad members and asked, "What would your mothers say if they could see you right now?"

His soldiers stopped in their tracks. Looking ashamed, they stopped their jeers and photography, and they gave proper respect to the fallen.

On another occasion Tommy and another soldier were ordered to secure prisoners. His soldier led a bound and terrified young woman into the jungle and began taunting and insulting her. Tommy saw that he was preparing to rape her.

He approached his soldier, blocked access to the woman, and ordered his comrade, "Remember who you are!" Tommy talked the young soldier to his senses as his rage and confusion wore off, then helped the woman dress and recover.

In yet a third incident, Tommy was on an armored personnel carrier next to their track commander, a staff sergeant posted behind their .50 caliber machine gun. The APC halted directly in front of a peasant's hut. It had stood there for twenty minutes when an elderly Vietnamese man emerged, stood in front of the track, and extended a tiny two-cup tea service. The commander screamed racial insults and curses. He yelled that the old man intended to blow them up and would poison any GI dumb enough to accept his tea. Tommy argued with the gunner, whose rant only worsened. He described what happened next:

> Fearful that he [the gunner] might actually open up on the old fellow, I jumped down off the track, stood between the gun and the Gunga Din, exchanged a few soft words with the elder, and took a couple of sips of weak, green, indigenous tea. Thereupon the old gracious gentleman calmed right down and retired to his very humble house and hopefully lived happily ever after.

Thanks to Tommy's soldiering, the dead were not dishonored, a rape did not occur, a murder did not occur, atrocities were stopped, and the woman, old man, his soldiers, and Tommy all survived these encounters with cleaner memories and souls.

Nonetheless, Tommy had a difficult homecoming with decades of isolation, alienation, loneliness, and misunderstanding. He kept these stories to himself in order to protect his brothers from shame. "It still mystifies me," he says, "how dense or mean a person must be to behave the way that sergeant did. My most insidious feeling is the anger I've carried all these years about those behaviors."

After forty years Tommy attended several veterans' healing retreats. He felt safe and understood and trusted that no one present would condemn troops for going berserk in the war zone. He finally told his stories, released shame that was not his, and humbly accepted honor for his actions.

We recall the Biblical teaching: do not do anything in war you will later regret. From right actions in the combat zone combined with public confession and recognition at home, Tommy's memories and heart are cleansed.

HEALING FROM A KILLING IN IRAQ[2]

We can help restore meaning and exalt by honoring and grieving not only our own fallen but the enemy dead and war's innocent victims as well. Karl Marlantes suggests prayers "thanking these dead on both sides for their fully played part in this mysterious drama." NCOs (noncommissioned officers) and officers, he holds, "should be trained in conducting the rituals of forgiveness and healing" and he suggests a prayer for use in such a ritual.[3] In Afghanistan, Army Chaplain Chris Antal led his troops in praying for all dead and helped individual troops find ways to reconcile with the dead.

While stationed together at Kandahar Air Base, "as big as a city," a man named Angel appealed to Chaplain Antal because he had "felt haunted" ever since his deployment to Iraq six years earlier as a medic attached to combat engineers involved with explosives disposal. There, he said, "I betrayed my true self."

Angel's unit was on the move. A car came speeding toward them. Warning shots were fired. The car did not stop. GIs opened fire. Angel's vehicle pulled up next to the car. A man stumbled out of the driver's seat, blood pouring from gut wounds. His crying wife and children stood beside him. His eyes met Angel's. The soldier saw helplessness and despair as the man collapsed in front of him. Angel's Humvee drove on, and the soldiers watched the father bleed to death in front of his family. Angel and his comrades shouted obscenities and "flipped him off."

Angel had been raised with strong family ties and religious values. His father had taught him the parable of the Good Samaritan and said, "Be that man. Help anyone in need." In Iraq, he "betrayed myself by doing the exact opposite."

Angel called his "haunting" a "soul wound." He thought of the Iraqi man all the time. He saw his face during the day and had nightmares of him while trying to sleep. He drank bottles of hard liquor to blot out the image, but it always returned when he sobered up. He was frustrated with commanders, counselors, and friends because they did not acknowledge his pain, instead offering him medications and anger-management sessions—"quick fixes" that he rejected. "Medications are only a BandAid that suppresses the wound without first cleaning it out. That only makes the wound fester. I was afraid the eventual outcome would be worse if I accepted."

Chaplain Chris asked him about what troops call "crossing the river of fear"—that is, knowing the right thing and doing it. In Iraq, Angel said, "my heart became cold . . . I couldn't get back to the reality of who I was. I lived with a broken heart."

Though Chaplain Chris was not his own unit chaplain, Angel knew Chaplain Chris was someone who would deeply listen, witness his story, understand that he had been pierced—not try to fix him or make the pain go away. Chris reminded Angel that "relations with the missing and the dead, and with death itself, are at the core of the soul wound,"[4] then set out to restore right relations between Angel and his ghost.

Before leaving for Afghanistan, as battalion chaplain, Chris gave a willing contingent of his soldiers a pre-deployment spiritual retreat. They were supported by Vietnam vet Hugh Scanlen serving as elder warrior. Hugh shared his story of his relationship with a dead Vietnamese farmer whom he had shot. Like Angel, the dead farmer and his family had haunted Hugh. Years later those Hugh had killed as a helicopter gunner appeared in dreams asking, "Why did you shoot me?" Hugh had consulted a Native American elder. The medicine man told him to build an altar in his backyard in honor of the dead and visit it every day until the dreams stopped. Hugh did. After a month the haunting went away.

Chaplain Chris gained Angel's trust because he did what Job's comforters and Angel's helpers could not. "You listened to how I truly felt and how it affected me," Angel said. Angel had a gift for music and played the guitar. Chris told Hugh's story to Angel and suggested he restore honor to the man by writing a song for him.

In his song Angel confessed the entire story—the man's death, the family's suffering, his own culpability:

> Instead of helping out I chose to run.
> I followed the crowd with their evil deed,
> Driving by while I watched you bleed.

He addressed the man's soul directly:

> I could have stopped. I could have done a lot
> And now your memory I cannot block.
> I'm paying now for my mistake.

Over and over he implored, "Please forgive me . . . "

Angel used the song "to look into myself and stop lying to myself. I want to remember this always. I will honor this person I didn't help by remembering so that I always help the next person who needs me." After writing the song, Angel said, "I am no longer afraid to think about him. The song is dedicated to him so now I thank him for being in my life. He's a conscience for me because he's a reminder of who I am. Whenever my heart wants to turn cold, he reminds me—don't!" Angel shared his song with a congregation in Afghanistan, then recorded it to be available as a public service. Now Angel says his trauma is healed:

> It will never go away completely, but now I sleep well and wake up with a smile on my face. I can allow myself to have fun again. I can analyze my burden and realize it is something that can help me. I have no more self-hate. I am now the guy who will help whenever I can.

And Angel has a message he wishes delivered to all leaders and commanders:

> Just because soldiers come home unscratched on the surface does not mean that they are not cut inside. I say

to leadership, "Let soldiers speak and truly listen. Try to understand what they are going through. Stay with them in their hardships. Don't rush to heal. Listen."[5]

AN EXCHANGE OF LOVE AT DEATH'S DOORWAY

In 1968, Stan Hyman was a young radio operator on a forward observation team serving in Viet Nam's Central Highlands. Early one morning his unit cordoned off and surrounded a village to find suspected Viet Cong. Stan reported:

> A young woman in her late teens was thought to be the wife of one of their leaders. She was bound and made to join our ranks to be taken away for interrogation, escorted by foreign, armed, and dangerous men. As she passed me our eyes connected. I saw utter contempt and fear. "This is not who I am," I wanted to shout. But that was who I was in her eyes. Her reflection could not have been more incongruous with how I perceived myself. Who was I really? My mirror or hers—where was the truth?

This memory and many others haunted Stan. He decided long ago that the war was immoral and wrong. He was burdened with sorrow and ached to apologize to the Vietnamese people. The woman's eyes followed him through four decades:

> Her horror became my own as I could not rid myself of the sense of what it must have been like for her bound, surrounded by hostile men, and en route to an unknown destination and future. Forty-plus years later I am trying to reconcile who she saw and how I experienced myself. Sadly for me, it is as simple as intent and impact. I had no intention of harming her, but the impact on her life was far different. I am sorry for my participation and pray that she withstood this ordeal and forged a life of meaning for herself. This not knowing, I feel, is in some way every veteran's trauma and ghost.

Like the Afghani father whom Angel grieved, this woman became Stan's conscience. "That moment of our eyes connecting," Stan said, "is seared into my being, and her face is as familiar to me as my mother's."

In January 2013 Stan was diagnosed with Stage 4 esophageal cancer due to Agent Orange exposure. Like many others, his fate would be as the folksinger Kate Wolf sang, "Killed me in Viet Nam and I didn't even know." Stan's wish to return to Viet Nam to apologize seemed impossible.

In June Tran Dinh Song and his wife, Huynh Thi Lan, visited the United States.[6] Together we held Vietnamese—American reconciliation programs in New York, Massachusetts, Ohio, and Oklahoma. In New York City we took Song and Lan to their desired stops—to see the Statue of Liberty, then pray at Ground Zero and the State Vietnam Memorial. Then we met with a circle of veterans, Stan among them.

We spent a long evening with American and Vietnamese veterans and civilians sharing stories of war and its aftermath. Lan and Song freely mixed and shared with the Americans, most of whom never thought they would have an opportunity to unburden with their counterparts. Stan spent time alone with Lan and Song. To him, at death's doorway, they became representatives of all of Viet Nam.

After our evening Stan exchanged emails with Song and Lan.[7] Stan wrote:

> You and Lan enriched all who met you with your kindness, wisdom, willingness to forgive, and openness to expressions of remorse that many of us veterans have held on to with the hope that one day we might express them to a Vietnamese of the age that recalls our time in your country.

Lan does not speak English, and this was her first visit to America. She was a young teen in her village of Tam Ky during the war. Meeting Stan brought back her own wartime memory of walking past an American base on the way to school. Along her way every day a friendly GI gently beckoned to her, but she was frightened. Over time she trusted him. Finally, without a common language the GI showed her a photo of his own daughter at home, the same age as Lan. The last time she saw her GI friend, he gifted Lan with a hat.

Lan had never told this story, even to her husband, Song, until meeting Stan and in his eyes remembering the eyes of her first GI friend. In response to Lan's story Stan found courage to tell his. He said:

> This soul scar has been with me since 1969. It was not until our meeting that its grasp began to loosen its grip of sadness, remorse, confusion, and shame. While Lan and I were not able to verbally communicate, our eyes connected and her message of understanding and kindness magically replaced the unspoken message of decades ago from that young woman prisoner. I appreciate the kindness of soul reflected in Lan's eyes that afforded me a sense of peace that I previously thought was not available.

From Viet Nam Song sent this answer:

> Lan and I are so touched by your story. I translated it to Lan, and she came to tears. If that woman is still alive, she is about Lan's age now, and through Lan I believe that she now understands and forgives you as much as Lan does. Vietnamese women have loving and forgiving hearts. Karma has brought Lan to you and you two could understand one another without language. The message was from heart to heart. From now on you will be in the story Lan will tell her friends and relatives about an American who still carries the wounds of war after so many years. Lan and I and other Vietnamese who hear your story will pray for you. We love you.

As he prepared for his own death from that long-ago war, Stan shared the impact of this encounter:

> This experience imbued me with the deep meaning and understanding of the amorphous concepts of forgiveness and reconciliation. These were lofty concepts that felt right, yet I had no understanding of how to implement

> them in a practical way. They also frightened me as they inferred an openness that I did not know if I had the capacity to achieve or willingness to explore.
>
> Song and Lan allowed me a very powerful encounter not frozen in the past but alive and in the moment. They gave generously from the heart and their kindness. This has allowed me to integrate my sadness over Vietnam as an integral part of my being. Without this meeting I would have remained in a purgatory of wishing to express my regrets and sorrows without an ear to hear. The response of these casualties of our invasion enabled me to grasp the implications of my participation in their hardships. Their kindness could not have been more unexpected or touching.

Stan faced his demise with a newfound acceptance, equanimity, and repose. Shortly before his death he looked into my sad eyes, smiled, and said, "It's all right."

WITH THE WARRIORS OF THE AGES

Pilgrimage entails "praying with our feet." It is an ancient spiritual practice during which we travel many miles over a long period of time to visit sites where notable and sacred events occurred. Author Phil Cousineau defines pilgrimage as "a transformative journey to a sacred center . . . It must be rigorous, evocative, and open us 'to find deep meaning' through 'encountering what is truly sacred.'"[8] We may be touched and revitalized by these sites and their powers as others have been in times past.

Warriors may make pilgrimage with groups or on their own to deepen, strengthen, or heal their connection to the warrior tradition. While leading a 2011 journey to Viet Nam, our group met four American airmen on leave from Afghanistan. They chose to take R&R where their elders had served. The airmen expressed more honor to our Vietnam vets than they had received in America. They declared that as new troops they had it easier than these old warriors. "You poor devils really had to eat C-rations," they teased, "instead of the MREs [Meals Ready to Eat] that we get. Compared to our war, you fought under primitive conditions."

A few of our military chaplains stationed in Europe and responsible for receiving our wounded have offered healing pilgrimage. Chaplain Capt. Eric Dean conducted weeklong "Memorials of Faith" journeys to Rome for soldiers suffering PTSD. Dean wrote, "A growing number of clinical studies presents a compelling case for addressing the moral injuries of war through spiritual interventions . . . [Yet] effective spiritual solutions that can easily be implemented (regardless of religion, location or financial resources) are few."[9] Chaplain Capt. Richard Nevard likewise conducted three-day intensive immersion pilgrimages to Rome for chaplains from the United States, Britain, and Ireland. He wrote,

> I watched the change firsthand from a group of broken men and women absolutely negative and resentful for being made to go on this trip into restored people of God, open to God and one another, letting walls down, and embracing grace. I sat on two occasions with chaplains who wept as they shared their trauma and talked with others about issues they faced in Afghanistan; I observed chaplains sitting in churches across Rome, their shoulders jerking up and down, overwhelmed as they cried out for restoration. Paul admonishes us to gently restore our brothers and sisters to faith; we carry our own load, but when the load becomes a burden, we must bear that weight together. After two occasions of seeing the dramatic results, pilgrimage to Rome has become my passion.[10]

Pilgrimage can be an effective pastoral care response to trauma "meeting some of the spiritual and psychosocial needs of traumatized combat veterans."[11]

In addition to offering intensive retreats and reconciliation journeys to Viet Nam, Kate Dahlstedt and I lead warrior pilgrimages to relevant sacred sites on home soil. With warriors we have visited scattered old battlefields such as Saratoga Springs, New York, and famous sites such as Valley Forge, Gettysburg, the Vietnam Memorial, cemeteries and memorials anywhere. We also lead pilgrimages to Greece, sometimes focused solely or especially on warrior restoration.

We study Greece's importance as one root of Western civilization and their ancient warrior tradition and teachings about the cultural and spiritual dimensions of trauma. In 2002, I led a warrior's pilgrimage to Greece with World War II, Korean, and Vietnam War veterans and their spouses. Together on Veterans Day in the valley of Thermopylae where the 300 Spartans had resisted unto death the Persian invasion, we prayed, shared, grieved, and honored.[12]

In 2011, we returned to Greece with Vietnam vet Tommy Laughlin and Special Forces vet Colonel Paul Henderson. We visited Marathon, Thermopylae, Sparta, and other warrior sites to study and receive renewal from their tradition. Paul explained the importance of warrior traditions and pilgrimage:

> Ancient Greece has fascinated me since I was thirteen years old and first read the *Iliad*. The Western ideas and ideals around "warriorhood" developed among the Hoplites of Athens, Sparta, Thebes, and the other city-states, and those ideals carried through the ages were part of my heritage and who I was. I felt connected to the ancients and wanted to experience the land where they lived, fought, and died.

Our goal was to renew the spiritual Warrior archetype as fully as possible by conjuring it at the sites where it most powerfully emerged in ancient warriors. Paul continued:

> Thermopylae had the most profound effect on me. I stood on Kolonos Hill where the Spartans and Thespians made their last stand against the Persians and felt emotions surge within. I felt a sense of déjà vu. I felt anger that the Persians chose to pummel us with arrows and refused to come down and fight man-to-man. I went with Tommy to the memorial plaque that marks where these soldiers fell some 2,500 years ago. He readily agreed to join me in saluting these fallen comrades. We came to attention. I called, "Present Arms" and we saluted and held our salutes until I said, "Order Arms" and our hands returned to

> our sides. The centuries disappeared. We had the chance to honor our brothers who, like us, had followed the Warrior's Path. They had paid the ultimate price, and part of our duty to them and to all was to remember them with love and honor. Was I there in 480 BCE? Who knows? But the energy of that experience was undeniable and stays with me still as I live half a world and two and a half millennia away.

Toward the end of our journey we visited Mycenae, the home palace and fortified city of Agamemnon, the commander-in-chief of the Greek forces during the Trojan War. Our group climbed the high citadel and surveyed the ancient Mycenaean kingdom—stretching sun washed in all directions.

Our group had dubbed Paul *Geraki*, Greek for "hawk." On the citadel he saluted the hawks flying overhead as totems of his warrior spirit. Then we descended into the dark, high-domed, stone-lined tomb that was Agamemnon's. Tommy had other business.

Still angry and hurt for being misused for a war that did not protect our highest values, Tommy wanted audience with its leadership. He interpreted Agamemnon in the same light. Agamemnon had not had a personal quarrel with the Trojans. His brother, not he, had been betrayed. He had been a ruthless king: sacrificing his own daughter, taking other troops' booty for his own, stealing Achilles's beloved captive woman, insulting his soldiers, and acting brutally on the battlefield. To Tommy, Agamemnon was the General Westmoreland of the Trojan War.

Our group offered Tommy the name *Thersites*, the only common soldier, the only "grunt" mentioned in the *Iliad*. Early in the epic Thersites stood alone before the entire army and confronted the commander on the war's illegitimacy and his greedy behavior toward his own soldiers. He challenged, "Let him learn how much he depends on us." He was insulted and silenced by Odysseus.[13] We do not hear from another grunt during the entire epic.

Tommy ached for his say. I suggested he write a poem or speech to Agamemnon. As Thersites, taking his place in the epic of the world warrior tradition, what would he say?

We climbed downhill and entered the king's dank tomb, its beehive-shaped stonework towering above us. It was empty but for our group. The walls rang and echoed. Tall Tommy, wild gray hair pouring from beneath his cap, stood in the middle, shafts of light piercing the gloom and stretching along the dust toward his feet. His narrow eyes widened. He was confronting the ghost of Agamemnon, Westmoreland, and every commander who had betrayed the devotion and noble aspirations of his troops. He recited:

AGAMEMNON!

Agamemnon! Daughter-slayer and man-betrayer!

Come hence and I will render my judgment upon you!

In your greed and vanity you and your kind
have waged a war of great courage and long slaughter.

As brave combats and deep passions have raged around you,
your only cause has been the aggrandizement
of your own power and prestige.

You have betrayed your fellow warriors, the mean
and the haughty alike.

Even to begin your incessant war, you spilled the blood,
extinguished the life of your own beloved
and innocent child.

As ye have sown, so shall ye reap.

Your fate shall be far harsher than I might have delivered.

For this I thank the gods.

Though my bones may end bare and bleaching
in some forgotten corner of your realm,

they will stand and dance when Justice comes at last
to claim you and all your class.

Go now Agamemnon; mix no more your fate with mine.

It is that way wretched king, the way to Hell.[14]

Our group gathered around Tommy and held him as we cried together. His words of accusation echoed off the walls. We hoped they penetrated the distance and harshness between grunts and commanders that has stretched from ancient times to the present. Tommy emerged lightened and smiling. He proudly accepted the name Thersites as his own.

Paul and Tommy transcended the abandonment they felt from our country that did not honor them or the sacred warrior tradition. Now they were one with their ancient brothers, the warriors of the ages.

REDEMPTION OF THE WOUNDED WARRIOR

These stories witness warriors' redemption—protecting or recovering their souls through right action in the war zone or after and being witnessed and honored. Chaplain Col. Mike Lembke emphasizes "the sacred value of internal, personal reconciliation and the redemption that comes when wounded souls can speak openly—within the context of a caring community—of the secrets and trauma that haunt them." When survivors voice their stories before witnesses—whether before only one, a squad or clan, the souls of the slain—their hearts reopen. When we identify the wounds in the stories, we can identify the remedies needed to heal. When we accept responsibility for the stories and their consequences, survivors mature and are relieved from fixation in the wound.

Since his return from Afghanistan and release from active duty, Reverend Antal has preached in dozens of congregations about the responsibility of the community in redeeming the warrior and restoring our society. In his sermon called "Meeting the Shadow," he quoted

Dwight D. Eisenhower, who called for "an alert and knowledgeable citizenry" to keep the military-industrial complex aligned with "our peaceful methods and goals."[15] He also quoted M. Scott Peck, who resigned in 1972 as Assistant Chief of Psychiatry to the Surgeon General of the Army:

> If we must kill, let us honestly suffer the agony involved ourselves. Otherwise we will insulate ourselves from our own deeds, and as a whole people we will become . . . evil. For evil arises in the refusal to acknowledge our own sins.[16]

When the military-industrial complex is utilized for anything other than our peaceful methods and goals, Antal said, and when we morally, emotionally, and psychologically insulate ourselves from our killing, the result is a profound betrayal of the spiritual Warrior archetype.

During the service Reverend Antal lamented his own moral injury: "I came to Afghanistan to support a just war against terror, and arrived to discover that we are terrorizing civilians with our drone strikes." He heard Angel's song as a herald to all Americans who are "driving by watching the world bleed." He played Angel's song as an example of one who did meet and integrate his shadow in order to become more whole. Restoring the warrior and redeeming the soul wounds of war, Antal said, will only be complete when Americans become like Angel: alert, knowledgeable, and willing to personally suffer the agony of our killing.

This is the wisdom we need that will do us more good than weapons; this is the wisdom America needs to "buy back" its warriors.

Simultaneously war stories become a shared legacy carried by the community. The traumatic wound transforms into "my story" and the survivor feels blessed, made wiser, and responsible to give further service. Through shared efforts the broken contract between warriors and society is restored.

We restore our wounded souls by stepping into the spiritual Warrior archetype, sometimes using poetry, music, speaking the truth, taking right action. We allow it to guide, inspire, and fill us. This gives us religio-spiritual ways of worship and behavior aligned with our highest values, identities, and histories. Adopting this archetypal identity of the spiritual warrior and fulfilling its requirements "buys back the warrior's soul," reconstituting the fragmented psyche and bringing redemption.

REVEILLE

Of Warriors and Doves

In the camp I made a powerful discovery.
No power exists in the world that is capable
of destroying humans as spiritual beings.

KARL RÖDER, "Nightwatch," on his imprisonment
in Dachau Concentration Camp, 1933–45

Civic, moral, and spiritual vision and responsibility regarding war, veterans, and their return involve us all. We admit that war maims, distorts, and hurts—and we abandon denial. We affirm that there is a spiritual warrior's journey, and we develop a vision of the elder warrior and nurture it in returnees. We accept that responsibility for return does not rest solely on the veterans and their caregivers but is shared by the entire community and nation. We embrace the recipe for healing—spirituality in community. We practice the necessary path of return and work toward initiation of warriors. Veterans and all of us together move from absurdity to meaning, isolation to inclusion, being haunted to witnessing, being angry to forgiving, rejecting to affirming. We move from ignorance and innocence to experience with wisdom. Finally our veterans' wounds become blessings that have led them into new visions of who they are, new dimensions of honor and service, and the rest of us into honesty and responsibility for things done in our names.

Combat survivors can evolve from being ravaged by disturbance, illness, and disorder into returned elder warriors carrying an honorable wound in meaningful service, from destroyer to creator and preserver, from one who has been isolated, neglected, excluded to one who serves for life in the center of the community as elder and teacher, carrying wisdom and blessing for all.

Chaplain Lembke evoked Isaiah's vision of the suffering servant as a fit description of the warrior "on the path of sacrifice in armed conflict." The servant:

> endured the suffering that should have been ours,
> the pain that we should have borne . . .
> because of our sins he was wounded . . .
> He was . . . led off to die
> And no one cared about his fate . . . [1]

We return to Isaiah to understand the servant's journey from derision, disability, and scorn to honor and redemption.

As our servant, the warrior suffers the consequences of war so that the rest of us remain unbothered, unscathed, and protected: "We are healed by the punishment he suffers . . . the Lord made the punishment fall on him, the punishment we all deserve."[2] Having given all, we can understand through his suffering "things we had never known" and the servant is promised redemption:

> But now many nations will marvel at him,
> And kings will be speechless with amazement . . .
> After a life of suffering, he will again know joy;
> He will know that he did not suffer in vain . . .
> So I will give him a place of honor . . . [3]

How do we provide this place of honor and blessing for our survivors? Iraq veteran Jeremy Berggren asks, "What will our memorial look like?"

> I hope it isn't for a war. I hope it is for a warrior.
> I hope it isn't only for loss. I hope it is for what you can find.
> I hope it isn't cold and lifeless. I hope it is real. I hope it is warm.
> I hope it isn't for lies. I hope the contents are our collective truths.
> I hope it isn't just another memorial. I hope it is an altar.

A living, changing, transformational altar . . .
all you beautiful people carrying our weight encircling the warrior,
protecting the warrior, watching the warrior,
and praying for and with the warrior.[4]

This journey is portrayed in combat veteran Brian Delate's new play *Memorial Day* in which a vet about to commit suicide spends an entire "dark night of the soul" reliving his combat tour to emerge with the dawn finally able to salute himself in the mirror with a new and affirming identity. It is the journey from curse to blessing. It is the journey from being a servant of Ares, the god who delights in slaughter, to a servant of Athena, the protectoress of civilization who grieves our losses. It is the journey from Psalm 22, when forsaken David cries out, to Psalm 23, when he passes through the valley of the shadow of death with faith restored. It replicates the ordeal of Jesus on the cross, from his despair at being forsaken to his descent into Hell and his triumphant acceptance of his destiny and mission. It is the journey from being rendered a disabled veteran to returning to international service as a spiritual warrior. It is the journey from soul wounding to soul restoration, from PTSD to Soldier's Heart and home. To the degree that we achieve this restoration in our warriors and ourselves, the traumatic wound evaporates and its space in the soul fills with the spiritual warrior.

"THE MOST PEACEFUL PLACE ON EARTH"

There are always stories to tell, remember, and share that make our world better and give meaning to the suffering we have contemplated. They are stories that we rarely hear and do not even imagine possible. They help us grasp a vision, not only for the wounded but also for what we learn with them, from them, and cannot know without them. These stories tell, as Job learned, of "things too wonderful for me, which I did not know."

My Lai is the site of the Vietnam War massacre of civilians, the worst known atrocity of that war. My Lai is actually a collection of four interlinked hamlets of thatch huts, emerald rice paddies, and tall palm trees just a little inland from the Eastern Sea. Three hamlets live today as they have for millennia, fishing and farming rice. My Lai 4, destroyed by

Charlie Company on March 16, 1968, is now a memorial museum and peace park. People from all over the world travel there, as to Hiroshima or Auschwitz, to contemplate and pray.

We wandered among dirt house-mounds and the remains of huts the GIs burned. We read names and ages of the family members who died in each one or who were buried in scattered grassy mounds that are small mass graves. We peeked into crude earthen bomb shelters. We stood beside the irrigation ditch in which over 100 villagers were killed. Bullet holes scar tall palms, but their bases show new growth.

In the small museum we read the names of all 504 victims and their ages—1, 3, 9, 68, 47, 75, 12—on the memorial wall. We saw their belongings—a cane, sandals, cooking pots. We saw blow-ups of Ron Haeberle's photos of the massacre and of some GIs who participated—then and later. We saw an exhibit honoring Hugh Thompson and his helicopter crew who landed their chopper in front of marauding GIs and saved villagers.

Outside are long rows of shrubs and flowers interspersed with sculptures depicting Vietnamese villagers in frozen postures. In the center of the park is a great marble statue of a Vietnamese woman holding her dead baby yet standing upright among the wounded and despairing. She rises out of the ashes like the phoenix, one of Viet Nam's four sacred animals, out of the ashes, tall and noble and in the victory of rebirth.

In front of this statue is a humble carved altar. We lit incense and prayed. The fumes floated over the stone effigies and into the bright blue sky.

My groups visit My Lai on most of our annual journeys to Viet Nam. Many veterans believe it is the most important place for them to visit; a few refuse to get off the bus. Bill, an African-American Ranger, had been through the hamlet days before the attack and had reported a peaceful and safe village. Outraged, he cried with our guide, who had lost family members and worked there as her memorial service.

During one visit I watched a stooped elderly woman weeding and tending shrubbery with a pair of rusty scissors. Gray haired and scrawny, she looked to be in her seventies. Her thin face was drawn and lined. She could have been there.

"*Ba*, Grandmother," I said, "I would be honored if you shared your story, your connection to this place."

The woman had indeed survived the massacre, but all her family members—parents, husband, children, and siblings—were killed.

"*Ba*, my heart breaks for you. Can you tell me what it has been like for you to survive all these years since?"

"In Viet Nam family is the most important thing. I have lived all these years alone. I am always sad. I wish I had died that day with my family. It would have been easier." Her exhausted face showed what her words told.

"I understand, *Ba*. But I am an American. My country did this. How do you feel about Americans?"

"Please don't misunderstand. You must not stay away," she said. "It is most important that you come here and share our stories."

"*Cam on*. Thank you, *Ba*. That is why I am here. But how do you feel about our veterans? Some of them might have been here or done terrible things to your people elsewhere."

The tiny woman looked directly at me. Her eyes were soft, sad, very old, and gentle. "It is especially important that your veterans come here," she said. "I have come to understand that the purpose of my survival was so I could live into this distant time when I could meet American veterans, take their hands, look into their eyes, forgive them, and help them forgive themselves."

Combat veteran Bob Cagle was with me. Broad and tall with a gentle face, he is a hospital respiratory therapist, so every working day he still lives on the knife-edge of life and death. On our return journey he grieved on his old remote battlefield, vomited up old war poisons at Dragon Mountain, and cried in relief at a temple in Tay Ninh. At the Buddhist pagoda on Lady Black Mountain, Bob held a ceremony for the soul of the young Viet Cong soldier he had killed. There he had a vision of the boy coming to him at peace, arms extended, pledging eternal alliance.

At My Lai, Bob wandered alone. He walked the old pathways in the footsteps of villagers and GIs. He prayed before the house memorials and lit incense at the statue. He reports,

> I was about to take a picture of two graves just in front of me. I was focusing my camera when the entire surroundings turned a beautiful yellow. Looking back through the lens I saw this girl just standing there. Small,

> beautiful, and just watching me. I tried to speak to her but could not. She walked away and I could not find her again. She seemed to be at peace.

Bob has kept the girl's photo on his study wall, looking across the room at him, for the last fourteen years.

After wandering, Bob sat on a garden bench and watched the grandmother weeding and pruning with her scissors. I joined him. "You okay, brother?"

Bob's round face was beaming. He wore a beatific smile. His misty eyes looked into mine. As he recalls it,

> The spirits of the dead were there that day in My Lai. They were sorrowful for the loss of their family members and all the people they grew up with. They seemed to have found peace of heart. None were angry or mad. They just were. This was one place we visited where I was not on guard or apprehensive. The spirit of the entire village was one of peace, forgiveness, and love for humanity.

That day, after retracing his wartime journey through Viet Nam, staying open to all that had been buried in his heart, and finally sitting among the spirits at My Lai, Bob declared, "For me, this is the most peaceful place on earth."

OF WARRIORS AND DOVES

Since time immemorial, life-risking service as a warrior for one's people accomplished ends without which a society collapses from within. Service provided initiation and transformed immature, self-centered youths into mature, aware, and self-sacrificing adults. It was the path by which one became a "citizen," recognized as "one of us" with rights and responsibilities to care for the people.

Consider the consequences to a society when military service shatters the character, wounds the soul, and alienates the warrior so that he or she cannot become, does not believe in, or does not want to become society's elder. Then, instead of wise and compassionate elders guiding, protecting, and leading us, we have millions of angry, alienated, shattered souls scattered across the landscape. These wounded often cannot achieve or imagine return. They become society's disabled and outcast, or when functioning may interpret personal and public events in hostile or distorted ways. They are treated as broken burdens rather than people suited to better society.

Meanwhile society and its leadership lack mature elders. Instead we have too many immature, unworthy people grabbing and manipulating power in abusive and greedy ways. Theirs is the behavior of the uninitiated. Such adults manifest the shadow warrior instead of the spiritual warrior, the child ruled by an immature, self-centered psyche rather than the adult caring for his or her people.

Where are the warriors who protect us from the predators within? Whose witness is so loud, strong, and determined that predation upon distant others and each other at home is checked? We do not wish them to impose peace by force; we are at the end point of the 5,000-year history of that tragic and failing strategy. Rather, our warriors must remind us of what is truly important, lead us in shared sacrifice, restore that "first casualty, truth" so that we have a chance at "the just and lasting peace between us and all nations" that Abraham Lincoln dreamed.

We don't treat a mental illness or disorder. We don't heal PTSD. We restore the soul and the spirit. We reconnect to community, history, and cosmos. We reconcile with former adversaries and take actions at home and abroad so that we make peace with life and the world. We honor scars and wounds and plumb them for their wisdom. We re-create a person's identity from disabled veteran into spiritual warrior. We travel from shame to honor, wound to gift, and curse to blessing. The wound is blessed and transforms from PTSD to Soldier's Heart.

Even after such times in hell as banish the soul, we can achieve restoration to a new, better, wiser identity and spirit. As the individual warrior carries the wound of the nation, so restoring our warriors and their truth restores the nations and planet. We can restore one soul. We can restore many. In spite of our centuries and millennia of difficult and violent history together, we can help restore the soul and spirit of our nation and all nations.

Trauma, the wound that afflicts us all, the wound that underlies much of human and natural suffering, must become the wound that unites us all.

Our wounded roots offer oracles. In the Bible, after the flood Noah released the dove to seek dry land. In Greek myth, on his quest for the Golden Fleece, Jason and his ship *Argo* followed the dove safely through the clashing rocks. She only lost a tail feather. In the tradition that predates both, the dove was the representative of the Great Goddess. Mother Mary carries and offers her to this day.

To restore after apocalypse, follow the dove. To complete warrior ordeals that would crush us, follow the dove.

We call for this. We call for restoration of the spiritual warrior, the re-creation and revivification of this archetype, this collective Soldier Soul, after its 5,000-year history of denigration and betrayal. We call today's warriors and survivors to evolve out of their soul wounds, and into elders who serve the world community through the wisdom, skill, and guiding pain in their Soldier's Hearts. We call for communities everywhere to embrace their witness, tend their wounds, and share their burdens. We call all citizens to become involved in warriors' return. We call for our military to model and fulfill the spiritual warrior ideal and for our politicians to so honor it that they would never misuse or betray it. A nation's wars and warriors belong to everyone. Out of the devastation of 5,000 years, we call for this rebirth.

Trauma response expert John Becknell affirms, "Soul is found in unexpected places. Today I found her in the Temple of Mars."[5]

Veteran and healer Roger Brooke declares, "The transformation of combat trauma into spiritual meaning is the warrior's archetypal calling."[6]

After decades as a Green Beret, Greg Walker declares, "The warrior's journey ends when he becomes a healer."

Buddha guides, "A holy man turns the curses of fate into blessings."

And Plato teaches, "Even the God of War is no match for Love."

Acknowledgments

We can only return truth to the war experience and bring healing to its wounded through high doses of love, compassion, courage, honesty, and inner strength. I give great thanks to all the warriors, veterans, and survivors I have worked with over the last thirty-five years who exemplify these qualities and have included me within their circles of trust. This book and this work are for all of you.

A great many supporters in the military, veteran, and civilian worlds have contributed to this work. While they are too numerous to mention, many are quoted in this book. A few deserve special mention. My agent, David Nelson, devoted great effort and attention to finding this work its proper home, and nurtured it into book form. The entire staff at Sounds True has been remarkably devoted, attentive, responsive, and responsible. In particular, editorial director Haven Iverson brought great skill to guiding this project toward its final form. While many active duty troops and veterans contributed, the US military and Veterans Administration Chaplain Corps have been especially supportive and responsive. Our nonprofit organization Soldier's Heart, Inc. and its community of several thousand veterans and civilians across the country has been an ongoing source of strength and commitment—a laboratory in which we could develop this work to perfect it and a clinic in which we could practice the healing described in this book. My wife and Soldier's Heart cofounder, Kate Dahlstedt, as well as our children Jeremy, Gabriel, and Sappho, are eternal sources of love, strength, and commitment. I give my gratitude and love to all.

And to all my fallen, we did it; we made it mean something.

Notes

INTRODUCTION: A CALL TO THE NATION

1. As a psychotherapist for forty years, I have worked with many non veteran men who feel that they lack vitality, strength, confidence, discipline, or purpose. They sometimes idealize the military they did not serve in as a source of these traits. They are in a midlife search to awaken and develop their inner warriors.
2. Paula Caplan, *When Johnny and Jane Come Marching Home* (Cambridge, MA: MIT Press, 2011).
3. For the full story of this veteran's successful healing and of my first five years of work with combat veterans, see Edward Tick, *Sacred Mountain: Encounters with the Vietnam Beast* (Santa Fe: Moon Bear Press, 1989). See chapter 1 for this veteran's story.

PART 1: THE WAR AFTER THE WAR

1. I'm indebted to John Wesley Fisher for the title of this section. Dr. Fisher is a Vietnam combat veteran who has extensively documented his war and healing stories and worked with me on veteran healing and with Viet Nam on reconciliation. His first two novels were *Angels in Vietnam* and *Not Welcome Home.* This section's title is taken from his most recent book, John Wesley Fisher, *The War After the War: A Warrior's Journey Home* (Greybull, WY: Pronghorn Press, 2011).

CHAPTER 1: THE UNIVERSAL WARRIOR

1. *Once a Warrior Always a Warrior* is the title of a book by Col. Charles W. Hoge, MD (Guilford, CT: Globe Pequot Press, 2010). Colonel Hoge's book also demonstrates that behaviors judged as symptomatic at home are normative in the combat zone and may give the survivor the very skills needed to transform and thrive after war. "Once a warrior" is such a common expression among veterans and warriors old and new that it can rightly be attributed to them; Colonel Hoge honors them and gives them voice with his title, insights, and significant guiding book.
2. Herbert Masson, trans.,*Gilgamesh: A Verse Narrative* (New York: Mentor, 1972), 49.
3. James Hillman, *A Terrible Love of War* (New York: Penguin Press, 2004), 17. This number only counts wars with decisive outcomes. There have been many more with no clear victor.
4. "Military-industrial-government complex" was the original phrase that President Dwight Eisenhower wrote into his farewell address to the nation, warning against the collaborative powers coming together in the modern world to guide us toward waging endless wars for profit. His advisors successfully convinced him to take the word "government" out of his warning.
5. Conversation between Lt. Col. van Rooyen and Prof. Roger Brooke, South African paratroop veteran and now professor of psychology, Duquesne University. Used with permission.
6. Shannon French, *The Code of the Warrior* (Lanham, MD: Rowan & Littlefield, 2005), 10.

7. Lt. Col. David Grossman, *On Killing: The Psychological Cost of Learning to Kill in War and Society* (Boston: Little, Brown and Co., 1995), 95.
8. Al Carroll, *Medicine Bags and Dog Tags* (Lincoln: University of Nebraska Press, 2008), 152.
9. William R. Arnold, "Afterword," *Jewish Holy Scriptures* (Washington: US Government Printing Office, 1942), 514. The italics added within the excerpt are mine.
10. Socrates's courageous military history and his service at Potidaea, Amphipolis, and Delium are briefly mentioned in his *Apology*, 28e, his trial defense available in numerous translations. His individual courage in battle is attested by the testimony of Alcibiades in Plato's *Symposium*, also available in many translations. One summary of Socrates's military service and its relation to his life and philosophy is found in A. E. Taylor, *Socrates* (Garden City, NY: Doubleday Anchor, 1952), 92–94.
11. Allan Nevins, "Foreword" to John F. Kennedy, *Profiles in Courage* (New York: Signet, 1963), xii.
12. Brian Delate, *Soldier's Heart: The Movie* (New York: Soldier's Heart Productions in association with Liberty Studios, 2008), soldiersheartthemovie.com.
13. Tick, *War and the Soul*, 177 and 179.
14. Andrew Bacevich, *Breach of Trust: How Americans Failed Their Soldiers and Their Country* (New York: Metropolitan Books, 2013), 14.
15. *An Intermediate Greek-English Lexicon: Founded upon Liddell and Scott's Greek-English Lexicon* (Oxford: Oxford University Press, 1995), 815.
16. Richard Boes, *The Last Dead Soldier Left Alive* (New York: iUniverse, Inc., 2007), 81.
17. *An Intermediate Greek-English Lexicon*, 815.
18. Richard A. Oppel, Jr., "Falluja's Fall Stuns Marines Who Fought There," *New York Times*, Jan. 9, 2014, A.
19. C. G. Jung, *On the Psychology of the Unconscious*, in C. G. Jung, *Collected Works*, Vol. 7 (Princeton: Bollingen Series, 1979), 72.

CHAPTER 2: THE WAR AFTER WAR

1. A short phrase from one of the most disturbing and prophetic songs of the Vietnam War era: Jim Morrison, "The End," *The Best of the Doors*, Electra Records, 1985.
2. Mike Brewer, "Vietnam Veterans Fast a Dying Breed," TucsonCitizen.com, Oct. 3, 2009, tucsoncitizen.com/veteranveritas/2009/10/03/vietnam-veterans-fast-a-dying-breed. Data from *The VFW Magazine,* the Public Information Office, and the HQ CP Forward Observer and elsewhere. Accessed Feb. 24, 2011.
3. Spencer Reece, "The Manhattan Project," *Poetry*, 198:4 July/August 2011, 294.

CHAPTER 3: WAR WOUNDS US ALL

1. Leo Shane III, "Vet groups tackle bigger issue than benefits cuts: How to stay relevant," *Stars and Stripes*, Jan. 7, 2014.
2. *New York Times*, March 13, 1862, as quoted in Doris Kearns Goodwin, *Team of Rivals* (New York: Simon and Schuster, 2006), 430.
3. Andrew Slater, "As Far as He Can Go Inside: Kevin Powers, War Poet," *Poets and Writers*, 42:2, March/April 2014, 49.
4. Most people believe that the massive benefits given the World War II generation in their GI Bill is the American norm for veteran support and assume only vets since WW II have been neglected. In fact, the treatment of the WW II generation was an anomaly in American experience; neglect of veteran support traces back to the Revolutionary War and has been contentious and withheld ever since.
5. Kate Dahlstedt, "Sentry," unpublished poem used at Soldier's Heart healing retreats. Used with permission here.

6. Ayelet Berman-Cohen, "PTSD—A Confession," unpublished poem, used with permission.
7. Leila Levinson, *Gated Grief: The Daughter of a GI Concentration Camp Liberator Discovers a Legacy of Trauma* (Brule, WI: Cable Publishing, 2011), 192.
8. Jason Moon, *Trying to Find My Way Home*, Full Moon Music, 2010.
9. The first suicide case was reported by a family member; the second was reported by a National Guard soldier from the same unit who was personally acquainted with the couple. Names withheld for confidentiality.
10. Bill Glauber, "Experts tackle suicide prevention among combat veterans: Doctors, social workers here join VA's drive for awareness" *Milwaukee Journal Sentinel,* March 1, 2007, jsonline.com/story/index.aspx?id=572352. The Veterans Administration's *Suicide Data Report 2012* estimates the rate at 21 percent of all suicides in the nation, though veterans represent only 7 percent of the population.
11. Associated Press, "Deployments strain troops' mental health: Pentagon panel warns overburdened system could fail to meet needs," May 4, 2007, msnbc.msn.com/id/18488585.
12. CNN News, "Study: Suicide risk double among male U.S. veterans," June 11, 2007, cnn.com/2007/HEALTH/06/11/vets.suicide/index.html. A recent study tracking American veteran and civilian males from World War I through 1994.
13. Robert D. Gibbons, C. Hendricks Brown, and Kwan Hur, "Is the Risk of Suicide among Veterans Elevated?" *American Journal of Public Health,* 102, no. S1, March 2012, S17–S19.
14. "Statistical information about casualties of the Vietnam Conflict," The National Archives, Electronic and Special Media Records Services Division Reference Report, archives.gov/research/vietnam-war/casualty-statistics.html, accessed Aug. 19, 2007.
15. The number of Vietnam veterans committing suicide was estimated to have surpassed the number of troops killed in action by the late 1980s. W. H. Capps, *The Unfinished War: Vietnam and the American Conscience* (Boston: Beacon Press, 1982). It topped at least 100,000 by 1998: Daniel Hallock, *Hell, Healing, and Resistance: Veterans Speak* (New York: Plough Publishing Corp., 1998); and perhaps even topped 150,000. See Chuck Dean, *Nam Vet* (Portland, OR: Multnomah Press, 1990).
16. Jeff Hargarten et al., "Suicide rate for veterans far exceeds that of civilian population," Center for Public Integrity, publicintegrity.org/2013/08/30/13292/suicide-rate-veterans-far-exceeds-civilian-population accessed Jan. 8, 2014.
17. Ilona Meagher, *Moving a Nation to Care: Post-Traumatic Stress Disorder and America's Returning Troops* (Brooklyn: Ig Publishing, 2007). As of 2007, Meagher cited reports of suicides of Iraq veterans from Illinois (p. 66), Missouri (p. 83), Connecticut (p. 92), Great Britain (94–5), Ohio (p. 100 and 119–120), California (102–3), Iraq (p. 105), Georgia (111–15), and many others from nonspecified locales.
18. Ibid., 92.
19. Jennifer Kerr, "The battle within: Iraq vet suicides," Associated Press, posted on *The Marine Corps Times,* Monday, May 28, 2007, marinecorpstimes.com/news/2007/05/ap_iraq_mentaldistress_070528/.
20. "'06 Suicide Rate for Soldiers Sets a Record for the Army," *New York Times,* Aug. 17, 2007, A15. These numbers "translate to a suicide rate of 17.3 per 100,000, the highest since the Army started counting in 1980."
21. Kevin Freking, "Veteran Suicide Rate at 22 Each Day, Department of Veterans Affairs Report Finds," *Huffington Post,* Feb. 1, 2013, 1.
22. Nicholas Kristof, "A Veteran's Death, the Nation's Shame," *New York Times, Opinion Section,* April 14, 2012; Ed Pilkington, "For US Soldiers, Suicide Now More Lethal Than Combat," *Guardian,* UK, Feb. 3, 2013, readersupportednews.org/news-section2/323-95/15849-for-us-soldiers-suicide-now-more-lethal-than-combat.

23. Mary Ann Boyd, Wanda Bradshaw, and Marceline Robinson, "Mental Health Issues of Women Deployed to Iraq and Afghanistan, *Archives of Psychiatric Nursing*, 27:1, Feb. 2013, 10–22.
24. Greg Zoroya, "Suicides Rare among Soldiers at Some Foreign Outposts," *USA Today*, Feb. 19, 2013, 3A.
25. Penny Coleman, *Flashback: Post-Traumatic Stress Disorder, Suicide, and the Lessons of War* (Boston: Beacon Press, 2007), 146. Based upon their own clinical observations, NATO military colleagues have reported this phenomenon to me among British veterans of the Falklands War, Portuguese veterans of Angola and Mozambique, and Dutch veterans of Indonesia.
26. Pilkington, "For US Soldiers, Suicide Now More Lethal Than Combat.
27. David Brown, "Motor vehicle crashes: A little-known risk to returning veterans of Iraq and Afghanistan," *Washington Post*, May 05, 2013, articles.washingtonpost.com/2013-05-05/national/39048053_1_motor-vehicle-crashes-two-wars.
28. Moni Blau, "Why Suicide Rates among Veterans May Be Higher Than 22 a Day," CNN, cnn.com/2013/09/21/us/22-veteran-suicides-a-day/, accessed Jan. 8, 2014.
29. Nancy Mayfield, "US Executes Gulf War Veteran," Reuters, first published March 18, 2003, available at commondreams.org/headlines03/0318-09.htm.
30. Gethin Chamberlain, "Gulf War Veteran Charged with Murders," *The Scotsman*, June 11, 2006, news.scotsman.com/topics.cfm?tid=1034&id=1008912006.
31. Dana Hull, "Veterans 'Psychic Wounds' Untended, Critics Say," *ContraCosta Times*, Mar. 23, 2007, veteransforcommonsense.org/articleid/7311.
32. Christopher Mumola, "Veterans in Prison or Jail," US Department of Justice, Bureau of Justice Statistics, Jan. 2000, ojp.gov/bjs/pub/pdf/vpj.pdf.
33. Margaret E. Noonan and Christopher Mumola, "Veterans in State and Federal Prison, 2004," US Department of Justice, Bureau of Justice Statistics, May 2007, ojp.usdoj.gov/bjs/pub/pdf/vsfp04.pdf.
34. US Department of Justice statistics, "What Providers Should Know," *Health Progress* (May–June, 2013): 11.
35. V.I.P., Veterans in Prison, June 12, 2004, vetsinprison.org.uk.
36. V.I.P., Veterans in Prison, April 15, 2007, vetsinprison.org.uk/index.php?option=com_content&task=blogcategory&id=1&Itemid=26.
37. Maria Cheng, "UK Study: Violence More Likely among Vets, Troops," March 15, 2013, news.yahoo.com/uk-study-violence-more-likely-among-vets-troops-000634030.html, accessed July 29, 2013.
38. "Substance Use, Dependence and Treatment among Veterans," *National Report on Drug Use and Health*, Substance Abuse and Mental Health Services Administration, Nov. 10, 2005, oas.samhsa.gov/2k5/vets/vets.htm.
39. "Alcohol Use and Alcohol Related Risk Factors Among Veterans," Substance Abuse and Mental Health Services Administration, updated July 27, 2007, oas.samhsa.gov/2k5/vetsAlc/vetsAlc.cfm.
40. "Male Veterans with Co-Occurring Serious Mental Illness and a Substance Abuse Disorder," Substance Abuse and Mental Health Services Administration, updated July 27, 2007, oas.samhsa.gov/2k4/vetsDualDX/vetsDualDX.cfm.
41. Leo Shane III, "Researchers: Alcohol Use, Divorce Rates, Higher among Returning Troops," *Stars and Stripes*, Mideast edition, December 9, 2005, estripes.com/article.asp?section=104&article=32730&archive=true.
42. Ibid.
43. Eliza K. Pavalko and Glenn H. Elder, Jr., "World War II and Divorce: A Life-Course Perspective," *American Journal of Sociology*, 95: 5, March 1990, 1213–34.
44. Janie Blankenship, "War's toll on marriage: study proves war veterans have higher divorce rate, but Vietnam vets have lower rate than public perception," *VFW Magazine*, March 2003, findarticles.com/p/articles/mi_m0LIY/is_7_90/ai_98829332.

45. Ibid.
46. Zahava Solomon, *Combat Stress Reaction* (New York: Springer, 1993), 117.
47. David S. Riggs, Christina A. Byrne, Frank W. Weathers, and Brett T. Litz, "The Quality of the Intimate Relationships of Male Vietnam Veterans: Problems Associated with Posttraumatic Stress Disorder," *Journal of Traumatic Stress*, 11:1, Jan. 1998, 87–101.
48. Gregg Zoroya, "Soldiers' divorce rate drops after 2004 increase," *USA Today*, Jan. 1, 2006, usatoday.com/news/nation/2006-01-09-soldier-divorce-rate_x.htm.
49. Donna Miles, "Programs Aim to Reduce Military Divorce Rates," *American Forces Press Service*, June 9, 2005, af.mil/news/story.asp?id=123010746.
50. "Mental Health Problems among Iraq and Afghanistan Veterans," Iraq and Afghanistan Veterans of America, June 29, 2007, 4, optruth.org/documents/Mental_Health.doc.
51. Virginia Olsen Baron, *Women in the Wake of War* (New York: Service Center, Church Women United, 1977), 2.
52. Andrea Stone, "At camp, military kids bear scars of their own," *USA Today*, June 21, 2007, usatoday.com/news/nation/2007-06-20-camp-cover_N.htm?csp=34.
53. Robert Davis and Gregg Zoroya, "Study: Child abuse, troop deployment linked," *USA Today*, May 7, 2007, usatoday.com/news/nation/2007-05-07-troops-child-abuse_N.htm, quoted in "Mental Health Problems among Iraq and Afghan Veterans."
54. Alison Williams, "Child Abuse in Military Families Up," *Minneapolis-St. Paul Star Tribune*, startribune.com/484/story/1336191.html. Deployment of one spouse led to a 60 percent increase in the rate of moderate to severe abuse of children. Overall, the rate of maltreatment—mild, moderate, and severe—for both males and females increased 40 percent when one spouse was deployed.
55. Rezak Hukanovic, *The Tenth Circle of Hell*, trans. Colleen London and Midhat Ridjanovic (New York: Basic Books, 1993), 123–24.
56. See Edward Tick, *War and the Soul* (Wheaton, IL: Quest Books, 2005), 71–73, for a complete survey of the war damage to the Vietnamese population, infrastructure, and ecology.
57. Of his many books on the subject, the best known is Roger Woolger, *Other Lives, Other Selves: A Jungian Psychotherapist Discovers Past Lives* (New York: Bantam, 1988). His most recent is *Healing Your Past Lives* (Boulder, CO: Sounds True, 2010).
58. Dr. Roger Woolger, personal communication, used with permission. This story has not appeared in Dr. Woolger's writings. In them he presents his own and other cases in which patients had imagistic memories of previous lives spent as soldiers or victims of war. He demonstrates how the themes of these "remembered" lives replicate life issues patients struggle with today. Whether or not one believes in literal past lives, Dr. Woolger demonstrates that "psychic residues" from earlier experiences of war and violence affect adult lives today. Dr. Woolger died while I was writing this book. I honor his memory and contributions.
59. Tick, *Sacred Mountain*, 68–70.
60. Sharon R. Cohany, "Employment and Unemployment among Vietnam-Era Veterans," *Monthly Labor Review*, April 1990, 22–29.
61. "Unemployment among Gulf War Veterans," US Department of Labor, Bureau of Labor Statistics, June 1, 2006, bls.gov/opub/ted/2006/may/wk5/art03.htm.
62. Rudi Williams, "Veterans Affairs Strives to Find Jobs for Iraq, Afghanistan War Vets," US Department of Defense, American Forces Press Service, Aug. 8, 2007, defenselink.mil/news/newsarticle.aspx?id=18082.
63. "Unemployment Rate for Young Veterans Hits 21.1%" *Washington Post*, Sat. March 13, 2010, washingtonpost.com/wp-dyn/content/article/2010/03/12/AR2010031204123.html.

64. US Department of Labor Statistics, released March 20, 2013, "What Providers Should Know,"*Health Progress*, 11.
65. Meagher, *Moving a Nation to Care*, 126.
66. National Coalition for Homeless Veterans, "Background and Statistics," June 2007, nchv.org/background.cfm.
67. US Department of Housing and Urban Development statistics, "What Providers Should Know,"*Health Progress*, 10.
68. William Welch, "Veterans More Likely to Be Homeless, Study Says," *USA Today*, Feb. 10, 2011, usatoday.com/news/nation/2011-02-10-1Ahomelessvets10_ST_N.htm.
69. National Coalition for Homeless Veterans, "Veterans and Homelessness Report," fas.org/sgp/crs/misc/RL34024.pdf.
70. Ibid.
71. Congressional Research Service, "Veterans and Homelessness Report," fas.org/sgp/crs/misc/RL34024.pdf.
72. Ibid., 127.
73. V.I.P., Veterans in Prison, April 15, 2007, vetsinprison.org.uk/index.php?option=com_content&task=blogcategory&id=1&Itemid=26.
74. Daniella David, MD, Claudia Woodward, PhD, Jose Esquenazi, MD, and Thomas A. Mellman, MD, "Comparison of Comorbid Physical Illnesses among Veterans with PTSD and Veterans with Alcohol Dependence," *Psychiatric Services*, American Psychiatric Association, Jan. 2004, psychservices.psychiatryonline.org/cgi/content/full/55/1/82.
75. "What Providers Should Know," *Health Progress*, 11.
76. U. Nalla, B. Durai, et al. "Exposure to Trauma and Post-Traumatic Stress Disorder Symptoms in Older Veterans Attending Primary Care: Comorbid Conditions and Self-Related Health Status,"*Journal of the American Geriatric Society*, 59:6, 2011, 1087–92.
77. *New York Times*, May 9, 2013, A1.
78. Robert Reiter, Veterans Service Officer, Rensselaer County, New York, personal communication, 2012.
79. Kerr, "The battle within: Iraq vet suicides."
80. Meagher, *Moving a Nation to Care*, 65.
81. Ibid., 72.
82. Joseph Stiglitz, interview: "The War is Bad for the Economy," *Spiegel Online International*, April 5, 2006, spiegel.de/international/spiegel/0,1518,409710,00.html.
83. "US Wars Fact Sheet," Department of Veterans Affairs, va.gov/opa/publications/factsheets/fs_americas_wars.pdf⊠, accessed January 8, 2014.
84. Miguel Rivera, personal communication.
85. Humberto Ak'abal, "The Yellow Flowers of the Graves," in *Tejiendo Las Huellas,* Jorge Aramburu and Humberto Ak'abal, translated by Miguel Rivera with Fran Quinn, Linardi y Risso, 2006. Used with permission.
86. Miguel Rivera, personal communication.
87. Meagher, 20. A long list of previous names for the wound appears in *Moving a Nation to Care*, 163–64.
88. George Tyger, *War Zone Faith: An Army Chaplain's Reflections from Afghanistan* (Boston: Skinner House Books, 2013), xiv.
89. Fisher, *The War After the War*, 22–23.
90. Lu Lun, "On Meeting a Sick Soldier," in Robert Payne, ed., *The White Pony: An Anthology of Chinese Poetry* (New York: Mentor, 1947), 231.

CHAPTER 4: ARENA FOR THE SOUL

1. Aeschylus probably also fought at Plataea, Salamis, and Artemisium. Richard Lattimore, "Introduction to the Oresteia," in Grene and Lattimore, eds., *The Complete Greek Tragedies: Vol. I: Aeschylus* (Chicago: University of Chicago Press, 1991), 1.
2. These epithets for war are taken directly or glossed from Aeschylus, *Seven Against Thebes,* Grene and Lattimore, 264, 271, 283. Epithets such as these appear throughout Aeschylus's seven surviving plays and could have been glossed from any. The prevalence of such descriptions demonstrates the degree to which Aeschylus and his society experienced the horrors of combat and used the expressive arts for its expression and catharsis.
3. Lisa Gale Garrigues, "Healing the Past," *Yes!* #66, Summer 2013, 49–50.
4. This number is actually much higher when we count the so-called IndianWars, which began when the United States was still a colony and lasted until the 1890 Wounded Knee massacre, as separate wars against distinct indigenous nations.
5. This figure counts combat and noncombat in-service deaths combined. "Fact Sheet—America's Wars, 1775–1991," US Department of Veterans Affairs, va.gov/opa/publications/factsheets/fs_americas_wars.pdf, accessed May 29, 2013.
6. Geoffrey Perret, *A Country Made by War* (New York: Random House, 1989).
7. Brigadier General William Menninger was the Army's Chief Neuropsychiatry Consultant during World War II. He cites General Eisenhower in W. C. Menninger, *Reactions to Combat: Psychiatry in a Troubled World* (New York: MacMillan, 1948), 134-52, 532.
8. Professor Russell has founded the Institute of War Stress Injuries, Recovery, and Social Justice at Antioch University Seattle for study and public education regarding preventable psychological war wounding.
9. Joseph Campbell, *Myths to Live By* (New York: Bantam, 1988), 181 and 183.
10. To be accurate, Moses, David, and the other early ancestors of our civilization were Hebrews. The word *Jew* for descendants of the tribe came into wide usage as derived from Judah, one of only two of the original twelve tribes to survive the Assyrian conquest and exile around 600 BCE. Before then, "Jew" referred to a member of the tribe of Judah and Judea was one of the two ancient kingdoms of the Hebrew people. The Jews are the remnants of the Hebrews who survived and evolved to carry the legacy that stretches back to Abraham.
11. Deuteronomy 7:1–6.
12. Genesis 4:13.
13. Genesis 7:22.
14. Genesis 9:25.
15. Genesis 8:21.
16. Campbell, *Myths to Live By*, 182.
17. Samuel 25:30–31.
18. Proverbs 6 16–19.
19. Genesis 14 1–24.
20. For a full analysis of this interpretation by combat veterans, see Tick, *War and the Soul*, 270–72.
21. Walt Whitman, "The Wound Dresser," *Complete Poetry and Selected Prose*, ed. James Miller (Cambridge: Riverside Press, 1959), 222.
22. Whitman, "Old War Dreams," *Complete Poetry and Selected Prose*, 335–36.
23. Tick, *War and the Soul*, 271.
24. Genesis 49:5–7.
25. Herodotus, *The Histories*, trans. Aubrey de Selincourt (Middlesex: Penguin Books, 1954), 494–95.

26. Jonathan Shay, *Achilles in Vietnam: Combat Trauma and the Undoing of Character* (New York: Athenaeum, 1994). Also: Jonathan Shay, *Odysseus in America: Combat Trauma and the Trials of Homecoming* (New York: Scribner, 2002).
27. Shay, *Achilles in Vietnam*, xiii.
28. See especially Shay, *Achilles in Vietnam*, 77–99; and Tick, *War and the Soul*, 36–38, 90, 178.
29. Shay, *Achilles in Vietnam*, 20–21.
30. Tick, *War and the Soul*, 88–89.
31. J. F. C. Fuller, *The Second World War: 1939—45* (New York: Duell, Sloan and Pearce, 1949), 401, 402, 398.
32. French, *The Code of the Warrior*, 60.
33. Parts of this encounter were filmed and appear in the documentary, Stephen Olsson, *Healing a Solder's Heart* (Sausalito, CA: CEM Productions, 2013).
34. Chris Hedges, "In Training War Leaders, Lessons from Poetry," *New York Times*. Jan. 17, 2003, Metro Section, 2.
35. Quoted in Robert N. Rosen, *The Jewish Confederates* (Columbia: University of South Carolina Press, 2000), 257.
36. II Samuel 22:44 and 48–49.
37. Psalm 69:1–3, 19–20.
38. Tyger, *War Zone Faith*, 53.
39. Peter's quote is in response to recent commemorations of the fortieth anniversary of the end of the Vietnam War and reinterpretations of that war, and is used with permission. As a survivor of both Vietnam combat and the Kent State shootings, he is a unique witness. See Peter Winnen, "Kent State: Reaching Beyond 'Them' and 'Us,'"*Akron Beacon Journal*, July 27, 1986, D1 and 4.
40. Our lectures were at 2012 Chaplain Annual Sustainment Training (CAST) conferences that the Army provided all its United Ministry Teams (UMTs), consisting of 2,000-plus chaplains and chaplain assistants. I was the Army's 2012 CAST expert trainer in PTSD. These annual retreats were the only group renewal activities for our chaplains. They were ended after 2012 to save federal money. Their training, renewal, and support will no longer be available to ministry teams, leaving them more vulnerable to emotional and spiritual breakdown. Many confessed that they are traumatized, others that they are thoroughly exhausted: all feel great need of support and hurt from its absence.
41. "All soldiers" is slightly overstated. The one personality type that has been determined not to change during military and combat experience is the antisocial personality—psychopathic or sociopathic. For these people, about 2 percent of the population, the conditions of combat match the conditions of their psyches. All others will change as a result of combat exposure. See Richard Gabriel, *No More Heroes: Madness and Psychiatry in War* (New York: Hill and Wang, 1987), 88; Tick, *War and the Soul*, 77.
42. Karl Marlantes, *What It Is Like to Go to War* (New York: Atlantic Monthly Press, 2011), 3.
43. *Geronimo: My Life*, as told to S. M. Barrett (Mineola, NY: Dover, 2005), 34.
44. Ibid., 18, 34, and 108.
45. Sigfried Sassoon, "The Prince of Wounds," 7.
46. N. Duncan Sinclair, *Horrific Traumata: A Pastoral Response to the Post-Traumatic Stress Disorder* (New York: Haworth Press, 1993), 65.
47. Ibid., 66–72.
48. Ibid., 67.
49. Job 41:9.
50. Ayelet Berman-Cohen, "PTSD–A Confession."

CHAPTER 5: THE JOURNEY THROUGH HELL

1. Marlantes, *What It Is Like to Go to War*, 1 and 3.
2. H. G. Evelyn-White, trans., "Hymn to Ares," *Hesiod, the Homeric Hymns, and Homerica* (Cambridge, MA: Harvard University Press, 1977) (1914 reprint), 433–35.
3. Owen, "Fragment: Cramped in that Funneled Hole," 109.
4. W. D. Erhardt, "'That Damned Bad,' Fragments from the Life of Robert James Elliott," *American Poetry Review*, 42:3, May/June 2013, 13.
5. Tyler Boudreau, *Packing Inferno* (Port Townsend, WA: Feral House, 2008).
6. Gen. William Tecumseh Sherman, Letter of May 1865.
7. Gen. William Tecumseh Sherman, Speech to the Graduating Class, Michigan Military Academy, 1879. Reportedly more than 10,000 people attended to hear him speak on this occasion. Sherman gave many versions of his "War is hell" speech over the years. It was a message he could not rest from expounding.
8. Quoted in Goodwin, *Team of Rivals*, 418.
9. Fuller, *The Second World War*, 402.
10. Grossman, 93.
11. Medea Benjamin, *Drone Warfare: Killing by Remote Control* (New York: OR Books, 2012), 214–15.
12. Brian Turner, "Sadiq," *Here, Bullet* (Farmington, ME: Alice James Books, 2005).
13. Kevin Powers, "Field Manual," *Letter Composed during a Lull in the Fighting* (New York: Little, Brown, and Co., 2014).
14. I met the Beast in the very first Vietnam-era veteran I worked with in the mid-1970s and countless times since. See Tick, *Sacred Mountain*, especially chapter 1.
15. *Agamemnon*, I, 48.
16. Philip Wheelwright, *Heraclitus* (New York: Atheneum, 1968), fragment 122, p. 102.
17. Ibid.
18. Aeschylus, *The Eumenides, The Complete Greek Tragedies: Vol. I: Aeschylus*, trans. Richard Lattimore, (Chicago: University of Chicago Press, 1992), 144–47.
19. Edith Hamilton, *Mythology* (Boston: Little, Brown and Co., 1950), 40.
20. Thomas Bulfinch, *Bulfinch's Mythology* (Garden City, NY: Garden City Publishing Co.), 13; Hamilton, *Mythology*, 40; Shay, *Achilles in Vietnam*, 5.
21. *Eumenides*, 146–47.
22. Captain Frank Hill, "MASH Today: Medicine, War, and Writing," *Explore: The Journal of Science and Healing*, 3:1, Jan./Feb. 2007, 61.
23. Joseph Epes Brown, *The Sacred Pipe: Black Elk's Account of the Seven Rites of the Oglala Sioux* (Baltimore: Penguin, 1971), 92.
24. Wilfred Owen, "The Next War," in C. Day Lewis, ed., *The Collected Poetry of Wilfred Owen* (New York: New Directions, 1963), 86.
25. Siegfried Sassoon, "Memory," in Rupert Hart-Davis, ed., *Siegfried Sassoon: The War Poems* (London: Faber and Faber, 1999), 106.
26. Tyger, *War Zone Faith*, 36.
27. Larry Winters, *Brotherkeeper* (New Paltz, NY: Lawrence Winters, 2013). I also highly recommend Larry's earlier book *The Making and Unmaking of a Marine: One Man's Struggle for Forgiveness* (New Paltz, NY: Mill Rock Writers Collective, 2007).
28. Roger Brooke, "An Archetypal Perspective for Combat Trauma," *Bulletin of the American Academy of Clinical Psychology*, 13:1, Fall 2012, 6.
29. I Samuel 9:2.
30. I Samuel 14:23.
31. I Samuel 14:52.
32. I Samuel 15:3.
33. I Samuel 16:23.

34. I Samuel 28:16–18.
35. I Samuel 18:10. See also 16:14 and 19:9.
36. Ruth Beebe Hill, *Hanta Yo* (New York: Warner Books, 1980), 969.
37. Ibid., 1047.

CHAPTER 6: THE INVISIBLE WOUND TODAY

1. Kevin Turner, "Nobody Knows," unpublished song, quoted with permission.
2. Gen. Douglas MacArthur, "Farewell Speech to the Corps of Cadets at West Point," May 12, 1962.
3. This famous quote has been attributed to both philosophers Plato and George Santayana. It is a favorite adage of veterans.
4. The DSM-5 now pays more attention to the behavioral symptoms that accompany PTSD and proposes four distinct diagnostic clusters. PTSD is also more developmentally sensitive for children and adolescents.
5. Gay Bradshaw, *Elephants on the Edge: What Animals Teach Us about Humanity* (New Haven: Princeton University Press, 2009).
6. Some of the material in the following sections of this chapter previously appeared in shorter form in Tick, *Wild Beasts and Wandering Souls: Shamanism and Post-Traumatic Stress Disorder* (Salt Lake City, UT: Elik Press, 2007). Reprinted in *Vietnamese Studies*, 4, 2007, 39—71; *Spirited Medicine*, Society of Shamanic Practitioners, 2013. An abridged version appears in *Journal of Shamanic Practice*, 4:1, Spring 2011.
7. I Samuel 16:14, 18:10, and 19:9.
8. Richard Gabriel, *Man and Wound in the Ancient World* (Washington, DC: Potomac Books, 2012), 155.
9. Josephus, *The Jewish War and Other Selections from Flavius Josephus*, trans. H. St. J. Thackeray and Ralph Marcus, (New York: Washington Square Press, 1965), 155.
10. Mark DeWolfe Howe, ed., *Touched with Fire: Civil War Letters of Oliver Wendell Holmes, Jr. 1861–1864* (New York: Fordham University Press, 2000), 149.
11. Tim Cook, "The Great War of the Mind," *Canada's History*, June/July 2010, 24.
12. Gabriel, *Man and Wound in the Ancient World*, 155.
13. For a history of the wound and its names see, among others, Richard Gabriel, *No More Heroes: Madness and Psychiatry in War* (New York: Hill and Wang, 1987), especially 16, 43–44; Meagher, *Moving a Nation to Care* 161–62; Tick, *War and the Soul*, especially 97–103.
14. Letter to his mother quoted in Douglas Kerr, "Introduction," *The Works of Wilfred Owen* (Hertfordshire: Wordsworth Poetry Library, 1994), vii.
15. Owen, "Insensibility," *The Works of Wilfred Owen*, 21-22.
16. Owen, "And I Must Go," *The Works of Wilfred Owen*, 58.
17. Leila Levinson, *Gated Grief: The Daughter of a GI Concentration Camp Liberator Discovers a Legacy of Trauma* (Brule, WI: Cable Publishing, 2011), 224.
18. "Britain: Soldier Executed in 1916 Pardoned," *New York Times*, Aug. 16, 2006, A7. Relatives of one, Pvt. Harry Farr, sued for and finally received his pardon due to shell shock—in August 2006, ninety years after his execution.
19. Gen. George S. Patton, Diaries, quoted by Meagher, *Moving a Nation to Care*, 12.
20. Catharine Arnold, *Bedlam: London and Its Mad* (London: Simon & Schuster Pocket Books, 2009), 253–60.
21. Martin Stone, "Shellshock and the Psychologists," *The Anatomy of Madness, III*, 245, quoted Arnold, *Bedlam*, 260.
22. "Principal Wars in Which the United States Participated: US Military Personnel Serving and Casualties," US Department of Defense, siadapp.dior.whs.mil/personnel/Casualty/WCPrincipal. National Institute of Mental Health, 2002, at Statistics,

Mental Illness Research Association, miraresearch.org/understanding/statistics.htm. Gabriel, *Man and Wound in the Ancient World*, 72–77.

23. Jennifer Price, "Findings from the National Vietnam Veterans' Readjustment Study, A National Center for PTSD Fact Sheet," US Department of Veterans Affairs, National Center for PTSD, ncptsd.va.gov/facts/veterans/fs_NVVRS.html.
24. Gabriel, *No More Heroes: Madness and Psychiatry in War*, 77.
25. Michael Korda, *Ulysses S. Grant: The Unlikely Hero* (New York: HarperCollins, 2004), 77.
26. Gary Paulsen, *Soldier's Heart* (New York: Dell Laurel Leaf, 1998), 103.
27. "Fact Sheet—America's Wars, 1775–1991," US Department of Veterans Affairs, va.gov/opa/publications/factsheets/fs_americas_wars.pdf, accessed June 26, 2013.
28. Vietnam was a war of attrition, hence the importance of the "body count" and a reason for so much civilian slaughter. One vet said, "I was just killing baby Charlies [Viet Cong], not children." The Vietnamese had the resilience to endure this unstated US strategy. Ho Chi Minh said, "For every one of us you kill, ten more are waiting to take their place," and, "You will kill many of us. We will kill a few of you. You will lose your will first. We will win."
29. Quoted in Goodwin, *Team of Rivals*, 685.
30. Sidney Andrews, *Boston Advertiser*, quoted in Rosen, *The Jewish Confederates*, 309.
31. Korda, *Ulysses S. Grant*, 102.
32. Norman Solomon, *War Made Easy* (New York: John Wiley, 2005), especially 184–226.
33. John Grant, "The Battle over PTSD," April 14, 2011, thiscantbehappening.net/node/561, accessed May 10, 2011.
34. Indications are that this trend will continue and expand as the military continues to shrink its general forces while increasing reliance on Special Forces and advanced technology. Thom Shanker and Helene Cooper, "Pentagon Plans to Shrink Army to Pre–World War II Level," *New York Times*, Feb. 23, 2014, A1.
35. This presentation is not meant to be critical or dismissive of the many clinicians and healers offering their services and techniques to returning troops. Most tending can help. Symptom reduction, especially through holistic means, is critical to homecoming. Here we seek the most holistic vision for restoration after war and evaluate most helping strategies as aiming at symptom reduction, cognitive retraining, lifestyle readjustment, and stress and anger management.
36. Caplan, *When Johnny and Jane Come Marching Home*, 85.
37. Wang Han, "The Song of Liangchow," Payne, *The White Pony*, 229.
38. Evan S. Connell, *Son of the Morning Star: Custer and the Little Big Horn* (San Francisco: North Point Press, 1984), 361–62 and elsewhere.
39. It is generally believed in the addictions field that patients must attain sobriety before working on deeper issues. Vince's story stands in contrast to this philosophy. It is sometimes the case that people abusing substances can be so "saturated" and numb that their history and feelings are inaccessible and we cannot do deeper work until they are sober. The critical point is that we do not in any way deny war experiences but communicate to the veteran that we will give his or her military history priority, no matter when or how we deal with substance use.
40. Psalm 70:5.
41. Psalm 22: 1, 6–7, 14–15, 20.
42. I Samuel 16:18.
43. On the importance of rites of passage in becoming warriors, see also Tick, *War and the Soul*, chapter 3, "War as a Rite of Passage," 45–62.
44. I Samuel 27:9. See also 27:11.
45. II Samuel 8:2, 4–5, 13, 14.
46. Sassoon, *Sigfried Sasson: The War Poems*, 131.

47. II Samuel 22:35–38 and 42. Same as Psalm 18.
48. Chris Adsit, *The Combat Trauma Healing Manual* (Newport News, VA: Military Ministry Press, 2008), 166–70.
49. II Samuel 23:3–5, 6–7.
50. Adsit, *The Combat Trauma Healing Manual*, 165.

CHAPTER 7: WAR TRAUMA AND THE SOCIAL CONTRACT

1. *Douglass' Monthly*, April, 1863, as quoted in Goodwin, *Team of Rivals*, 549.
2. Langston Hughes, "Beaumont to Detroit: 1943," *The Collected Letters of Langston Hughes* (New York: Alfred A. Knopf, Inc., 1994).
3. Tomas Young, "Dying Iraq War Veteran, Pens 'Last Letter' to Bush, Cheney on War's 10th Anniversary," huffingtonpost.com/2013/03/19/tomas-young-letter-iraq_n_2908335.html.
4. Mary Catherine Bateson, "It's the System!" *Center Post*, 24:2, Spring/Summer 2013, 5.
5. For interested readers, Ed Bloch found peace and redemption through writing about the atrocity and ensuring it is recorded in history, by serving wounded veterans, and finally in his late eighties by making a trip back to the village in China where the atrocity occurred. Those interested in his complete story can find it in Edward Tick, "Atonement Practices after War," in Phil Cousineau, ed., *Beyond Forgiveness: Reflections on Atonement* (San Francisco, CA: Josey-Bass, 2011). Ed's writings are referenced there. That chapter contains many stories of individual atonement practices by World War II and Vietnam veterans and their families. Atonement can be practiced individually or collectively.
6. Many nonveterans have never been initiated, creating a culture of boy-men who have not been honed and matured through ordeals in the people's service. The consequences of this lack of initiated adults, especially men, are dire and extreme, and they affect every aspect of our lives. It is well to remember that these inexperienced, untested, and uninitiated people often become the adults who make and shape our decisions regarding warfare, veteran treatment, and the needs of society.
7. Sen. John McCain, "Foreword," in David Halberstam, *The Best and the Brightest* (New York: Random House, 2002).
8. Homer, *The Iliad*, trans. Robert Fitzgerald (Garden City, NY: Doubleday, 1974), 414.
9. *Sayings of Buddha* (Mt. Vernon, NY: Peter Pauper Press, 1957), 32.
10. Stanley Vestal, *Sitting Bull: Champion of the Plains* (Norman, University of Oklahoma Press, 1989), 77.
11. Sophocles, *Ajax*, in *The Complete Greek Tragedies: Vol. II: Sophocles*, trans. John Moore (Chicago: University of Chicago Press, 1992), 233.
12. Ibid., 222.
13. Ibid., 221 and 227.
14. Shared after his funeral by his battle buddy and best friend. Names withheld.
15. Shay, *Achilles in Vietnam*, 13–14.
16. Thucydides, "The Funeral Oration of Pericles," ed. M. I. Finley, *The Greek Historians* (New York: Viking, 1959), 271–72.
17. Ibid., 239.
18. This assertion is based upon my visits to and reports from social workers, counselors, veterans, law enforcement officials, and Native healers on various reservations and in traditional communities in the Northeast, Midwest, Upper West, Pacific Coast, and Alaska.
19. Harold Napoleon, *Yuuyaraq: The Way of the Human Being* (Fairbanks, AK: University of Alaska, 1991) 15.

20. Sun Tzu, *The Art of War* (London: Hodder and Stoughton, 1995), 87.
21. Robert M. Utley, *The Lance and the Shield* (New York: Ballantine, 1993), 91.
22. This quote is frequently attributed to Sitting Bull and cited in many speeches, writings, and on websites. However, no direct reference is known. It may be gleaned from his other observations or evolved and attributed to represent the Lakota ethos on warriors.
23. Douglas MacArthur, quoted in Paul Fussell, *Thank God for the Atom Bomb* (New York: Ballantine, 1988), 25.
24. This quote is cited as Washington's in many speeches, writings, and on veteran websites. However, no direct reference is known. It may be gleaned from other Washington observations or, like the cherry tree, be representative rather than actual.
25. Kennedy, *Profiles in Courage*, 14.
26. Ibid., 16.
27. Ronald Lee Orem, *Jungle Dreams: A Collection of Essays on War*, unpublished manuscript, 3.
28. Earl Shorris, *The Death of the Great Spirit* (New York: Signet, 1972), 45.
29. For a comprehensive accounting of war wounding to Vietnamese military, civilians, infrastructure, and the environment—and a comparison with American losses—see Tick, *War and the Soul*, 72–73.
30. Unless otherwise noted, this and all quotes and references to Vietnamese experts and veterans are direct personal communications.
31. Nguyen Duy, *Distant Road: Selected Poems of Nguyen Duy*, trans. K. Bowen and Nguyen Ba Chung (Willimantic, CT: Curbstone Press, 1999), 83–85.
32. Sun Tzu, *The Art of War*, 15–17 and 66.
33. Le Van Hao (Viet Nam) and Monica Martinez (Spain), "The Consequences of Psychological Trauma of Veterans Who Are Exposed to Agent Orange." Article presented at the International Conference "Psychological Trauma among Agent Orange Affected Victims in the Vietnam War," Ha Noi, March 19, 2010.
34. Personal communication, Feb. 20, 2014.
35. Unofficially, all members of Vietnamese society now accept each other and are reconciled. ARVNs and southern-force veterans now hold respectable jobs, their children freely intermarry, and people from both sides are best friends. But officially ARVN veterans are still disenfranchised by the government, not given benefits, not buried in military cemeteries, and their mothers are not counted among the Heroic Mothers. This causes some American veterans additional grief as they judge that we abandoned our allies to a difficult fate. The issue continues today as some veterans of the Iraq and Afghanistan Wars fear for and protest the fates of their abandoned translators and troop allies in the Middle East whose lives are at risk for supporting the United States and among whom very few have been repatriated to America.

CHAPTER 8: THE WOUND: A HOLISTIC UNDERSTANDING

1. Hillman, *A Terrible Love of War*, 32.
2. Ibid.
3. Quoted in Hansel, Steidle, Zacek, and Zacek, eds., *Soldier's Heart: Survivor's Views of Combat Trauma* (Lutherville, MD: Sidran, 1995), xiii.
4. Slater, "As Far as He Can Go Inside: Kevin Powers, War Poet," 48.

CHAPTER 9: WOUNDING AND IDENTITY

1. For recent inquiries into moral injury: WBUR (Boston NPR), "Moral Injury: An Invisible Wound of War," wbur.org/series/moral-injury; Shira Maguen, PhD, and

Brett Litz, PhD, "Moral Injury in the Context of War," ptsd.va.gov/professional/pages/moral_injury_at_war.asp; National Center for PTSD, "Moral Injury in Veterans of War," *PTSD Research Quarterly*, 23:1, 2012; Rita Nakashima Brock and Gabriella Lettini, *Soul Repair: Recovering from Moral Injury after War* (Boston: Beacon Press, 2012). Though moral injury has only recently gained significant attention, some practitioners and veterans have been speaking of moral trauma for decades. See, among others: Larry Dewey, *War and Redemption* (Burlington, VT: Ashgate Publishing, 2004); William P. Mahedy, *Out of the Night: The Spiritual Journey of Vietnam Vets* (New York: Ballantine, 1986); Peter Marin, "Living in Moral Pain," *Freedom and Its Discontents* (South Royalton, VT: Steerforth Press, 1995); Shay, *Achilles in Vietnam* and *Odysseus in America*; Tick, *Dream Healing*, especially 10–13; Tick, *War and the Soul*, especially 59, 110–14, 169–71, 276. We will examine how concern over moral trauma stretches back to ancient religions and civilizations.

2. Euripides, *The Trojan Women*, in *Three Greek Plays*, trans. Edith Hamilton, and intro (New York: Norton, 1937), 37, 39, 43.
3. Tick, *The Practice of Dream Healing*, 10–11. For a complete presentation and analysis of *The Trojan Women* and the use of this play for war healing, see 3–14.
4. Mahedy, *Out of the Night*, 155, 179, and elsewhere.
5. Boudreau, *Packing Inferno*.
6. Dewey, *War and Redemption*, especially 73ff.
7. Jeff Schogol, "Pentagon: No Purple Heart for PTSD," *Stars and Stripes*, January 6, 2009, stripes.com/news/pentagon-no-purple-heart-for-ptsd-1.86761, accessed May 11, 2011.
8. See, for example, Tick, *War and the Soul*, 74–79, 101–2 for accurate versus reported casualty reports from recent wars. A few examples: the United States counted only 148 combat deaths and 467 wounded in the Gulf War (1990–91). A decade later the Veterans Administration had recognized over one-quarter million disabled vets and over 10,600 dead of combat-related injuries since the end of that war, making the US casualty rate for the first Gulf War almost 31 percent: see *War and the Soul*, 74. Or consider the suicide rates for veterans, reported in chapters 1 and 2. What would be the casualty rates of these wars if veteran suicide were linked to military experience and aftermath, and they included the 100,000-plus suicides of Vietnam vets or the 30,000-plus of Iraq and Afghanistan War vets?
9. McCain, "Foreword," in *The Best and Brightest*.
10. Brian Delate, *Soldier's Heart: The Movie* (New York: Soldier's Heart Productions in association with Liberty Studios, 2008), soldiersheartthemovie.com.
11. Campbell, *Myths to Live By*, 176.
12. Tran Quang Quy, "Gift," trans. Nguyen Phan Que Mai and J. Fossenbell, reprinted in *Peace Poems from the Two Sides* (Ha Noi, Viet Nam: privately printed, 2010), 53.

CHAPTER 10: THE TRANSFORMATIONAL JOURNEY

1. All of Joseph Campbell's works deserve study, but the fullest synthesis of the hero's journey is presented in *The Hero with a Thousand Faces* (New York: Bollingen Foundation, 1949).

CHAPTER 11: LESSONS FROM THE CHIEFS OF OLD

1. The portrait and history of General Ridgway as well as his quotes are taken from David Halberstam, *The Coldest Winter: America and the Korean War* (New York: Hyperion, 2007), 487.

2. Ibid., 490.
3. Ibid., 490.
4. Hillman, *A Terrible Love of War*, 31.
5. Ruwan M. Jayatunge, MD, *Post-Traumatic Stress Disorder (PTSD)—A Malady Shared by East and West: A Sri Lankan Look at Combat Stress and Trauma,* (Fort Leavenworth, KS: Foreign Military Studies Office, 2013), 17.
6. Roger Brooke, "An Archetypal Perspective for Combat Trauma," *Bulletin of the American Academy of Clinical Psychology*, 13:1, Fall 2012, 2.
7. Carroll, *Medicine Bags and Dog Tags*, (Lincoln: University of Nebraska Press, 2008) 210.
8. Ibid., 216–17.
9. See examples in Tick, *War and the Soul.* Art's story opens the book and is retold in detail there. See "my soul has fled," 11–16.
10. Those who may find this notion of "seven souls" strange are invited to compare the Eastern system of the seven chakras, the Western psychological concept of "sub-personalities," or various polytheistic cultures' beliefs in contending deities. There are many interpretations of our internal divisions and intrapsychic conflicts.
11. All information about Sri Lanka above is summarized from Dr. Jayatunge's article cited in chapter 11, note 5. His quote is on page 19.
12. Information on the Xhosa supplied by Dr. Roger, professor of psychology at Duquesne University and former South African paratrooper. I am grateful to Dr. Brooke for research on traditional peoples and practices from his homeland and for his support, contributions, insights, and healing he has shared regarding the warrior's journey.
13. Information on the Shangaan supplied by Dr. Roger Brooke from his field research in South Africa, summer 2013.
14. For a full analysis of the intimacy that results after killing, see Tick, *War and the Soul*, especially chapter 7, "Eros and Aesthetics in Hell." For strategies for completing the healing and reconciliation with the dead, see Tick, "Atonement Practices for Veterans" in Cousineau, *Beyond Forgiveness.*
15. To view the *haka* performed as a farewell for a fallen warrior from his unit, see youtube.com/watch?v=xI6TRTBZUMM&feature=share. I am grateful to both Fr. Michael Cicanato and Bud Mahoney for their assistance in Maori research. Fr. Michael visited New Zealand in 2013 to interview Maori people and leaders today. Bud Mahoney lived in New Zealand and among the Maori twice for a total of six years. He worked with Maori to achieve significant presence in the national museum.
16. Jae-sung Chung is currently webmaster of the Republic of Korea Vietnam veterans (ROKs) website. The site can be accessed for excellent information and contact about the Korean experience in Viet Nam: rokfv.com. I am grateful for help in this research on Korea to both Jae and Vietnam veteran Michael "Magoo" Phillips, who introduced me to Jae and traveled to South Korea to research the impact of war on, and to build bridges with, ROKs.
17. The ceremony and its history can be viewed in a film by Eleanor Cox, producer, and Liz Thompson, director, *Breaking Bows and Arrows: A Search for Reconciliation and Forgiveness* (Firelight Productions and Tiger Eye Productions, 2001) The summary and commentary is from Kate Dahlstedt, "Burying the Stone: Rituals and Ceremonies of Atonement," in Cousineau, *Beyond Forgiveness.* The quotes are from pages 61–72.
18. Personal account by Roger Shourds and taught by elder Johnny Arlee and recorded in Johnny Arlee, *Over a Century of Moving to the Drum: Salish Indian Celebrations on the Flathead Indian Reservation* (Pablo and Helena, Montana: Salish Kootenai College Press and Montana Historical Society, 1998), especially 28–30. I express my gratitude and honor to Nupkus and his people for keeping the sacred traditions, for serving their

people and all Americans with great devotion, and for trusting us to share the practices of their tribe so that we may learn and heal as one.

19. Joseph J. Ellis, *His Excellency George Washington* (New York: Vintage, 2004). Early military history: 12–24; quote: 22.
20. George Washington, General Order, New York, July 29, 1776.
21. As of July 2013, one Lt. Colonel chaplain and one Master Sergeant chaplain assistant had committed suicide during that year. Information supplied by Chaplain Colonel Scott Sterling, Fort Polk, July 24, 2013.

CHAPTER 12: RELIGION AND SPIRITUALITY FOR WAR HEALING

1. Numbers 19.
2. Numbers 26:2.
3. Numbers 31:50–52.
4. Numbers 35:33.
5. St. Basil the Great, Epistle 188.13.
6. Deuteronomy 23:9–14.
7. Deuteronomy 24:5.
8. Deuteronomy 20:5–8.
9. Gabriel, *Man and Wound in the Ancient World*, 114.
10. Deuteronomy 20 1–5, 10–20.
11. Psalm 7:3–4.
12. Mahedy, *Out of the Night*, 152. Earlier we heard from Siegfried Sassoon and other WW I poets who identified with the crucified, abandoned Christ.
13. Archibald MacLeish, *J.B.* (Boston: Houghton Mifflin, 1958).
14. *The Gatekeepers*, Phillippa Kowarsky Productions, Dror March Productions and Les Films du Poisson, SARL, 2012.
15. Ryan Smithson, *Ghosts of War: The True Story of a 19-Year-Old GI* (New York: Collins, 2009), 307–9.
16. See Galatians 1:13–14; Philippians 3:6; Acts 8:1–3.
17. For an analysis of the Just War theory and its influence, see Tick, *War and the Soul*, 39–40.
18. Siegfried Sassoon, "The Redeemer," *The War Poems* (London: Faber and Faber, 1999), 4–5.

CHAPTER 13: THE PATH OF WARRIOR RETURN

1. Four of these steps—purification, storytelling, restitution, and initiation—were initially presented in *War and the Soul*. Through my research and healing practices since its 2005 publication, I have expanded that model; two additional steps as presented herein. Readers are referred to *War and the Soul*, especially part III, for complete chapters on each of the first four steps.
2. Numbers 31:19–20.
3. Numbers 31:21–24.
4. Carroll, *Medicine Bags and Dog Tags*, 205.
5. Dr. Fisher retells his family history, its influence on him, and his quest to carry it in *The War After the War*, 265–87. The Civil War incidents: 268–70. Quotes: 265 and 278.
6. Marie-Louise Sjoestedt, *Celtic Gods and Heroes* (Mineola, NY: Dover, 2000 [orig. 1949]), 65–66. Quote: 65.

7. Vanessa Gera, "Austrian children learn of Holocaust from survivors," lubbockonline.com/stories/020604/wor_020604091.shtml, accessed July 26, 2013.
8. Edward Tick, "Atonement Practices after War," in Cousineau, *Beyond Forgiveness*, 116.
9. Ibid., 127.
10. Ibid., 133–34.
11. Fisher, *The War After the War*, 289.
12. This description of our Soldier's Heart war healing retreats, which our organization has been conducting across the nation since 2006, can be found on our website, soldiersheart.net/retreats. The written description was originally published in Kate Dahlstedt, "Breaking Bows and Arrows," Cousineau, in *Beyond Forgiveness*, 68–72.

CHAPTER 14: SPIRITUAL COMFORT AND HEALING FOR THE WAR-WOUNDED

1. An earlier version describing this ceremony was published as Edward Tick, "Afterword" to "Wild Beasts and Wandering Souls," *Journal of Shamanic Practice*, 18.
2. Marlantes, *What It Is Like to Go to War*, 1.
3. Proverbs 16:7.
4. Kennedy, *Profiles in Courage*, 205.
5. Whitman, "Reconciliation," *Complete Poetry and Selected Prose*, 229.
6. Levinson, *Gated Grief*, 31 and 246. Leila's book is the most comprehensive to date in recording and analyzing the experiences of American concentration camp liberators and the impact of this service on their later life histories and families.
7. Christal Presley, *Thirty Days with My Father: Finding Peace from Wartime PTSD* (Deerfield Beach, FL: Health Communications, Inc., 2012).
8. An exhibit of Steven Ross's Iraq photography is on permanent display in our Soldier's Heart offices in Troy, New York.
9. Linda G. Myers and Arthur H. Myers, *Return to Viet Nam: One Veteran's Journey of Healing* (Bloomington, IN: Author House, 2011).
10. Isaiah 58:12.
11. John Becknell, *Listening to War*, PhD dissertation, Pacifica Graduate Institute, 2013, chapter 4.

CHAPTER 15: REDEMPTION OF THE WOUNDED WARRIOR

1. Dewey, *War and Redemption,* various.
2. This story was provided from the Army Ministry of Chaplain Chris Antal during his deployment in Afghanistan from 2012 to 2013. Angel recorded his song "Driving By as I Watch You Bleed" and an interview with Chaplain Chris Antal in Afghanistan in December 2012 after they accomplished the healing described. Used with permission of Angel (last name withheld by request), Chaplain Chris Antal, and Vietnam vet and mentor Hugh Scanlen.
3. Marlantes, *What It Is Like to Go to War*, 79.
4. Tick, *War and the Soul*, 140.
5. Mark Timpany, a member of Chaplain Antal's congregation in Kandahar, put the song and interview on his blog. It is available at bamiyan.us/wordpress/?p=737.
6. Song, a veteran of the southern air force, is our Soldier's Heart representative in Viet Nam and our in-country guide.
7. Following are excerpts from their actual letters. This story and their writings are used with permission of all parties. I express my honor and gratitude to all. Tragically,

Stan died shortly after this section was written, leaving permission to share his story and a bequest to do charitable works in Viet Nam in his memory. His reconciliation continues beyond his death.

8. Phil Cousineau, *The Art of Pilgrimage* (Berkeley, CA: Conari Press, 1998), xxiii, xxvii–xxviii.
9. Eric O. Dean, *Spiritual Pilgrimage as a Ritual of Healing for Warriors in Transition Suffering from Post Post-Traumatic Stress Disorder*, doctoral dissertation, Erskine Theological Seminary. April 2013, 6.
10. Richard Nevard, "After Action Report," and "A Spiritual Pilgrimage to Rome," privately circulated, Sept. 2012.
11. Dean, *Spiritual Pilgrimage as a Ritual of Healing*, 172–73.
12. For a full report and Jungian analysis of this journey, see John Giannini, "A Pilgrimage to the Ancient Healing Sites of Greece: A Journey with Ed Tick," *San Francisco Jung Institute Library Journal*, 23:1, Feb. 2004, 75–91. Dr. Giannini is a World War II veteran.
13. *Illiad* Book Two, 211–77.
14. Tommy Laughlin, previously unpublished poem, used with permission.
15. Dwight D. Eisenhower, "Farewell Address," January 17, 1961.
16. M. Scott Peck, *People of the Lie: The Hope for Healing Human Evil* (New York: Simon & Schuster, 1983), 232–33.

REVEILLE: OF WARRIORS AND DOVES

1. Isaiah 53:4–8.
2. Isaiah 53:5–6.
3. Isaiah 52:15 and 53:11–12.
4. Jeremy Berggren, "Our Memorial," previously unpublished poem used with permission. This poem was written during a Soldier's Heart retreat and is now used during memorial ceremonies at every Soldier's Heart retreat.
5. Becknell, *Listening to War*.
6. Brooke, "An Archetypal Perspective for Combat Trauma," 5.

Index of Veterans' Testimonies

This is a list of veterans who are directly quoted in *Warrior's Return.* Full names are real names, used with permission. When only first names are offered, they are pseudonyms to protect confidentiality. Anonymous entries are direct quotes, and their requests to remain unnamed have been honored. When known, branches, ranks, countries, and places of service accompany each name.

Abattello, Michael: Marines, rifleman, Afghanistan, 3–6

Adams: Chaplain, Army, 85

Al: Army, Viet Nam, 155

Alberto: Army, Korea, 6–7

Angel: Army, medic, Iraq & Afghanistan, 240–43, 252

Anonymous: Afghanistan, 30, 40, 72, 84, 93, 105, 122, 142, 151, 171, 237

Anonymous: Army psychiatrist, Walter Reed Military Hospital, 173

Anonymous: Iraq, 14–15, 16, 17, 30, 72, 94, 125, 146–47, 174

Anonymous: Navy, 87

Anonymous: Special Forces, 125

Anonymous: Viet Cong, 133, 221

Anonymous: Viet Nam, 18, 145

Anonymous: World War II, 76

Antal, Chris: Chaplain (Capt.), Army, Afghanistan, 84, 157, 189–90, 240–43, 251–52

Bell, Terry: Captain, Army Ranger, Viet Nam, 29, 221–23

Ben: Marines, Viet Nam, 70

Berggren, Jeremy: Marines, mortuary detail, Iraq, 254–55

Berman-Cohen, Ayelet: Israeli Air Force, 39, 78

Bloch, Ed: Marines, rifleman, World War II, 49, 122–23, 227n5

Bob: Marines, helicopter door gunner, Viet Nam, 46

Brooke, Roger: Paratrooper, S. Africa, 10, 179, 181–82, 260, 280n12

Cagle, Bob: Army, Viet Nam, 257–58

Candy: Captain, Iraq, mental health officer, 28, 39, 40

Carl: Marines, Viet Nam, 154–55

Delate, Brian: Army, Viet Nam, 14, 153, 255

Daniel: Army, Iraq, convoy truck driver, 23, 25

Dave: Chaplain (Major), Army Reserves, Bosnia and Iraq, 188–89

David: Navy, Sea-Bee, Afghanistan, 44

Fisher, John: Army, Viet Nam, radio and telephone operator, xv, 55, 96, 153, 161, 209, 214,263n1

Gunny: Marines, Korea & Viet Nam, 123–24, 126–27

Hat: North Vietnamese Army (NVA), 201–2

Henderson, Paul: Lieutenant Colonel, Army Special Forces, Viet Nam & career, 11, 248–49, 251

Hill, Frank: Captain, Army, MASH Executive Officer, Afghanistan, 17, 89–90

Houde, Frank: Lieutenant Colonel, Air

Force, pilot, Viet Nam and career, 95
Huu Ngoc: Doctor, Viet Minh, 133
Hyman, Stan: Army, Viet Nam, 243–46

Jack: Marines, Viet Nam, 135
Jae-Sung Chung: Korean Army (ROK), Viet Nam, 184–85
Jim: Air Force pilot, Viet Nam, 27, 79–80, 83

Ken: Army, Afghanistan, 42

Laughlin, Tommy: Sargent, Viet Nam, Army, 238–40, 248–51
Lembke, Michael: Chaplain (Col.), Army, career, 13, 37, 251, 254
Lynn: Army, nurse, Viet Nam, 46

McHenry, Dick: Captain, Army, Viet Nam, 96
Michel, Wilbert: Army, Viet Nam, 146
Miller, Glen: Sargent, Army, Viet Nam, 160–61
Mitchell: Navy, USS Iowa, gunner's mate, 231–33
Myers, Art: Army, military police, Viet Nam, 228–29

Nelson, Sean: Army, Ranger, Somalia, 105, 108, 109
Nguyen Sin Phuc: Doctor, North Vietnamese Army (NVA), 132
Nguygen Tam Ho ("Mr. Tiger"): Viet Minh and Viet Cong, 69–70, 95, 133, 225
Nick: Army, National Guard, tank corps, Iraq, 70

Olsen, Eric: Chaplain (Col.), Army National Guard, career, 54

Pacello, Charles, Lieutenant, Air Force, Nuclear Weapons teams, 96–97, 100
Phillips, Michael "Magoo": Army, Viet Nam, truck driver, xvi–xviii, 281n16
Pierce, David: Navy, gunner's mate, Persian Gulf, 54

Ross, Steve: Army, Iraq, 228
Rothenstein, Louis: Sgt. Major, Army, Intelligence Officer, Viet Nam, 9–10
Roy: Marines, Viet Nam, helicopter door gunner, 66, 223, 224
Ruckles: Sargent, Marines, Iraq & Afghanistan, 122
Russell, Mark: Commander, Navy, psychiatrist, career, 60, 271n8

Saa, Bill: Liberian Civil War, 230–31
Sarah: Army, Iraq, 31
Scanlen, Hugh: Army, helicopter door gunner, Viet Nam, 223–24, 225, 232, 235–36, 241
Searcy, Chuck: Vietnam, 18–19
Shourds, Roger (Kwu Kak Nupkus): Marines, Vietnam, 12, 120–21, 188–89, 231
Sterling, Scott: Chaplain (Col.), Army, Iraq & career, 190–91, 198
Sue: Army, medical officer, 196–97

Tam Tien: Viet Cong, 133, 138, 225
Tina: Lieutenant, Army, chaplain, Afghanistan, 72
Tran Dinh Song: Lieutenant, ARVN (S. Viet Nam) air force personnel officer, 137–38, 244–46
Turner, Kevin: Chaplain (General), Army, career, special forces & chaplain, 10, 19, 73–74, 96

Uhl, Michael: PhD, Army, Viet Nam, xv

Van Rooyen: Lieutenant Colonel, Special Forces, South Africa, paratrooper, 9
Vince: Army, Viet Nam, 110–11, 203

Walker, Greg: Green Beret, career, 10–11, 156–57, 260

Walt: Army, Viet Nam, heavy equipment operator, 24–27
Willy: Marines, LRRP Squad Leader, Viet Nam, 86

Zemler, John: Doctor, Special Forces, 233–34

Index

abandonment, 47
Abatello, Michael, 3–6
aborigines, 15
Abraham, 63–64, 65, 66
acceptance of warrior destiny (step), 208–9, 215
accidental deaths, 41
Achilles, 17, 67–69, 70, 109, 124
Adams, Army Chaplain, 85
addiction, 44, 111
addictions, 276n39
Aeneas, 82
Aeschylus, 57–58, 86, 270n1, 270n2
The Persians, 150
Afghanistan, war in, xi, 18, 30, 43, 46, 72, 77, 84–85, 122, 240–43, 278n35. *See also under* veterans
African Americans, 120
African traditions, 210
Agag, 92
Agamemnon, 183, 249–51
"Agamemnon" (Laughlin), 250–51
Agent Orange, 25, 27, 46–47, 49, 70, 136–37, 199, 213, 244
aggression, 44–45
Air Force, 144
Ajax, 124, 125, 126, 127
Ajax (Sophocles), 124, 127
Ak'abal, Humberto, 51–53
Akedah, 64
Al, 155
Alberto, 6
alcohol abuse, 30, 43, 44, 47, 109–11
alienation, 138–39, 160, 226
American Psychiatric Association, 96
American Revolution, 102, 187, 188
anathema, 150–51
ancestors. *See also* transgenerational trauma
spirits of, 209
traumatized, 63–66
worship of, 138
Angel, 240–43, 252
anger, 30–31, 44–45
Antal, Chris, 84, 157, 189–90, 240–43
"Meeting the Shadow," 251–52
anxiety, 99–100
Apaches, 75
Ares, 130
"Are You Experienced" (Hendrix), 201
Aris, 221
Army Experience Center, 103–4
Army of the Republic of Viet Nam (ARVN), 137–38, 278n35
Arnold, William, 13
artistic programming, 159
atheism, 76
Athena, 67, 124, 125, 220
Athens, 15–16, 125–26, 150
atomic bomb, 29, 83
atonement, 212–13, 224, 228–29, 237, 252
"Atonement Practices after War" (Tick), 212–13
attachment disorder, 146
attachment/love wound, 147, 148
Augustine, St., 203
Australia, 213
Austria, 210–11
Austrian Holocaust Memorial Service, 211

Bacevich, Andrew, 16
Bà Me Viêt Nam Anh Hung, "Vietnamese Heroic Mothers,," 64
Banotai, Adam, 18
baptism, 210
Barry, 65
Bateson, Mary Catherine, 122

Bathsheba, 113
the Beast, 86
Becknell, John, 233, 260
belief, war and, 76
Bell, Terry, 29, 221–223
Ben, 70
Benjamin, Medea, 84
Berggren, Jeremy, 254–55
Berman-Cohen, Ayelet, 39, 78
the Bible, 60–61, 82–83, 194–99, 202–3, 260. *See also* New Testament; Old Testament; *specific books*
Bill, 256
binding, 64–65
birth defects, 46–47
Black Hawk Down, 105
Blake, William, 201
blessing, 235–36
Bloch, Ed, 49, 122–23, 277n5
Bob, 46
body, 95, 166
body politic, wounds affecting, 36
Boes, Richard, 17
Book of Numbers, 195
Bosnian war, 43
Boston Advertiser, 103
Boudreau, Tyler, 80, 151
Bradley, David, 42
Bradshaw, Gay, 98
breakdowns, 99–101
Brooke, Roger, 10, 179, 181–82, 260, 280n12
Buck Fever, 99
Buddha, 260
Buddhism, 128, 133, 213
buffalo, 130–31
the Bulge, Battle of, 64
Bush, George W., 42, 121, 128
Bushido, 10
"buying back" warriors, 237–38, 252–53

Cagle, Bob, 257–58
Cain, 62
Campbell, Joseph, 61, 63, 82, 153–54, 169, 169, 170, 171, 172
cancer, 25, 46
Candy, 28, 39, 40
Canvas Dance songs, 186
Caplan, Paula, xi, 107
care providers, 174
  goals for, 167
Carl, 154–55
Carlin, George, 144
casualty rates, 103–4, 279–80n8
catharsis, 221
"Ceremony of the Beast" (Willy), 86
chanting, 222
chaplains, 74, 77, 82, 85, 124–25, 151, 157, 167, 198, 224, 240–43, 247, 251–52, 272n40. *See also specific chaplains*
  retreats for, 207–8
  warrior medicine and, 187–89
character, 100, 123
Charleston, South Carolina, 103
Charlie Company, 256
Cheney, Dick, 121
"chiefs of old," ?, 219
child abuse, 46, 268n54
children, 31, 32, 44
child abuse, 46, 268n54
costs of war and, 45–47
  Warrior archetype and, 8
China, 110
"Christ and the Soldier" (Sassoon), 203
Chu Lai, 230–31
Chung, Jae-sung, 281n16
citizenship, military service and, 36–37, 258
civilians, ix
  killing of, 32, 102, 103–4
  lack of initiation among, 277n6
  social contract with warriors, 119–39, 147, 167
  as targets, 102
  as witness to warrior's journey, 233–34
Civil War, 65, 71, 80–81, 99. *See also under* veterans
  casualties of, 102–3
  mass technological warfare in, 102–4
  psychiatric casualties in, 107
  slaves serving in Union army during, 119–20
clinicians, goals for, 167

Cocks, Ray, 227
codes, 9–10, 69, 128, 133
cognitive dissonance, 14–15
Cohen, Leonard, 55
Cold War, 129
collapse, 157, 199
"collateral damage," 61
collective trauma, 36–37
colleges, veteran-friendly, 159
combat, 123. *See also* killing
"combat fatigue," 100
combat trauma, 142, 178–87
effect of, 145–46
protecting and redeeming the soul during, 238–40
Combat Infantryman's Badge (CIB), 160, 161, 214
comfort, 219
commanders, 134, 240
communal societies, 133. *See also* traditional cultures
communities, 166
community support, 135, 147, 158–59, 160, 163–64. *See also* social contract
goals for, 167
honor and, 126–27
restitution in the, 212–13
spirituality and, 163
witness in, 233–34
as witness to warrior's journey, 174
wounding and, 157–61
Compassion House, 228–29
concentration camps, 100, 101
confession, 210, 212, 224
confidence, 129
Confucius, 135
congenital defects, 46
conscience, 70
costs of war
accidental deaths, 41
children and, 45–47
criminality, 42–43
disability costs, 49–50
disability payments, 49–50
divorce, 44–45
health issues, 48–49. *See also specific health issues*
homelessness, 48
homicide, 42–43
marital difficulties, 44–45
substance abuse, 43–44
suicide, 39–41
unemployment, 47–48
courage, 130
A Course in Miracles, 231
Cousineau, Phil, 246
"cowardice," 100, 101, 105
creative arts, 159
creed, 9–10
criminality, 42–43
criminal justice system, veterans in the, 42–43, 159
Cú Chulainn, 210
culture, wounds to, 166
Cuong, Tran Van, 136
Custer, George Armstrong, 110

Da Costa, Jacob Mendes, 99–100
Da Costa's Syndrome, 99–100
Dahlstedt, Kate, xv, 163, 185, 207–8, 215–18, 220, 247
"Sentry," 37–38
Damascus, 203
Da Nang, 228
dancing, 222
Daniel, 23, 25
Dante, *Inferno,* 80
Dave, 188–89
David (veteran), 44
David (Biblical figure), 63, 71–72, 86, 91–93, 111–15, 180, 197–98, 255
and Goliath, 112–14
as "PTSD sufferer," 114
Day of Atonement, 210, 224
Day of Wandering Souls, 138
the dead, relations with, 146
Dean, Eric, 247
death, 80
reconciliation and, 243–46
relations with, 89–91, 146
death penalty, 42
dehumanization, 85, 138–39, 160, 227, 238
deities of war, 58, 83. *See also specific deities*
Delate, Brian, 14, 153
Memorial Day, 255

Department of Defense, 53–54, 152
Department of Labor, 47–48
Department of Veterans Affairs, 50, 102
departure, 169, *169, 170*
Deployment Blessing Ceremonies, 154
depression, 109
descent, 79–94, 171
Desert Storm, 144
despair, 30
detachment, 227
Deuteronomy, 197
"developmental fallacy," 108
"Devotion to Duty" (Sassoon), 113
Dewey, Larry, 151, 237
Diagnostic and Statistical Manual (DSM), 97–98, 274n4
dignity, 135
disability claims, 49
disability costs, 49–50
disability payments, 49–50
disappointment, 138
discipline, 17
dishonor, 124, 125–27
the Divine, 58–59, 74–77, 85, 91–93, 94, 125, 183, 189
divorce, 44–45
Donahue, Anne Marie, 214
donation, 213
Douglass, Frederick, 119–20
Dragon Mountain, 257
"drive-by caring," 233
driving while intoxicated, 44
drone warfare, 84
drop-on centers, 159
Dr. P., 105
drumming, 222
Dutthagamani, 181
duty, 224
Duy, Nguyen, 133

earth, wounds to, 166
Eastern Orthodox Church, 196
Ed B., 49
educational programs, 158
educators, goals for, 167
"the Effort Syndrome," 100
Eichmann, Adolf, 227
Eisenhower, Dwight D., 14, 252
elders
  elder warriors, 128, 134, 167, 214–15, 241, 253–54, 257–58
  lack of, 259, 260
Eleazar, 206–7
electric shocks, 67
Emerson, Ralph Waldo, 187
Emerson, William, 187
enemies
  honor of, 224–25
  as human beings, 145–46, 227–28
  respect for, 224–25
"enemy tepee," 225
Enola Gay, 83
environment, damage to, 103
Epic of Gilgamesh, 7
ethics, 9. See also codes; morality
Euripides, *The Trojan Women,* 150
evil, 199
experience, 201
expressive arts, 159, 222

faith, 129, 130
  lost, 225
  war and, 76
Falklands, war in the, 43
Fallujah, Iraq, fall of, 18
families, 166
  alienation and, 226
  community support for, 160
  honor and, 126–27
"father wound," 101
fear, 30–31
Fisher, John, xv, 55, 96, 153, 161, 209, 214, 263n1
"fog of war," 36
force, moral use of, 197–98
forgiveness, 223–24
Fort Bliss, 84–85
Franklin, Benjamin, 56
French, Shannon, 9, 69
French and Indian Wars, 187, 188
Freud, Sigmund, 221
Fuller, J. F. C., 68
the Furies, 86–89, 150–51

Gabriel, 8
Gabriel, Richard, 102
Genesis, 60, 62
Geneva Convention, 197
Geronimo, 75
Gettysburg, Battle of, 103
Gettysburg, Pennsylvania, 209
Gettysburg Address, 126
GI Bill, 265n4
"Gift" (Tran Quang Quy), 164
"global war," 61
Global War on Terror, 129
Goals for Clinicians, Educators, Care Providers, and Communities Serving Veterans, 167
Golden Fleece, 260
Gold Star Mothers, 64
"Golgotha" (Sassoon), 203
Goliath, 112–13, 114
Good Samaritan, parable of, 240
grandchildren, 46
grandparents, 31–33
Grant, Ulysses S., 103, 178
Great Britain, 42, 43
Great Goddess, 260
Greece, 19, 247–49
Greece, Ancient, 60–61, 124, 125–26, 150–51, 178, 248–51
  war trauma in, 66–70
Greek mythology, 82, 83, 86–89, 109, 150–51, 171, 183, 260
Greek tradition, 83
Green Berets, 124, 156
Greenfield, Irving, 119
grief, 138
Grossman, David, 11–12, 82
growth, xvi–xix
Growth Goals for Wounded Warriors, 166–67
Guatemala, 50–53
guilt, 86
Gulf War (first), 42, 43, 47–48, 49
Gulf War syndrome, 49, 199
Gunny, 123–24, 126–27
Gutheim, James, 71
Haeberle, Ron, 256
haka, 183–84
han, 184
Hao, Le Van, 136–37
Hat, 201–2
healing, xvi–xix, 144–45, 147, 181–82, 213, 219–36
  in the Bible, 194–99
"healing from our roots," 209
  indigenous, 178
  from killing, 240–43
  as peacemaking, 163
  religion and, 193–204
  spiritual, 162, 167, 193–204
  in traditional cultures, 147
healing and reconciliation journeys, 69–70
health issues, 48–49. *See also specific health issues*
health workers, 160
heart, 95, 166, 221
Hector, 68–69, 70
Hekabe, 150, 151
hell, journey into, 79–94
helplessness, 30–31
Hemingway, Ernest, 180
Henderson, Paul, 11, 248-49, 251
Hendrix, Jimi, "Are You Experienced?," 201
Hercules, 178
Herodotus, 18, 249
Histories, 66
Heroic Mothers, 278n35
"hero's journey," 169–74, *169, 170*
Hill, Frank, 17, 89–90
Hillman, James, 108, 142, 143, 179
Hiroshima, 83
Histories (Herodotus), 66
Ho, Nguyen Tam ("Mr. Tiger"), 69–70, 95, 133, 162, 225
Ho Chi Minh, 133, 275–76n28
Hoge, Charles W., 263n1
holidays, 158
holistic understanding, 95, 141–48, 276–35
Holmes, Oliver Wendell, 99
Holocaust, 210–11, 212
homecoming. *See also* return
  community support for, 160

failures of, 228–29
social contract and, 167
as source of trauma, 122–25, 142, 166
successful, 139, 142–43, 167
in traditional cultures, 147
two paths, 142–43
homelessness, 48, 228
Homer, 67, 123
Iliad, 17, 60, 61, 67–69, 70, 183, 248, 249
"Homeric Hymn to Ares," 80
homesickness, 56, 228
homicide, 42–43, 127, 128
honor, 124, 125–27, 128–29, 135, 224–25
communities and, 126–27
families and, 126–27
Hopi people, 179–80
hospice programs, 159
hotlines, 159
Houde, Frank, 95
Hughes, Langston, 120
human nature, in the Old Testament, 61–63
Hunkpapa Warrior Society, 176
Huu Ngoc, 133
Huynh Thi Lan, 244–46
Hyman, Stan, 243–46
"Hymn to Ares," 127

ideals, betrayal of, 93–94, 98–99
identity, 145, 167
evolution of, 231–32
identity crisis, 147, 148
identity disorder, 145
warrior's sacred, 220
wounding and, 149–64
IED burns, 199
"I-Feel-Like-I'm-Fixin'-to-Die Rag" (McDonald), 234
Iliad (Homer), 17, 60, 61, 67–69, 70, 183, 248, 249
indigenous cultures, 135, 175–76. *See also specific traditions and cultures*
combat trauma and, 178–87
rituals to attend to wounds, 153–54
Inferno (Dante), 80
"In Flanders Fields" (McRae), 65
infrastructure, damage to, 103
initiation, x, 15–17, 141, *141,* 144–45, 169, *169, 170,* 171, 258
interrupted, 142, 147, 148
lack of, 277n6
step in return process, 214–15
integrity, 130
invaders, 70
invisible wounds, 28, 95–115, 155, 166
among the Vietnamese, 132, 135–38
growing beyond, 166
as identity crisis, 145
misdiagnosis of, 109–11
naming of, 149
as result of operation stress, 147
as social disorder, 138–39
as war casualties, 28
Iraq, war in, xi, 18, 28, 30, 36, 43, 50, 67, 70, 121–22, 126, 128, 198, 234, 240–43, 278n35. *See also under* veterans
casualties of, 103
parents lost in, 46
Iraq and Afghanistan Veterans of America (IAVA), 35, 45
Irish mythology, 210
"irritable heart," 99–100
Isaac, 64
Isaiah, 231, 254
Ishmael, 64
isolation, 206–8, 210, 215
isolation and tending (step in return process), 206–8
Iverson, Haven, 261
iwis, 183

Jack, 135
Jackson, Reverend, 180–81
Jacob, 63, 66
Jae-sung Chung, 184–85
Jason, 260
Jayatunge, Ruwan M., 179, 181
J.B. (MacLeish), 200
Jeremy, 67
Jesus, 82, 202
Jewish Wars, 99
Jim, 27, 79–80, 83
Jo, 31, 32–33
Joan, 32
Job, 71–72, 73, 77, 171, 199–202, 241

Jonathan, 92
Jones, Louis, 42
Joseph, 63
Josephus, 98–99
Joshua, 63
journey, transformational, 163, 165–74
Jove, 98
Jung, Carl, 19
Just War argument, 203

kanene, 181–82
karma, 213
Kate, 8
Ken, 42
Kennedy, John F., 14, 129, 225
Kent State shootings, 73, 227, 272n39
Khe Sanh, siege of, 73
kidney cancer, 25
killing, 12–13, 17, 32, 74, 79–80, 123, 148, 151, 228. *See also* combat
  acceptance of, 103–4
  acknowledgment of, 252
  in the Bible, 128, 196
  detachment from, 83
  healing from, 240–43
  intimacy of, 145–46
  long-distance, 83–84
  moral justification for, 83
  in Native American tradition, 146
  religion and, 196, 197–98
  toll of, 105
  trauma of, 82–85, 170–71, 240–43
kinship systems, 133, 134
Kootenai tribe, 146
Korea, 184, 281n16
Korean War, 102, 177–78. *See also under* veterans
Kris, 31–32

labeling, resistance to, 149
Lady Black Mountain, 257
Lakota people, 180
Lan, Huynh Thi, 244–46
land and water reclamation projects, 213
land mines, 103, 232
Laughlin, Tommy, 238–40, 248, 249–51
Lazarus, 202, 203
Lazarus Rising, 203
learning disabilities, 46
Lembke, Michael, 13, 37, 251, 254
Lennox, William Jr., 70
Le Van Hao, 136–37
Levi, 66
Levinson, Leila, 225–26
Levinson, Reuben, 101
Liberian Civil War, 230
life after war, 23
limb losses, 199
Lincoln, Abraham, 36, 126
Lisa, 30
listening, 233–34
literary programming, 159
Little Bighorn, 110
long-distance killing, 83–84
Lot, 63–64, 77
love, 145–48, 161–62, 194, 231, 243–46, 260
Lynch, Jessica, 180
Lynn, 46

MacArthur, Douglas, 97, 128, 177
MacLeish, Archibald, *J.B.,* 200
madness, 124, 125
Mahavamsa, 181
Mahedy, William, 151, 199
mana, 183
Manhattan Project, 29
Maori, 183–84
Marathon, Battle of, 57–58, 178, 248
marijuana, 44
marital difficulties, 44–45
Marlantes, Karl, 75, 80, 220–21, 240
Mars, 98
Marshall Plan, 213
martial arts traditions, 134
Mary, 260
Massey, Calvin, 226
mass technological warfare, 102–4
mastery, 171
McCain, John, 123, 152–53
McCasland, Don, 203
McCullah, Jodi, 203

McDonald, Joe, "I-Feel-Like-I'm-Fixin'-to-Die Rag," 234
McHenry, Dick, 96
McNamara, Robert, 36
In Retrospect, 224
McRae, John, "In Flanders Fields," 65
McVeigh, Timothy, 42
meaning, 234, 240
medication, 109–11, 200
"medicine chiefs of warriors," 167, 176–78, 189
"Meeting the Shadow" (Antal), 251–52
Mekong Delta, 69
melancholy, 138
Memorial Day, 158
Memorial Day (Delate), 255
memorialization, 234
mental health workers, 160
mental illnesses, 43
mentors, 134, 159, 232
Mexican War, 103
MIAs, 138
Michel, Wilbert, 146
military culture, 104–5
military ethics, 9
"military-industrial complex," 8, 252, 264n1
military services
citizenship and, 36–37
as passage to citizenship, 119–20
Military Sexual Trauma (MST), xi, 23–24, 49
military training system, recreating, 160
Miller, Glen, 160–61
Milton, John, 28
mind, 95, 166
Minutemen, 187
misdiagnosis, 109–11
Mitchell, 231–33
Moabites, 113
Mohawk Warrior Society, 12
moral injury, xv, 54, 67, 93–94, 149, 149–50, 151–54, 247, 252
morality, 13–14, 93–94
moral shields, 69, 82
moral superiority, 69, 70
Moses, 63, 195, 206, 210
Mozambique, 182
Mr. Tiger. *See* Nguyen Tam Ho ("Mr. Tiger")
Munch, Edvard, *The Scream,* 148
mustard gas, 199
mutism, 67
Mycenae, 249
Myers, Art, 228–29
My Lai, 255–58
mythology, 58
Greek, 82, 83, 86–89, 109, 150–51, 171, 183, 260
Irish, 210
Norse, ix, 83
Roman, 82

nagi napayape, 180
napalm, 199
Napolean, Harold, 127
the nation
national purification practices, 210–11
national trauma, 50–53, 166
warriors and, 129–31
National Guard, 207
Native Americans, 120, 146. *See also* Native American tradition; *specific peoples*
Native American tradition, 9, 12, 16, 24–27, 75, 120–21, 134, 152, 160–61, 175, 186–87, 210, 219, 241. *See also specific peoples*
combat trauma and, 179–80
isolation of warriors in, 207
killing in, 146
Plains Indian Model, 130–32
respect for enemies in, 224–25
Nazis, 10, 14, 100, 119, 210
neglect, 122–25
Nelson, David, 261
Nelson, Sean, 105, 108, 109
Nevard, Richard, 247
New Testament, 202–3
New Zealand, 183–84
Ngoc, Huu, 133
Nguni people, 182
Nguyen Duy, 133
Nguyen Sinh Phuc, 132

Nguyen Tam Ho ("Mr. Tiger"), 69–70, 95, 133, 225
Nicholson, R. James, 48
Nick, 70
Nietzsche, 238
nightmares, 70, 85
Noah, 62, 260
"Nobody Knows" (Kevin Turner), 96
noncommissioned officers (NCOs), 240
"normalcy," 154, 155, 156
Norse mythology, ix, 83
Norse tradition, 67, 83
Northern Ireland, war in, 43
North Vietnamese Regular Army, 136–38, 201–2
nostalgia, 56, 99, 109, 228
nostos, 228

oaths, 10, 64–65
Odin, ix
Odysseus, 82, 124, 171, 249
officers, 240. *See also* commanders
Old Sergeant Syndrome, 99
Old Testament, 9–10, 13, 60–63, 72, 83, 91–93, 111–15, 128, 154. *See also specific books*
  violence in, 61–63
  war healing in, 194–99
Olson, Eric, 54
O'odham people, 207
operational stress, 98, 147
Operational Stress Disorder, 54
Orem, Ron, 129–30
Owen, Wilfred, 65, 76, 80, 100

Pacello, Charles, 96–97, 100
Pan, 178
Papua New Guinea, 185
parents, 31–33
Paris, 69
partners, 30–31, 160
pathologization, 55, 106–7, 122, 144, 145, 149, 179, 259
Patroclus, 67
Patton, George, 101
Patty, 30
peacemaking, as healing, 163
"The Peace Prayer of St. Francis," 193–94
Peck, M. Scott, 252
Peloponnesian War, 150
Pend d'Orielle people, 120–21, 186–87, 281n18
People's Army, 132
Pericles, 125–26
perpetrator PTSD, 83
Persians, 248–49
The Persians (Aeschylus), 150
Peter, 73
philanthropic organizations, 213
Philistines, 92, 93, 112
Phillips, Michael "Magoo," xvi–xviii, 281n16
Phuc, Nguyen Sinh, 132, 135–36
Pierce, David, 54
Piestewa, Lori, 180
pilgrimage, 246–51, 255–58
Plains Indian Model, 130–31
Plato, 100, 260
Plutarch, 67
political leaders, 70
politics, 200
post-service roles, 166
Post-traumatic Growth, xix, 143, 163, 164, 167
Post-traumatic Soul Distress, 144, 164
Post-traumatic Spiritual Development, 164, 167
Post-traumatic Stress, 54
Post-traumatic Stress Disorder (PTSD), xi–xii, xv–xvii, 14, 18, 30, 36, 53–55, 70, 78, 95, 102, 187, 199, 247, 259, 274n4
  costs of war and, 42, 44–45
  definition of, 147
  diagnosed as "nostalgia," 99
  disability claims and, 49
  in the DSM, 97–98
  entry into APA classification system, 96
  homecoming and, 142–43
  as an honorable and inevitable wound, 166
  as an identity, 155
  inadequacy of diagnosis, 144
  as "infection of the soul," 127
  as invisible wound, 23–24
  lack of among Vietnamese, 132, 136–38, 166

pathologization and, 53–55, 107, 144, 149, 179
perpetrator PTSD, 83
as proof of humanity, 166
Purple Heart and, 152
as a societal problem, 122
as a specifically American response to war trauma, 179
spirituality and, 77
susceptibility to other illnesses and, 49
treatment of, 161
use of the term, 53–55
Post-traumatic Stress Injury, 53–54
Powell, Colin, 128
Powers, Kevin, 85, 145
The Practice of Dream Healing (Tick), 150–51
President's Commission on Mental Health, 45
Presley, Christal, 45–46, 226
Preston, 27
prison-based programs, 159
protesting, 7–8, 227
protest movement, xiv
protest songs, 234
Proverbs, 154, 197–98
Psalms, 197–98, 255
Psalm 18, 113–14
Psalm 22, 112, 255
Psalm 23, 112, 255
"pseudo-empathy," 151
psychological warfare, 133
psychology, reparative, 200
punishment, 86
purification, 210–12, 224
confession and, 212
national purification practices, 210–11
transgenerational, 211
purification and cleansing (step in return process), 210–12, 215
purification fire ceremony, 210
Purple Heart, 152, 154
purpose, 123

Qa tutsawanavu, 180
Quang Tri province, 132, 133, 232
Quy, Tran Quang, "Gift," 164

radiation illness, 23, 25, 49
rape, 199
Ray, 27
rebirth, 141–42, 144–45
reconciliation, 226–27, 228–29, 243–46
"Reconciliation" (Whitman), 225
reconciliation programs, 159, 212, 247, 259
recruits, 17
Red Cow Ceremony, 195–96
redemption, 219–36, 237–38
Reece, Spencer, 29
reforestation projects, 213
regret, 196–97
rehabilitation programs, 110
rehumanization, 227
reintegration, 228–29
relationships, 166
relics, 219–20
religion, 57–78, 82–83. *See also* faith; spirituality
healing and, 193–204
killing and, 196, 197–98
trauma and, 71–73
religious programs, 158
rememberment, 144–45
repression, 85
Republic of Korea Vietnam veterans (ROKs), 281–16
resolve, 123
restitution, 212–15, 229–30
in the community, 212–13
Marshall Plan, 213
traditional cultures and, 213–14
two stages of, 212–13
Vietnamese and, 213
restitution in the community (step in the return process), 212–14, 215
restoration, x, xvi–xix, 37–38, 142, 157, 166, 172, 200, 214, 220, 229–30, 233, 255, 259, 260
of meaning, 240
restoration projects, 159
Soldier's Heart model, 163–64
Warrior archetype and, 252–53
restorative justice, 229–30
restorative service, 166
restraint, 127–28

retreats, 219, 222, 223, 232, 241, 247, 272–40, 283–12
for chaplains, 207–8
Soldier's Heart model and, 215–18
Soldier's Heart retreats, 210
return, x, 169, *169,* 170, 171–72, 208–9. *See also* homecoming
failures of, 228–29
necessary steps of, 206, 210–15
acceptance of warrior destiny step, 215
initiation step, 214–15
isolation and tending step, 206–8, 215
purification and cleansing step, 210–12, 215
restitution in the community step, 212–14, 215
storytelling and confession step, 211–12
path of warrior return, 205–18
practices of, 167
principles of, 167
Ridgway, Matthew, 177–78
Rifleman's Creed, 10
rituals, 75, 138, 153–54, 185, 207, 214, 219, 222. *See also* initiation
Rivera, Miguel, 50–53
Robin Hood, 10
Roman mythology, 82
Rome, 98–99
Ross, Steven, 228
Rothenstein, Louis, 9–10
Rotiskenrakete, 12
Roy, 66, 223
Ruckles, Sergeant, 122
Rumi, 200
Russell, Mark, 60, 271–8
Russia, 100
Russo-Japanese War of 1904–5, 100

Saa, Bill, 230–31
sacrifice, 13, 17, 64, 65, 237
safe havens, 158
Salamis, Battle of, 150
Sally, 174
Samuel, 92
Samurai, 9, 10
Sarah (veteran), 31,
Sarah (Biblical figure), 64
Sassoon, Siegfried, 76, 86
"Christ and the Soldier," 203
"Devotion to Duty," 113
"Golgotha," 203
"Vicarious Christ," 203
Satan, 82, 199
Saul, 91–93, 98, 112, 113, 114, 127, 202
Scanlen, Hugh, 223–24, 225, 232, 241
"Veteran's Prayer," 235–36
scars, 55–56
Schleup, John, 233–34
The Scream (Munch), 148
Searcy, Chuck, 18–19
Seethawaka Rajasinghe, 181
self-medication, 109–11
self-sacrifice, 130
"Sentry" (Dahlstedt), 37–38
September 11, 2001, 18
Serenity Prayer, 209
service, 231–32, 234, 258
"seven souls," 180, 280n10
sex offenders, 43
sexual abuse, 127, 146–47
sexual assault, 49
sexuality, 146–47
the shadow, 19
Shangaan, 182
Shay, Jonathan, 67, 68
"shell shock," 100, 101–2
Sherman, William Tecumseh, 80–81
Sherman's March, 103
Shiloh, Battle of, 102
Shourds, Roger (*Kwu Kak Nupkus*), 12, 120–21, 186, 230–31, 281n18
siblings, 31–33
"signature wounds," xi
Simeon, 66
Sinclair, N. Duncan, 77
singing, 222
Sitting Bull, 123, 128, 175, 176, 189–90
Slater, Andrew, 36
Smithson, Ryan, 202
social contract, 129, 131–32, 147, 167
broken, 174
restoration of, 157
war trauma and, 119–39
social disorder, 147, 148, 174

society. *See also*social contract; social
disorder, redemption and, 237–38
Socrates, 13–14, 264n10
soldiering
four truths of, 73–74
universal dimensions of, 74
Soldier's Creed, 10
Soldier's Heart (film), 153
Soldier's Heart (wound), 99–100, 144, 149, 153, 161–62, 188, 259, 260
Soldier's Heart, Inc., xv, xvii–xviii, 137, 138, 154, 157, 162–64, 185, 261, 283n12
founding of, 163
mission of, 163
model of restoration, 163–64
Soldier's Heart model, 163–64, 168–74
applying in retreat settings, 215–18
Soldier's Heart Transformational Model, 172, *172*
Soldier Soul, 260
Song, Tran Dinh, 137–38, 244–46
Sophocles, *Ajax,* 124, 127
SORCC (Southern Oregon Rehabilitation Center and Clinics), xvii–xviii
the soul, 13–14, 166
arena for, 57–78
protecting during combat, 238–40
redeeming, 238–40
soul's cry of anguish, 147, 210
universality of, 59–60
soul medicine, 176–78
soul wounds, xv, 96–97, 147, 148, 166, 241, 255
South Africa, 9, 181–82, 185
Sparta, 248
Spartans, 18, 66, 67, 248
Special Forces, 156
spirit, 95, 166
spiritual comfort, 219–36
"spiritual fitness," 187
spirituality, 162, 247
community and, 163
healing and, 193–204
Post-traumatic Stress Disorder (PTSD) and, 77
war and, 57–78
spiritual war healing, 167
spiritual warriors, 167
spouses. *See* partners
Sri Lanka, 181
St. Basil the Great, 196
Sterling, Scott, 190–91, 198
Stiglitz, Joseph, 50
storytelling, 107, 108, 209, 211–12, 215, 219
storytelling and confession (step in return process), 211–12
strength, 123
stress, 106–7
Stress and Anxiety Disorder, 147, 148
substance abuse, 43–44, 47, 109–11, 127, 276n39
Substance Abuse and Mental Health Services Administration, 44
Sue, 196–97
suicide, xi, 39–41, 127, 266n15, 279–80n8
Sun Tzu, 128, 134
survivor benefits, 49
Susie, 30
sweat lodges, 210
symptoms, 108
as language of soul wounds, 108
medication and, 111
reducing, 276n35

talking, as medicine, 226
Tam Ky, 244
Tam Tien, 133, 138, 225
tapu, 183
Tarantino, Tom, 35
Tay Ninh, 257
technology, 84
Ted, 7–8
Ten Commandments, 195
terrorism, collective impact of, 18
Terry, 221–22
Tet offensive, 228
Teton Lakota nation, 175
Themis, 150
therapeutic programs, 158
therapy, 105, 107–8
therapy groups, 27, 108
Thermopylae, 18, 66, 248
Thersites, 249

Theseus, 178
Tibbets, Paul, 83
Tick, Edward
"Atonement Practices after War," 212–13
The Practice of Dream Healing, 150–51
War and the Soul, xv, xvi, xvii, xix
Tick, Gabriel, 261
Tick, Jeremy, 261
Tick, Sappho, 261
Tien, Tam, 133, 138, 225
Tiger, Mr. *See* Nguyen Tam Ho ("Mr. Tiger")
Tina, 72
Tiro, 99
totems, 214
toxic herbicide, 49
traditional cultures, 134, 146, 147, 167, 175–76, 187, 248
combat trauma and, 178–87
expressive arts in, 222
healing in, 147
homecoming in, 147
initiation and, 141
path of warrior return, 205–18
restitution and, 213–14
rituals to attend to wounds, 153–54
warriorhood and, 169
warrior medicine and, 189
Tran Dinh Song, 137–38, 244–46
Tran Quang Quy, 164
transformation, 13, 165–74, 220
through pilgrimage, 246–51
through service, 231–32
transformational journey, 163, 165–74
transgenerational trauma, 37, 47, 61, 63–66
transgenerational warfare, 64
Tran Van Cuong, 136
trauma
in the Ancient Greek World, 66–70
collective, 36–37
combat trauma, 142
meaning of, 17–19
national, 50–53
popular approaches to, 106–9
religion and, 71–73
social contract and, 119–39
"spirit" of, 37
spirituality and, 76–78
transgenerational, 37, 47, 61, 63–66
uniting through, 260
universality of, 59–60
war and, 71–73. *See also* traumatic war wounding
Trauma and Stressor-Related Disorder, 148
trauma-healing strategies, xviii
trauma therapy, 105, 107–8
Traumatic Brain Injury (TBI), xi, 23–24, 49, 50, 110, 199
traumatic war wounding, xiv–xv, 67, 81
among the Vietnamese, 132, 135–38
medical model of, 106–9
in modern history, 98–104
pathologization of, 106–9
reduced to "stress," 107–9
Trojan War, 67–69, 82, 124, 127, 150, 171, 248–51
The Trojan Women (Euripides), 150
troops, xi
trust, 129, 130
truth, 130
war and, 57–58
Truth and Reconciliation Commission, 182, 212
tsawana, 179–80
Turner, Brian, 85, 94
Turner, General, 162
Turner, Kevin, 10, 19, 73–74
"Nobody Knows," 96
Tyger, George, 55, 73

Uhl, Michael, xv
Ukubula, 181–82
the Underworld, 82, 203
unemployment, 47–48
Union army, 119–20
Unitarian Universalist Association, 207–8
United Church of Christ, 207
United States, military engagements involving, 36, 59–60
Universal Warrior, 14
universal warrior, 3–22
University of Ha Noi, 132
uranium exposure, 49, 199
Uriah, 113
US Army, 72, 103

Soldier's Creed, 10
US Department of Justice, 42–43
US Eighth Army, 177
US Marines, 3–6, 80, 122–23
Rifleman's Creed, 10
US military, 10, 261. *See also specific branches*
minority groups serving in, 120
transitioning of, 16
USS *Cole,* terrorist attack on, 18
USS *Iowa,* 231, 232

Valley of Elah, 112
values, 129, 130, 166
Van Rooyen, Lt. Colonel, 9
vengeance, 93
veteran conservation corps, 232
veteran ministries, 158
veterans, xi, xiv, 132, 154–55, 156, 260. *See also specific veterans*
abandonment of, 121–22
accidental deaths and, 41
alienation of, 138–39, 160
benefits to, 265n4
children of, 45–47
community support for, 163–64
in the criminal justice system, 42–43, 159
dehumanization of, 138–39
divorce and, 44–45
as educators, 158
elder, 159, 231
families of, 28–33
as first responders, 232
grandparents of, 31–33
of Gulf War, 42, 43, 47, 50
homelessness and, 48
incarcerated, 159
invisible wounds of, 23–24
killing and, 83
Korean, 281n16
of Korean War, 6, 45, 123–24, 248
marginalization, 138–39
neglect of, 121–25
of North Vietnamese Regular Army, 136–38, 201–2
parents of, 31–33
partners of, 30–31
pathologization of, 144, 179
post-service roles of, 166
in prison, 42–43
psychology of, 160
return of, 122–25, 166
service by, 231–32
siblings of, 31–33
storytelling by, 107, 108, 159, 209, 211–12, 215, 219
suicide and, 40–41, 266n15, 279–80n8
therapy and, 83
transferring experiences of, 147
unemployment and, 47–48
of Viet Cong, 69–70, 132–33, 136–38, 221, 225
Vietnamese, 135–38, 164, 201–2, 228–29, 278n35
of Vietnam War, xiii, xvi–xviii, 9, 24–27, 29, 40, 43, 47, 66, 69–70, 73, 79–80, 95, 123–24, 132–33, 135–36, 146, 160–61, 164, 201–2, 212, 221, 224–25, 228–31, 238–41, 243–48, 255–57, 266n15, 278n35, 281n16
of war in Afghanistan, xi, 3–6, 30, 40–41, 44–45, 72, 77, 122, 212, 278n35
of war in Iraq, xi, 28, 30, 40–41, 44, 45, 67, 70, 121–22, 212, 232, 278n35
of World War I, 76, 265n4
of World War II, xiii, 45, 76, 122–23, 248, 265n4
Veterans Administration
loss of benefits and, 125
medical system, xi, 40
Veterans Administration, 109
disability claims and, 49
Veterans Administration Chaplain Corps, 261
Veterans Community Network, 161
Veterans Day, 158, 248
Veterans for Peace, 213
"Veteran's Prayer" (Scanlen), 235–36
Veterans Service Corp, 159
"Vicarious Christ," Sassoon, Siegfried, 203
Victory Song, 186
Viet Cong, 69, 132–33, 136–38, 243, 257
Viet Minh, 69, 133
Viet Nam, xvi, 47, 77, 138, 224, 246–47
birth defects in, 46–47
healing and reconciliation journeys to, 69–70
lack of traumatic breakdowns in, 132–39
pilgrimage to, 255–58

reconciliation in, 278n35
Vietnamese, 224, 244–46, 275–76n28
reconciliation among, 278n35
restitution and, 213
traumatic breakdown among the, 135–38, 166
"Vietnamese Heroic Mothers" *Bà Me Viêt Nam Anh Hung*, 64
Vietnamese tradition, 120, 138, 154, 180–81, 257
Viet Nam People's Army, 132
Vietnam War, xiii, xvi–xvii, 7–8, 40, 49, 65–67, 73, 79–80, 146, 180–81, 184, 224, 228, 230–31, 234, 238–40, 243–46, 255–58, 275–76n28, 278n35. *See also under* veterans
casualties of Vietnamese, 132
compared to Homer's epics, 67
effect on the Vietnamese, 132, 135–38
invisible wounds in, 132–33
Koreans in, 281n16
parents lost in, 46
partners lost in, 46
psychiatric casualties in, 102
restitution for, 213
Vijithapura, Battle of, 181
Vince, 110–11, 203
violence, 127
moral use of, 70, 197–98
in the Old Testament, 61–63
virtues, faith in, 129–30
vision quests, 210

Walkabout, 15
Walker, Greg, 10–11, 156–57, 260
Walt, 24–27
war, 165. *See also under* veterans; *specific wars*
in the Ancient Greek World, 66–70
archetype of, 58–59, 165
belief and, 76
controversial, 19
costs of, 39
faith and, 76
hidden tolls of, 104–6
legacy of, 61
as a moral arena, 93–94
moral versus immoral, 70
in the Old Testament, 61–63
religion and, 57–78, 82–83
as a sacred arena, 74–76
spirituality and, 57–78
trauma and, 71–73
truth and, 57–58
truths about, 165–66
universality of, 59–60
"War and Human Memory" conference, 210
War and the Soul (Tick), xv, xvi, xvii, xix
war casualties, counting, 28
warfare
drone, 84
mass technological, 102–4
psychological, 133
transgenerational, 64
unending, 129–30
universal dimensions of, 74
"war-illiterate society," xi
war in Afghanistan, xi, 18, 30, 43, 72, 84–85, 278n35. *See also under* veterans
accidental deaths and, 40–41
parents lost in, 46
suicide and, 40–41
trauma of killing and, 240–43
war in Iraq, xi, 18, 28, 30, 36, 43, 50, 67, 70, 121, 126, 128, 198, 278n35. *See also under* veterans
accidental deaths and, 40–41
parents lost in, 46
suicide and, 40–41
trauma of killing and, 240–43
war in the Falklands, 43
War of 1812, 102
"war path," 9
Warrior archetype, ix–x, 12, 19, 56–57, 75, 168, 170, 219–20, 237, 248
innate, 7–9
restoration and, 252–53
restoration of, 260
soul medicine and, 176–78
as Spiritual Form, 6
traits of, 11
universality of, 6–7
warrior chief, ideal of, 175–91
Warrior ethos, 56. *See also* codes
warriorhood, 9–10, 128, 142–43
codes and, 9–10
definition of, 15
initiation into, 15–17, 141–42, *141*
journey of, 168–74
modern reversal of, 127

sacrifice and, 13
transformation and, 13
Warrior ideal, 15
warrior medicine
chaplains and, 187–89
contemporary, 189–91
"medicine chiefs of warriors," 167, 176–78, 189
traditional cultures and, 189
"warrior preparedness training," 105
warrior return, path of, 205–18
warriors. *See also* warriorhood
definition of, 9–10
destiny of, 208–9
elder, 128, 134, 167, 214–15, 241, 253–54, 257–58
initiation of, 15–17, 141–42, *141*
journey of, 165–74
the nation and, 129–31
nurturing, x
path of, 168–74
qualities of, x
redemption of, 238–52
return of, 131–32, 142, 205–18. *See also* homecoming; return
social contract and, 129, 157, 167
in society, 127–29
spiritual, 167
state of mind of, 11
traits of, 11
warrior's code, 128. *See also* codes
Warrior's dance, 221–22
Warrior Self, 220
warrior's journey, 260
"Warriors Journey Home," 234
"warrior soul," 13–14
Warrior's Path, 9
warrior stories, 209
war survivors, portraits of, 38–39
war trauma, 166
social contract and, 119–39
as soul wound, 144
Washington, George, 24, 129, 154, 176, 187, 188
Western tradition, war in the, 60–61
Westmoreland, William, 249, 250
Whirlwind, 201
white phosphorus, 199
Whitman, Walt, 65
"Reconciliation," 225
will, 123
loss of, 100
Willy, "Ceremony of the Beast," 86
Winnen, Peter, 73, 272n39
witness in community, 233–34
Wolf, Kate, 244
women soldiers, 49
Woolger, Roger, 47, 269n58
World War I, 76, 80, 100. *See also under* veterans
casualties of, 103
mutism during, 67
psychiatric casualties in, 101–2, 107
World War II, xiii, 14, 68, 76, 100, 101, 119, 210–11. *See also under* veterans
African Americans serving in, 120
casualties of, 103
psychiatric casualties in, 101
wounded roots, 60–61
wounded spirit, witnessing, 35–38
"The Wounded Warrior," ED: Should this title be in italics?, 20
wounds, 35–56. *See also* moral injury
community and, 157–61
healing, 162
holistic understanding of, 141–48
honoring of, 158
identity and, 149–64
as inevitable, 152–54
invisible, ix, xi–xiv, xviii, 14, 23–24, 28, 95–115, 132, 135–39, 145, 147, 149, 155, 166
moral, 151–54
spirituality and, 162
transformation and, 166–67
witnessing of, 158
wrath, 68, 144
Wright, H. P., 100

Xhosa people, 181–82, 280n12

Yom Kippur, 210, 224
Young, Tomas, 121

Zarathustra, 238
Zemler, John, 233
"zombies," 100

About the Author

Edward Tick, PhD, is founding director of the nonprofit organization Soldier's Heart, Inc., created in response to the outpouring of concern for our nation's veterans and their psychological wounds. Honored for his groundbreaking work in the spiritual, holistic, and community-based healing of veterans and Post-Traumatic Stress Disorder (PTSD), Dr. Tick has been a psychotherapist for thirty-nine years, specializing in working with veterans since the 1970s. He is the author of *Sacred Mountain, The Practice Of Dream Healing, The Golden Tortoise, Wild Beasts and Wandering Souls* and the award-winning book *War and the Soul.*

Dr. Tick is an internationally recognized educator and expert on veterans, PTSD, and the psychology of military-related issues and has conducted trainings, retreats, and workshops across the country as well as overseas. He has lectured, trained staff, and worked with wounded warriors at West Point, Walter Reed Army Medical Center, Fort Hood, Fort Knox, Fort Bragg, Altus Air Force Base, and other Department of Defense facilities. The Department of Defense and VA facilities now use his pioneering work and he was the US Army's 2012 PTSD expert trainer for its annual Chaplain Sustainment Training.

As a tireless advocate for war-healing and peacemaking, Dr. Tick lectures around the world and leads semiannual educational, healing, and reconciliation journeys to Viet Nam and Greece.

Dr. Tick is a gifted healer, teacher, and guide specializing in using psychospiritual, crosscultural, and international reconciliation practices to bring healing and hope to veterans, communities, and nations recovering from the traumas of war and violence.

About Sounds True

Sounds True is a multimedia publisher whose mission is to inspire and support personal transformation and spiritual awakening. Founded in 1985 and located in Boulder, Colorado, we work with many of the leading spiritual teachers, thinkers, healers, and visionary artists of our time. We strive with every title to preserve the essential "living wisdom" of the author or artist. It is our goal to create products that not only provide information to a reader or listener, but that also embody the quality of a wisdom transmission.

For those seeking genuine transformation, Sounds True is your trusted partner. At SoundsTrue.com you will find a wealth of free resources to support your journey, including exclusive weekly audio interviews, free downloads, interactive learning tools, and other special savings on all our titles.

To learn more, please visit SoundsTrue.com/freegifts or call us toll free at 800-333-9185.